Oracle E-Business Suite 12 Financials Cookbook

Take the hard work out of your daily interactions with E-Business Suite financials by using the 50+ recipes from this cookbook

Yemi Onigbode

[PACKT] enterprise

PUBLISHING

professional expertise distilled

BIRMINGHAM - MUMBAI

Oracle E-Business Suite 12 Financials Cookbook

First published: August 2011

Production Reference: 1090811

Livery Place
35 Livery Street
Birmingham B3 2PB, UK.

ISBN 978-1-849683-10-4

www.packtpub.com

Cover Image by Tony Shi (shihe99@hotmail.com)

Credits

Author

Yemi Onigbode

Reviewers

Ola Tubi

Paul Wilkinson

Acquisition Editor

Dhwani Devater

Technical Editor

Merwine Machado

Copy Editor

Leonard D'silva

Project Coordinator

Leena Purkait

Proofreader

Aaron Nash

Indexer

Rekha Nair

Production Coordinator

Shantanu Zagade

Cover Work

Shantanu Zagade

About the Author

Yemi Onigbode has experience of over a decade in ERP systems development and maintenance. He has progressed from the early days of the mainframe-based systems to the present day of web-based distributed systems.

Yemi is a hybrid techno-functional (Functional and Technical) independent Oracle consultant. He is a hands-on Project Manager, Business Architect, and Trainer/Instructor, specialized mainly in Financials and Supply Chain models. He has assisted a number of businesses to find solutions to complex business issues using various technologies. Yemi is also a keen believer in self-development and research–he is at par with the current developments in the IT and communications industry. He is currently developing and implementing e-business solutions for large and medium-sized companies, fully integrating their business applications with the Internet, and providing a totally integrated solution. He has been a developer in Java since 1996 and implementing Oracle Applications since 1997.

Yemi is a Fellow of the Association of Chartered Certified Accountants. He has a Bachelor of Science (Honors) degree in Mathematics. Yemi is also a technical writer on Accountancy and IT issues, and presents at Accounting and IT seminars. He motivates and mentors young adults on career management and planning. In his spare time, Yemi loves to study the Holy Bible, write, and is learning to play musical instruments. He authors a number of blogs including www.i-oracle.com, www.mentorbuilders.com, and www.cementors.com.

Special thanks go to all the members of the editorial team at Packt Publishing, especially Dhwani Devater and Leena Purkait. You guys are great, even when things didn't seem to go in the right direction you were patient with me, so thank you for your support.

I would also like to thank Lata Basantani, Stephanie Moss, Rashmi Phadnis, and Wilson D'souza of Packt Publishing for your contributions in the early stages. Thank you.

I also want to thank all my colleagues and trainees at E-Consulting Limited and Cementors Limited for your assistance over the years in the Oracle and Java world, without you there would be no one to train, and no one to work with. The future is great!

About the Reviewer

Paul Wilkinson was born in New Zealand and qualified as a Chartered Accountant. He is a former employee of Price Waterhouse, The Hertz Corporation, and Oracle Corporation. In 1999, he became an independent Oracle Consultant specializing in Training Manager and Delivery roles. Paul is currently employed by the Ricoh Corporation Plc. as the UPK Administrator, assisting with the creation of over 1000 e-learning topics across the APRO, Dexterra, Click, Cognos, Hyperion, Oracle, and Siebel Applications. This includes translation into French and German.

Paul has worked with Yemi Onigbode for over 10 years and has thoroughly enjoyed reviewing the book. The market needs a book of this nature to link processes with the application.

www.PacktPub.com

Support files, eBooks, discount offers and more

You might want to visit www.PacktPub.com for support files and downloads related to your book.

Did you know that Packt offers eBook versions of every book published, with PDF and ePub files available? You can upgrade to the eBook version at www.PacktPub.com and, as a print book customer, you are entitled to a discount on the eBook copy. Get in touch with us at service@packtpub.com for more details.

At www.PacktPub.com, you can also read a collection of free technical articles, sign up for a range of free newsletters, and receive exclusive discounts and offers on Packt books and eBooks.

http://PacktLib.PacktPub.com

Do you need instant solutions to your IT questions? PacktLib is Packt's online digital book library. Here, you can access, read, and search across Packt's entire library of books.

Why subscribe?

- ► Fully searchable across every book published by Packt
- ► Copy and paste, print, and bookmark content
- ► On demand and accessible via web browser

Free access for Packt account holders

If you have an account with Packt at www.PacktPub.com, you can use this to access PacktLib today and view nine entirely free books. Simply use your login credentials for immediate access.

Instant Updates on New Packt Books

Get notified! Find out when new books are published by following @PacktEnterprise on Twitter, or the *Packt Enterprise* Facebook page.

Table of Contents

Preface

Oracle E-Business Suite 12 Financials is a solution that provides out-of-the-box features to meet global financial reporting and tax requirements with one accounting, tax, banking, and payments model, and makes it easy to operate shared services across businesses and regions. You may have read what EBS Financials does, but with this book on your work desk you will see how to do it.

There are many ways of configuring and using E-Business Suite 12 Financials. This cookbook demonstrates how to use E-Business Suite 12 Financials in a way that will enable you to understand the core functionalities of the main Financials modules. Each recipe is presented as a scenario-based topic that details typical business scenarios.

You will start by creating Items in Inventory, and then purchase Items in Procurement. Supplier invoices are entered and paid in Payables and Assets created and managed.

Items are sold and shipped to customers in Order Management, and funds received from customers in Receivables. Cash is managed and transactions transferred to the General Ledger through the Subledger Accounting with the corresponding tax calculations. The periods are then closed in the final chapter. Let's look at each chapter in brief summaries.

What this book covers

Chapter 1, Creating Items in Inventory, includes recipes for creating Items and exploring the Item attributes. It then continues with creating Item templates and exploring Item controls and concludes with adjusting Items in Inventory and classifying Items into categories.

Chapter 2, Purchasing Items in Procurement, covers the Requisition-to-Receiving flow, with recipes covering raising and approving Requisitions, creating Suppliers, Purchase Orders, and receiving Items. The chapter then concludes with reviewing the Procurement Accounting transactions.

Chapter 3, Paying Supplier Invoices in Payables, covers the Invoice-to-Payment flow, with recipes covering entering and managing various types of Invoices. The recipes then cover payment to Suppliers, and conclude with a review of the Payables Accounting transactions.

Chapter 4, Managing Assets, covers adding and adjusting assets. The recipes then cover depreciating and retiring assets and conclude with a review of Asset Accounting transactions.

Chapter 5, Selling Items to Customers in Order Management, covers the Orders-to-Invoice flow, with recipes covering creating customers and different types of sales orders. The recipes then cover adding Items to a Price List, reviewing Order Management workflow, and the management, releasing, and shipping of orders, and then conclude with creating invoices for customers.

Chapter 6, Receiving Funds in Receivables, covers the Invoice-to-Receipt flow, with recipes covering creating and adjusting invoices, entering receipts, and managing debts. It concludes with reviewing the Receivables Accounting transactions.

Chapter 7, Managing Cash, covers creating a bank account, and entering and reconciling bank statements. It then goes on to creating Cash Forecasts, and concludes with a review of Cash Accounting transactions.

Chapter 8, Defining Transactions for the General Ledger, covers defining the Chart of Accounts, and setting up the ledger. It then covers defining Subledger Accounting and concludes with defining E-Business tax accounting.

Chapter 9, End of Period Processing, covers closing Payables, Purchasing, Receivables, Inventory, and the General Ledger.

What you need for this book

You will need access to the standard Oracle E-Business Suite 12 demonstration Vision database. This can be downloaded from `http://edelivery.oracle.com`.

Who this book is for

This book is for E-Business Suite Financials specialists who want a broader understanding of particular areas of the Financials modules. Businesses can use this book to identify key functionalities of the financial modules, and very quickly demonstrate a pilot to obtain the core requirements.

If you are a business analyst, functional consultant, technical consultant, project sponsor, project manager, project team member, system accountant or solution designer, testing team member, training team member or support team member, then this book is for you.

This book assumes that you have basic navigation skills and you understand some key E-Business Suite terminology.

Conventions

In this book, you will find a number of styles of text that distinguish between different kinds of information. Here are some examples of these styles, and an explanation of their meaning.

New terms and **important words** are shown in bold. Words that you see on the screen, in menus or dialog boxes for example, appear in the text like this: "Search for the **PRD20001** Item."

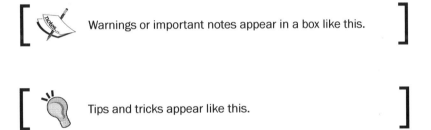

Warnings or important notes appear in a box like this.

Tips and tricks appear like this.

Reader feedback

Feedback from our readers is always welcome. Let us know what you think about this book—what you liked or may have disliked. Reader feedback is important for us to develop titles that you really get the most out of.

To send us general feedback, simply send an e-mail to feedback@packtpub.com, and mention the book title via the subject of your message.

If there is a book that you need and would like to see us publish, please send us a note in the **SUGGEST A TITLE** form on www.packtpub.com or e-mail suggest@packtpub.com.

If there is a topic that you have expertise in and you are interested in either writing or contributing to a book, see our author guide on www.packtpub.com/authors.

Customer support

Now that you are the proud owner of a Packt book, we have a number of things to help you to get the most from your purchase.

Errata

Although we have taken every care to ensure the accuracy of our content, mistakes do happen. If you find a mistake in one of our books—maybe a mistake in the text or the code—we would be grateful if you would report this to us. By doing so, you can save other readers from frustration and help us improve subsequent versions of this book. If you find any errata, please report them by visiting http://www.packtpub.com/support, selecting your book, clicking on the **errata submission form** link, and entering the details of your errata. Once your errata are verified, your submission will be accepted and the errata will be uploaded on our website, or added to any list of existing errata, under the Errata section of that title. Any existing errata can be viewed by selecting your title from http://www.packtpub.com/support.

Piracy

Piracy of copyright material on the Internet is an ongoing problem across all media. At Packt, we take the protection of our copyright and licenses very seriously. If you come across any illegal copies of our works, in any form, on the Internet, please provide us with the location address or website name immediately so that we can pursue a remedy.

Please contact us at copyright@packtpub.com with a link to the suspected pirated material.

We appreciate your help in protecting our authors, and our ability to bring you valuable content.

Questions

You can contact us at questions@packtpub.com if you are having a problem with any aspect of the book, and we will do our best to address it.

1
Creating Items in Inventory

In this chapter, we will start with recipes for creating Items. We will cover:

- ▶ Creating Items
- ▶ Exploring Item attributes
- ▶ Creating Item templates
- ▶ Exploring Item controls
- ▶ Adjusting Items in inventory
- ▶ Classifying Items

Introduction

An organization's operations include the buying and selling of products and services. Items can represent the products and services that are purchased and sold in an organization. Let's start by looking at the Item creation process.

The following diagram details the process for creating Items:

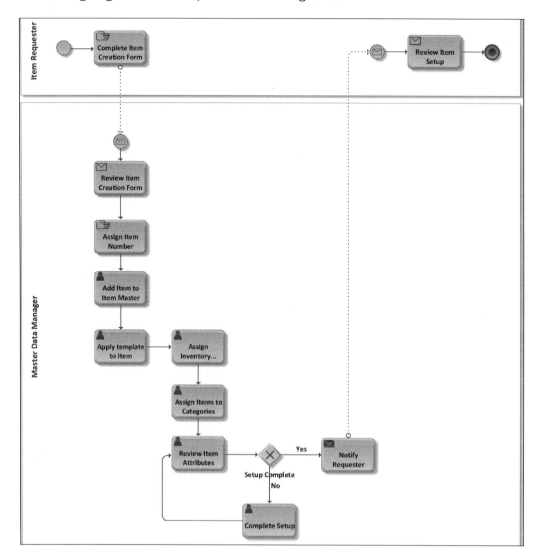

1. The **Item Requester** (the person who requests an Item) completes an **Item Creation Form**, which should contain information such as:

   ❑ Costing information

   ❑ Pricing Information

   ❑ Item and Product Categories

   ❑ Details of some of the Item attributes

   ❑ The inventory organization details

2. Once complete, a message is sent to the **Master Data Manager** (the person who maintains the master data) to create the Item. The message could be sent by fax, e-mail, and so on.

3. The **Master Data Manager** reviews the form and enters the details of the Item into Oracle E-Business Suite by creating the Item. Once complete, a message is sent to the **Item Requester**.

4. The **Item Requester** reviews the Item setup on the system.

Let's look at how Items are created and explore the underlying concepts concerning the creation of Items.

Creating Items

Oracle Inventory provides us with the functionality to create Items. Sets of attributes are assigned to an Item. The attributes define the characteristics of the Item. A group of attributes values defines a template, and a template can be assigned to an Item to automatically define the set of attribute values.

An Item template defines the Item Type. For example, a **Finished Good** template will identify certain characteristics that define the Item as a finished good, with attributes such as "Inventory Item" and "Stockable" with a value of "Yes". Let's look at how to create an Item in Oracle Inventory. We will also assign a **Finished Good** template to the Item.

Getting ready

Log in to Oracle E-Business Suite R12 with the username and password assigned to you by the System Administrator. If you are working on the Vision demonstration database, you can use OPERATIONS/WELCOME as the USERNAME/PASSWORD:

1. Select the **Inventory Responsibility**.

2. Select the **V1 Inventory Organization**.

How to do it...

Let's list the steps required to create an Item:

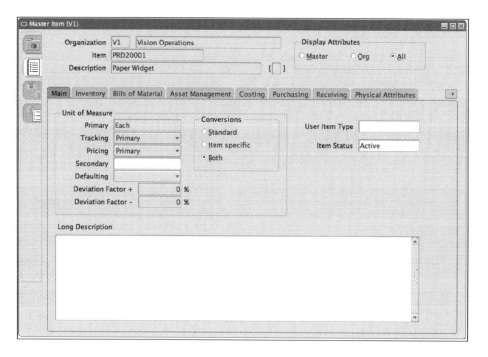

1. Navigate to **Items | Master Items**. Please note that Items are defined in the Master Organization.

2. Enter the **Item code**, for example, **PRD20001**.

3. Enter a description for the Item:

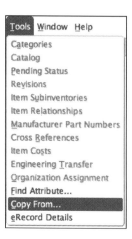

4. Select **Copy From** from the tools menu (or press *Alt+T*). We are going to copy the attributes from the **Finished Good** template:

5. We can also copy attributes from an existing Item.

6. Enter **Finished Good** and click on the **Apply** button (or press *Alt+A*) and click on the **Done** button.

7. Save the Item definition by clicking on the **Save** icon (or press *Ctrl+S*).

How it works...

Items contain attributes and attributes contain information about an Item. Attributes can be controlled centrally at the Master Organization level or at the Inventory Organization level.

There's more...

Once the Item is created, we need to assign it to a category and an inventory organization.

Assigning Items to inventory organizations

For us to be able to perform transactions with the Item in the inventory, we need to assign the Item to an inventory organization. We can also use the organization Item form to change the attributes at the organization level. For example, an Item may be classified as raw materials in one organization and finished goods in another organization.

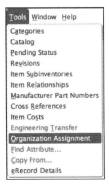

1. From the **Tools** menu, select **Organization Assignment**.

2. Select the inventory organization for the Item. For example, **A1–ACME Corporation**. Click on the **Assigned** checkbox.

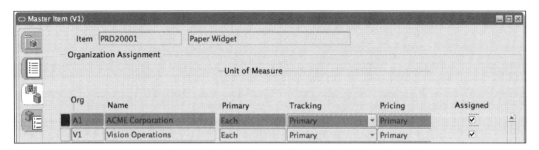

3. Save the assignment.

Assigning Items to categories

When an Item is created, it is assigned to a default category. However, you may want to perform transactions with the Item in more than one functional area, such as Inventory, Purchasing, Cost Management, Service, Engineering, and so on. You need to assign the Item to the relevant functional area. A category within a functional area is a logical classification of Items with similar characteristics.

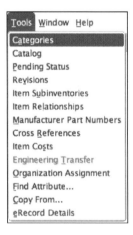

1. From the **Tools** menu, select **Categories**.

2. Select the **Categories Set**, **Control Level**, and the **Category** combination to assign to the Item:

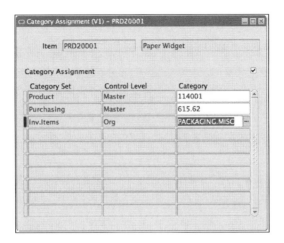

3. Save the assignment.

See also

Classifying Items recipe in this chapter

Exploring Item attributes

There are more than 250 Item attributes grouped into 17 main attribute groups. In this recipe, we will explore the main groups that are used within the financial modules.

How to do it...

Let's explore some Item attributes:

1. Search for the **Finished Good** Item by navigating to **Items | Master Items**:

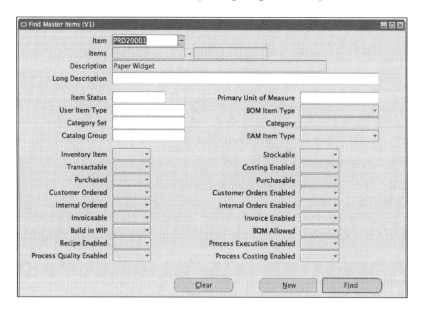

2. Click on the **Find** icon. You then enter the Item code and click on the **Find** button to search for the Item.

3. Select the tabs to review each of the attributes group:

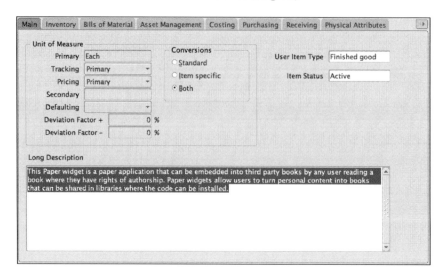

4. In the **Main** tab, check that the **Item Status** is **Active**. We can also enter a long description in the **Long Description** field.

5. The default value of the primary **Unit of Measure (UOM)** can be defined in the **INV: Default Primary Unit of Measure** profile option. The value can be overwritten when creating the Item. The Primary UOM is the default UOM used in other modules. For example, in Receivables it is used for invoices and credit memos.

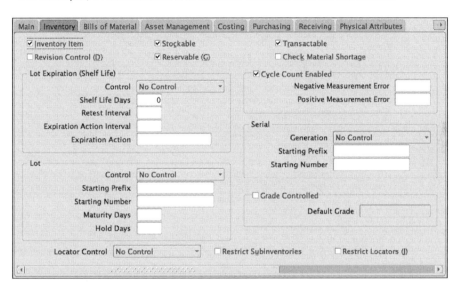

6. In the **Inventory** tab, check that the following are enabled:

    ❑   **Inventory Item**: It enables the Item to be transacted in **Inventory**. The default **Inventory Item** category is automatically assigned to the Item, if enabled.

    ❑   **Stockable**: It enables the Item to be stocked in Inventory.

    ❑   **Transactable**: Order Management uses this flag to determine how returns are transacted in Inventory.

    ❑   **Reservable**: It enables the reservation of Items during transactions. For example, during order entry in Order Management.

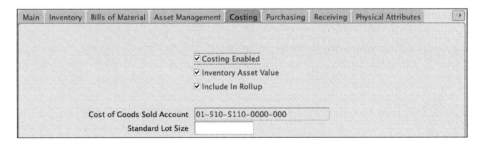

7. In the **Costing** tab, check that the following are enabled:

   ❑ **Costing**: Enables the accounting for Item costs. It can be overridden in the Cost Management module, if average costing is used.

   ❑ **Cost of Goods Sold Account**: The cost of goods sold account is entered. This is a general ledger account. The value defaults from the Organization parameters.

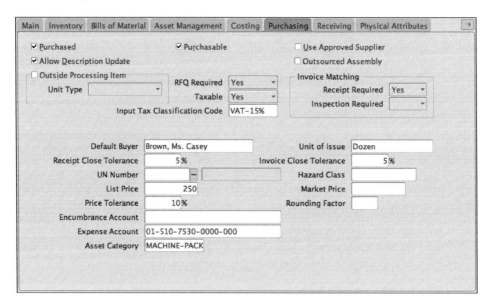

8. In the **Purchasing** tab, enter a **Default Buyer** for the purchase orders, a **List Price**, and an **Expense Account**. Check that the following are enabled:

   ❑ **Purchased**: It enables us to purchase and receive the Item.

   ❑ **Purchasable**: It enables us to create a Purchase Order for the Item.

   ❑ **Allow Description Update**: It enables us to change the description of the Item when raising the Purchase Order.

   ❑ **RFQ Required**: Set this value to **Yes** to enable us to require a quotation for this Item.

   ❑ **Taxable**: Set this value to **Yes** with the Input Tax Classification Code as **VAT–15%**. This can be used with the default rules in E-Tax.

   ❑ **Invoice Matching**: Receipt Required–**Yes**. This is to allow for three-way matching.

9. In the **Receiving** tab, review the controls.

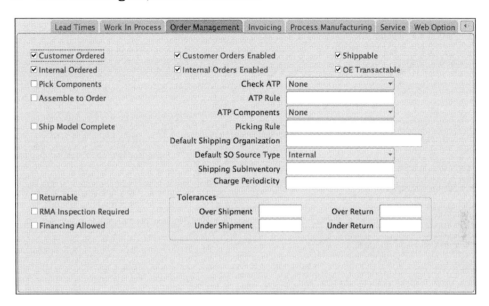

10. In the **Order Management** tab, check that the following are enabled:

   ❑ **Customer Ordered**: This enables us to define prices for an Item assigned to a price list.

   ❑ **Customer Orders Enabled**: This enables us to sell the Item.

   ❑ **Shippable**: This enables us to ship the Item to the Customer.

   ❑ **Internal Ordered**: This enables us to order an Item via internal requisitions.

   ❑ **Internal Orders Enabled**: This enables us to temporarily exclude an Item from internal requisitions.

   ❑ **OE Transactable**: This is used for demand management of an Item.

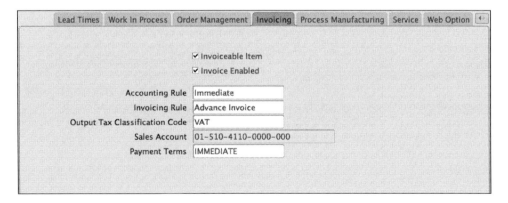

11. In the **Invoicing** tab, enter values for the **Accounting Rule, Invoicing Rule, Output Tax Classification Code**, and **Payment Terms**. Enter the **Sales Account** code and check that the **Invoiceable Item** and **Invoice Enabled** checkboxes are enabled.

Creating Item templates

An Item template is a set of attributes that enable the 'quick' creation of an Item. In this recipe, we will create an Item template that can be used to create many similar Items. We will copy from the **Finished Good** template to our new template called **ACME Finished Good**.

Getting ready

Log in to Oracle E-Business Suite and select the Inventory responsibility.

How to do it...

Let's list the steps required to create an Item template:

1. Navigate to **Setup | Items | Templates**.
2. Select the Inventory Organization.

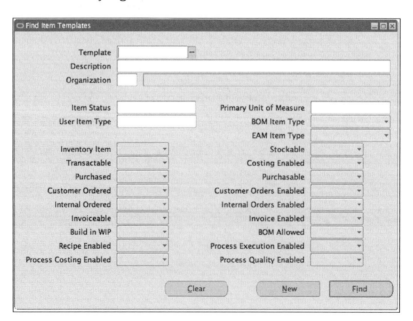

3. From the **Find Item Templates** form, click on **New** button or press *Alt+N*.

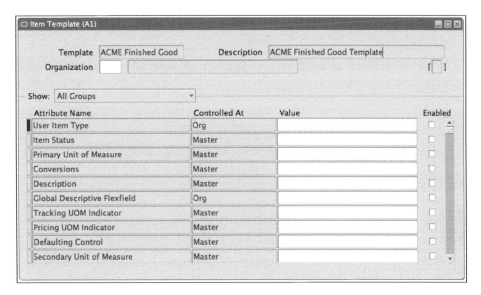

4. In the **Template** field, enter the name of the new template; for example, enter **ACME Finished Good**.

5. In the **Description** field, enter a suitable description, for example, enter **ACME Finished Good Template**.

6. Select **Copy Template** from the **Tools** menu.

7. We can use this form to select the attributes groups that we want to copy from the **Finished Good** template.

8. Click on the **Apply** button.

9. Click on the **Done** button.

10. In the dialog box presented to us, with the message **"Do you want to save the changes you have made?"**, click on the **Yes** button.

How it works...

Item templates can be created from scratch. To make the template creation process easier, Oracle has provided us with a number of seeded templates as a starting point to copy from. We can also combine templates and manually amend the attributes to define our template. When we copy from an existing template, we have choices that determine how the copy will occur.

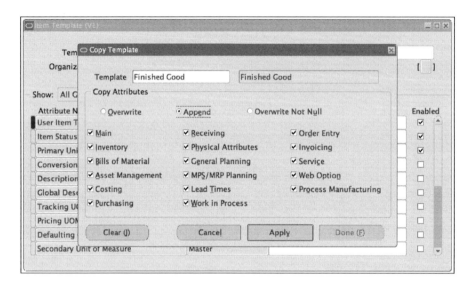

The three main choices are as follows:

1. **Overwrite**: All selected attribute values are copied to the new template and any values that we have manually created will be overwritten.

2. **Append**: Attributes that have no value will be copied across to our template. This mode is useful if you are using a combination of templates.

3. **Overwrite Not Null**: Only the selected attributes that contain values will be copied.

There's more...

Let's amend the template to allow us to automatically populate the template with some default values. Let's create an Item and apply the amended template to the Item.

Amending the template

Let's search for the template and amend the templates to include some of the default values:

1. Search for the **ACME Finished Good** template by navigating to
   Setup | Items | Templates.

2. Enter **ACME Finished Good** in the **Template** field and click on the **Find** button.

3. Click on the **Open** button to view the template.

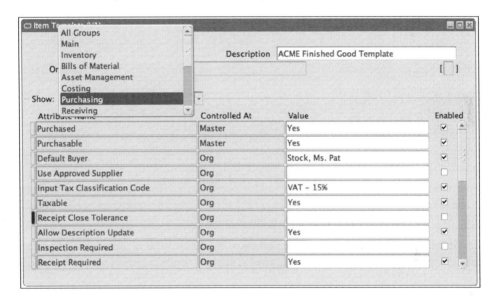

4. In the **Attributes Group** region, select **Purchasing** and enter some default values, for example:

   - **Default Buyer**: **Stock, Ms. Pat**

   - **Input Tax Classification Code**: **VAT-15%**

   - **Taxable**: **Yes**

   - **Allow Description Update**: **Yes**

   - **Receipt Required**: **Yes**

5. Save the template.

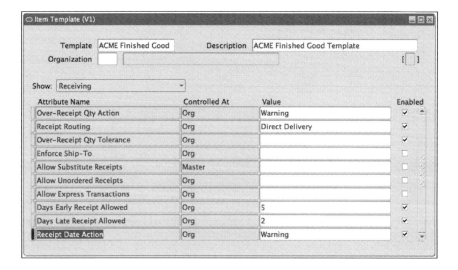

6. In the **Attributes Group** region, select **Receiving** and enter some default values, for example:

   ❑ **Over-Receipt Qty Action: Warning**

   ❑ **Receipt Routing: Direct Delivery**

   ❑ **Days Early Receipt Allowed: 5**

   ❑ **Days Late Receipt Allowed: 2**

   ❑ **Receipt Date Action: Warning**

7. Save the template.

8. In the **Attributes Group** region, select **Invoicing** and enter some default values, for example:

   ❑ **Accounting Rule: Immediate**

   ❑ **Payment Terms: Immediate**

9. Save the template.

Creating an Item and applying the template to the Item

Let's create an Item and apply the template to the Item:

1. Navigate to **Items | Master Items**.

2. Enter the Item code and description.

3. Select **Copy From** in the **Tools** menu.

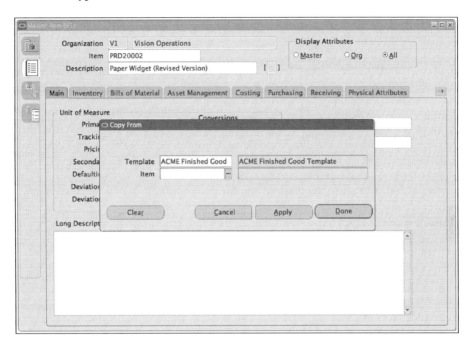

4. Click on the **Apply** button.

5. Click on the **Done** button. This action will validate the template created.

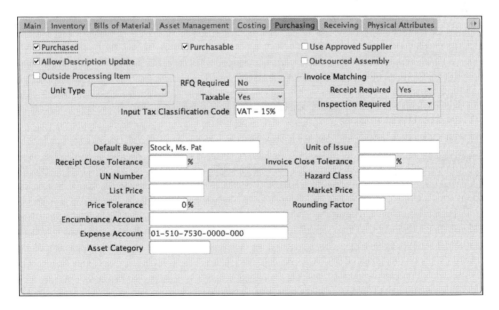

6. Click on the **Purchasing** tab to review the default values of the attributes assigned automatically by the template.

7. Save the Item.

Exploring Item controls

During the creation of Items, we may decide to restrict the use of the Items by controlling Items within an Inventory Organization. When an Item is defined, it is defined in the Item Master Organization and can then be assigned to other Inventory Organizations. Items are then held in Subinventories, which can contain Locators. Locator, Serial number, Lot number, and Revision number within a Subinventory can be used to control Items. In this recipe, we will explore some of the control parameters for Items.

Getting ready

Log in to Oracle E-Business Suite and select the Inventory responsibility.

How to do it...

Let's explore the following Item controls:

1. **Item Status**

2. **Item Attribute**

The Item Status is the status of an Item and it determines the actions that can be performed on an Item. For example, an obsolete Item may not be sold to the customer, but can be used as parts for repairs and can still be stockable. Let's create an Item status for obsolete Items.

1. Navigate to **Setup | Items | Status Code**.

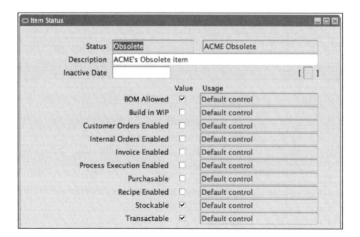

2. In the **Status** field, enter **Obsolete** and **ACME Obsolete** in the **Translated Status** field.

3. Enter a **Description**, for example, **ACME Obsolete** Items.

4. Enable the following attributes:

   ❏ **BOM Allowed**

   ❏ **Stockable**

   ❏ **Transactable**

5. Save the form.

The levels that the attributes can be controlled at are set in the Item Attribute Controls form. Let's look at some of the **Item Attribute Controls**:

1. Navigate to **Setup | Items | Attribute Controls**

2. From the menu, select **View | Query By Example | Enter** (or press *F11* on the keyboard).

3. In the **Group Name** field, enter **Main%.**

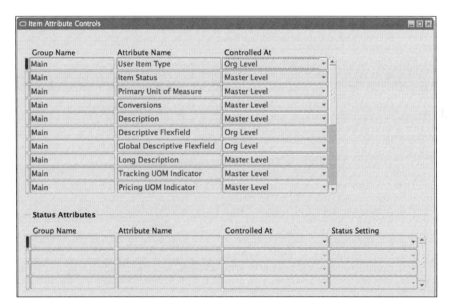

4. From the **Menu**, select **View | Query By Example | Run** (or press *Ctrl+F11* on the keyboard).

5. Observe that some attributes are controlled at the **Master Level** and some at the **Org Level**.

6. Close the form.

There's more...

Items are stored in a Subinventory and can be controlled using a locator. Items can be identified by lot and by serial numbers.

Storing Items by Subinventories

Subinventories are distinct separations of Items within an Inventory Organization. Subinventories can be physical or logical. Items within an Inventory Organization must reside in a Subinventory.

Transactions are performed from the Subinventories. Examples of Subinventories include: finished goods, van, stores, staging area, and fast moving goods. Let's create a finished goods Subinventory and restrict an Item to the Subinventory.

1. Navigate to **Setup | Organizations | Subinventories**.

2. Click on the **New** button.

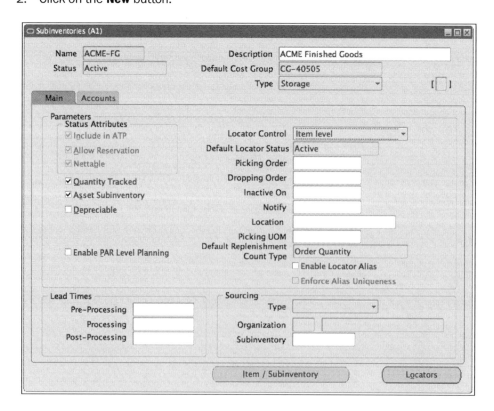

3. In the **Name** field, enter **ACME-FG**.

4. In the **Description**, enter **ACME Finished Goods**.

5. In the **Locator Control** field, select **Item level**. This will enable the Inventory transactions for this Subinventory to use locator control, which we define at the Item level.

6. Save the record.

Let's restrict an **Item** to the **Subinventory**:

1. Navigate to **Items | Organization Items**.

2. Search for the **PRD20001** Item.

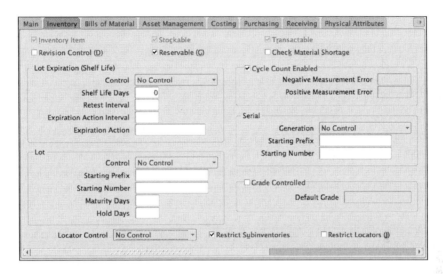

3. Select the **Inventory** tab and select the **Restrict Subinventories** checkbox.

4. Save the record.

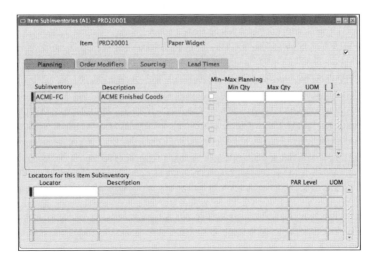

5. In the **Tools** menu, select **Items Subinventories**.

6. Select **ACME-FG** in the Subinventory field.

7. Save the record.

Storing Items by locators

Stock locators identify the physical areas where Items are stored. Additional controls can be placed on the Items in stock locators. For example, we can control the shelf life of an Item with stock locators. Stock locators are usually defined as Row, Rack, and Bin. Let's create three stock locators for the ACME Finished Goods Subinventory and restrict an Item by locator control:

1. Navigate to **Setup | Organizations | Subinventories**.

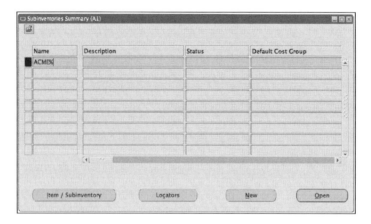

2. Search for the **ACME-FG** Subinventory (press *F11* on the keyboard, and enter the search mask **ACME%**, then press *Ctrl+F11* on the keyboard).

3. Click on the **Locator** button to enter the locator details.

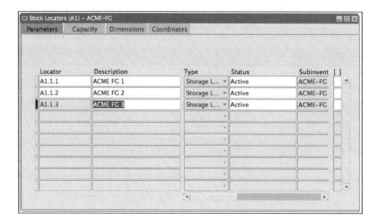

4. Enter **A1.1.1** in the **Locator** field.

5. In the **Description** field, enter **ACME FG 1**.

6. In the **Type** field, select **Storage Locator**.

7. Enter another row for **A1.1.2**, **ACME FG 2**, with **Storage Locator** in the **Type** field.

8. Repeat for **A1.1.3**, **ACME FG 3**, with **Storage Locator** in the **Type** field.

9. Save the record.

The structure of the stock locator is defined in the stock locator Flexfield structure and can be defined to fit your business requirements. Locator Control can be "prespecified" before they are used or can be defined dynamically as Items are received or shipped.

Let's restrict an Item to the **Locator**:

1. Navigate to **Items | Organization Items**.

2. Search for the **PRD20001** Item.

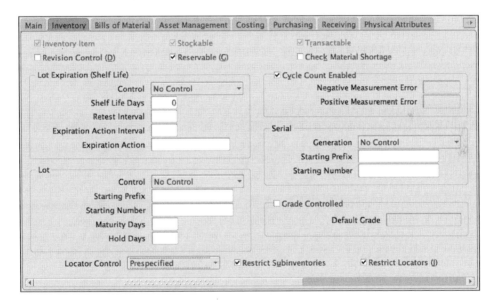

3. Select the **Inventory** tab, select the **Restrict Locators** checkbox, and then select the **Locator Control** as **Prespecified**.

4. Save the record.

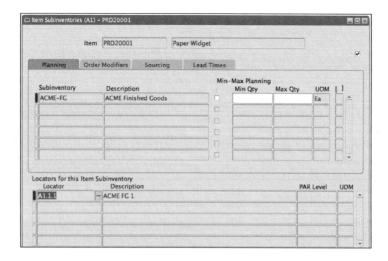

5. In the **Tools** menu, select **Items Subinventories**.
6. Select **A1.1.1** in the **Locator** field.
7. Save the record.

Identifying Items by lot control

A lot of numbers can be used to identify Items that share the same specifications. For example, lot numbers can be used to specify the expiry period of an Item. Let's look at how to use lot numbers to control Items. We will impose a shelf life of **30** days on the Item and assign lot numbers to the Item:

1. Navigate to **Items | Organization Items**.
2. Search for the **PRD20001** Item.

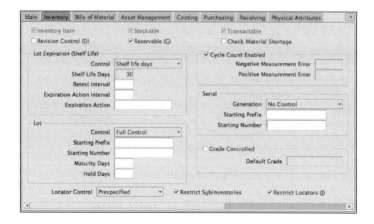

3. Select the **Inventory** tab.

4. In the **Lot Expiration (Shelf Life)** region, select the **Control** field and select **Shelf Life Days**.

5. Enter **30** as the number of days.

6. In the **Lot** region, select **Full Control** in the **Control** field.

7. Save the record.

Tracking Items using serial control

Serial numbers can be used to track an Item. A serial number is assigned to each unit of the Item, if serial control is used:

1. Navigate to **Items | Organization Items**.

2. Search for the **PRD20001** Item.

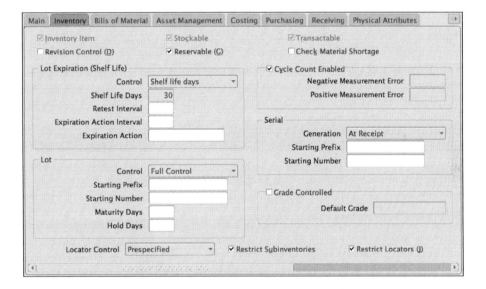

3. Select the **Inventory** tab.

4. In the **Serial** region, select the **Generation** field, and select **At Receipt**. This will allow us to specify the format of the serial numbers at the time of receipt.

5. Save the record.

Controlling Items using revisions

Items can have versions. Item versions are controlled using revisions. For example, we can decide to make the **PRD20002** revision controlled, and have another version of the Item. Let's change the attribute to revision controlled and add a revision **B** to the Item:

1. Navigate to **Items | Organization Items**.

2. Search for the Item **PRD20002**.

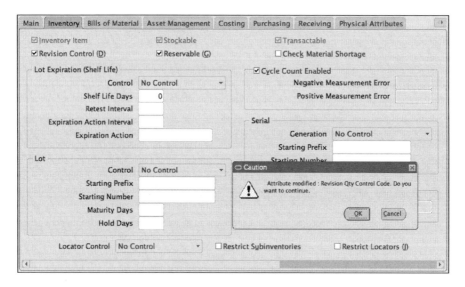

3. In the **Inventory** tab, enable the **Revision Control** checkbox.

4. In the displayed message, select **OK**.

5. Save the Item.

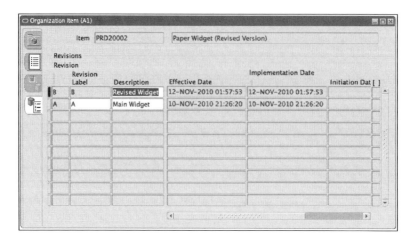

6. From the **Tools** menu, select **Revisions**.

7. Add a line for **Revision B** of the Item with the description **Revised Widget**.

8. Save the record.

Adjusting Items in Inventory

Item quantities can be adjusted in Inventory. In this recipe, we will use miscellaneous transactions to adjust Items. Let's try to enter transactions on some of the controls we have set up. We will try and enter a **Miscellaneous Transaction** for five paper widgets into Inventory.

How to do it...

1. Navigate to **Transactions | Miscellaneous Transactions**.

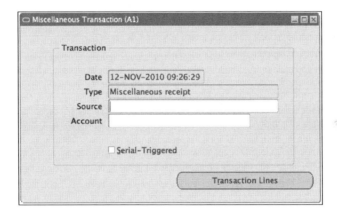

2. In the **Type** field, select **Miscellaneous receipt** from the list of values.

3. Click on the **Transaction Lines** button to enter the receipt.

4. Search for the **PRD20001** Item in the Item field.

5. Select the **Subinventory** list of values and the field should be automatically populated with **ACME-FG**.

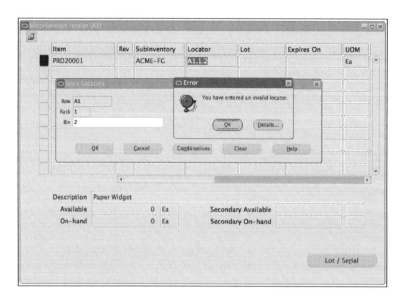

6. In the **Locator** field, enter **A1.1.2**.

7. The system should display an **Error** message to indicate that an invalid locator has been entered.

8. Click on **OK** and enter **A1.1.1**–the system should accept this value.

9. Enter a value of **5** in the **Quantity** field.

10. In the account field, enter **01-000-1410-0000-000**. This is the account that will be charged for the Inventory transaction.

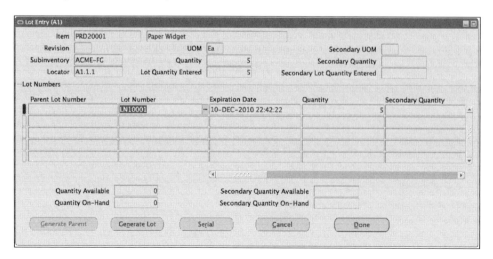

11. Select the **Lot / Serial** button.

12. Enter the **Lot** number–**LN10001**.

 The expiration date is generated based on the setting in the Item definition.

13. Enter the quantity of **5**.

14. Click on the **Serial** button.

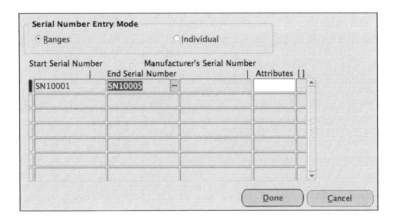

15. Enter **SN10001** in the **Start Serial Number** field and press *Tab* on the keyboard.

16. The **SN10005** should be automatically populated in the **End Serial Number** field.

17. Click on the **Done** button.

18. Click on the **Done** button again in the next screen.

19. Save the record.

There's more...

Let's search for the Items in Inventory.

Searching for Items

We will use the material workbench to search for the Items:

1.   Navigate to **On-hand | Availability | On-hand Quantity**.

2.   Enter **PRD20001** in the **Item / Revision** field.

3.   Click on the **Find** button.

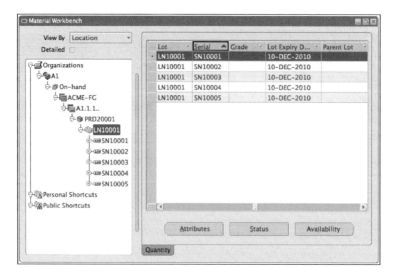

4. **Expand** the **Organizations** tree to show **LN10001.**

5. Review the Item details.

6. Close the form.

Classifying Items

Items are grouped into logical classifications through categories. Categories can be further grouped into category sets. A default category set can be assigned to a functional area. When an Item is created, it is automatically added to the default category set.

The groupings are mainly used for reporting purposes. Let's look at how to classify Items using categories.

How to do it...

Let's list the steps required to create category codes:

1. Navigate to **Setup | Items | Categories | Category Codes**.

2. Click on the **New** button to enter the **Category**.

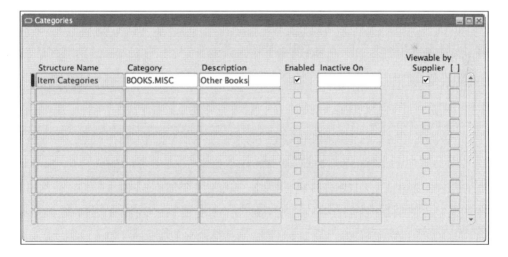

3. In the **Structure Name**, select **Item Categories**.

4. In the **Category** field, enter **BOOKS.MISC**.

5. In the **Description** field, enter **Other Books**.

6. Save the record.

Let's now create the **Category Set**, add the **Category Codes** to a new set called **ACME Books**, and assign it to the **PRD20001** Item:

1. Navigate to **Setup | Items | Categories | Category Sets**.

2. Click on the **New** button to enter the category set.

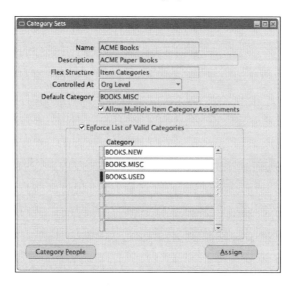

3. In the **Name** field, enter **ACME Books**.

4. Enter a description, for example, **ACME Paper Books**.

5. Select **Item Categories** for **Flex Structure**.

6. Select **Controlled At** as the **Org level**.

7. Enter **BOOKS.MISC** as the **Default Category**.

8. Select the checkbox **Allow Multiple Item Category Assignments**.

9. Add the following **Category Codes** to the list:

   ❑ **BOOKS.MISC**

   ❑ **BOOKS.NEW**

   ❑ **BOOKS.USED**

10. Save the record.

Let's now assign the categories to the **PRD20001** Item:

1. Navigate to **Items | Organization Items**.

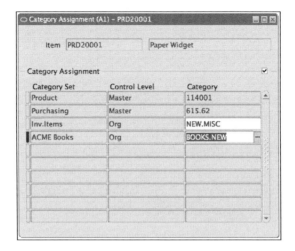

2. From the **Menu**, select **Tools** and then **Categories**.
3. Select **ACME Books** in the **Category Set**.
4. Enter **BOOKS.NEW** in the **Category** field.
5. Save the record.

How it works...

The structure of the Item category is defined in the Item Flexfield structure and the values are held in the individual Value Sets. The combination of the individual values forms the category code. For example, the structure we used previously is made of two segments, defined in the Flexfield structure. The segments are Family and Class. BOOKS is a value in Family and MISC, NEW, and USED are individual values in Class.

There's more...

Let's look at how the Item Flexfield structure is constructed and how values are added to the structure.

Viewing the Item Categories structure

1. Navigate to **Setup | Flexfields | Key | Segments**.

2. Search for **Item Categories** in the **Flexfield Title** field.
3. Select the **ITEM_CATEGORIES** code.
4. Click on the **Segments** button.

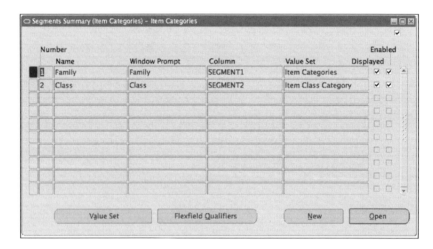

5. The **Items Categories** we have used has two segments, namely, **Family** and **Class**. The **Item Category** structure can be configured to have a maximum of 20 segments.

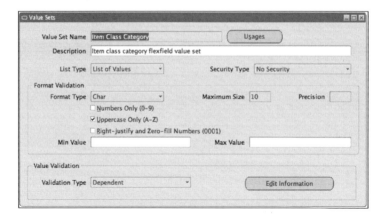

6. Click on the **Value Set** button to view the validation format of the data that can be stored in the **Value Set**. The **Class Segment** uses the **Item Class Category** value set, this segment has a **Validation Type** of **Dependent**. It is dependent on another segment for the validation of the values that can be stored.

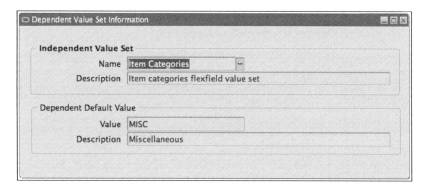

7. Click on the **Edit Information** button to view the independent value set that it depends on. This is the Item Categories value set.

8. Close the forms.

Viewing the values in the structure

Let's look at the values in the structure. We are also going to add a new value for Rare Books in the Item category. We are also going to add the new code to the category codes:

1. Navigate to **Setup | Flexfields | Key | Values**.

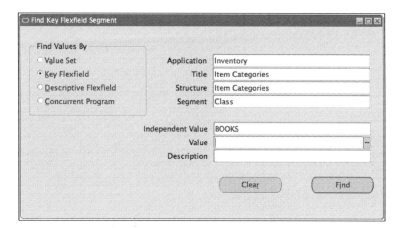

2. Enter the following search criteria:

   ❑ In the **Application** field, select **Inventory**.

   ❑ In the **Title** field, enter **Item Categories**.

   ❑ In the **Structure**, enter **Item Categories**.

   ❑ In the **Dependent Segment**, enter **Class**.

   ❑ In the **Independent Value**, enter **Books**.

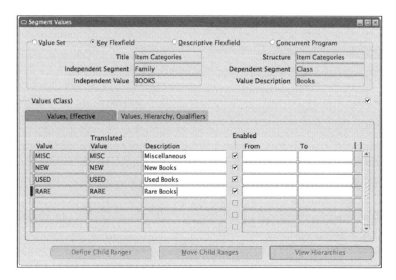

3. Click on the **Find** button.

4. In the **Value** field, enter **RARE**, and **Rare Books** in the **Description**.

5. Save the record and click on **OK** in the note to compile the record.

6. Navigate to **Setup | Items | Categories | Category Codes**.

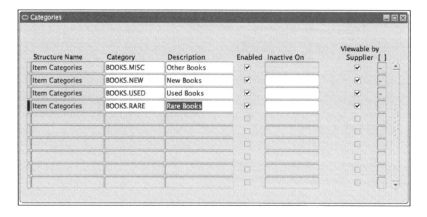

7. Click on the **New** button.

8. Search for the existing **BOOKS** codes by using **BOOK%** as the search criteria in the **Category** field.

9. Add a new line for **BOOKS.RARE** and **Rare Books** as the **Description**.

10. Save the record.

Items can also be grouped into logical catalogs. Let's look at how this is done.

Creating catalogs

Catalogs are used to add descriptive information to Items that share common characteristics. For example, paper can have size, color, and weight. Let's look at how to create Item catalogs for **ACME Books**, with descriptive elements for size, color, and weight:

1. Navigate to **Setup | Items | Catalog Groups**.

2. From the **Menu**, select **File** and then **New**.

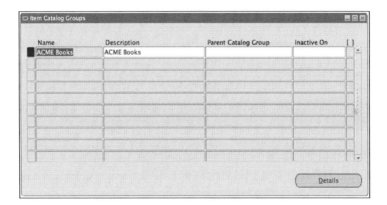

3. In the **Name** field, enter **ACME Books**, and enter **ACME Books** in the **Description**.

4. Click on the **Details** button.

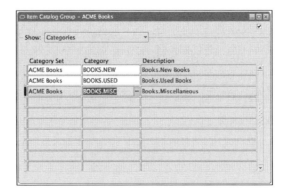

5. Enter the following **Descriptive Elements**:

   ❏ **Size**

   ❏ **Color**

   ❏ **Weight**

6. Select **Categories** and enter the following categories for **ACME Books**:

   ❏ **BOOKS.NEW**

   ❏ **BOOKS.USED**

   ❏ **BOOKS.MISC**

7. Save the record.

Assigning a catalog description to an Item

Let's find the **PRD20002** Item and assign the catalog:

1. Navigate to **Items | Master Items**.

2. Search for the **PRD20002** Item.

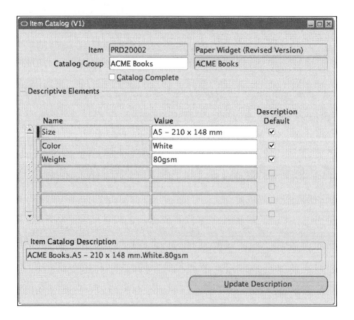

3. Select **Catalog** from the **Tools** menu.

4. In the **Catalog Group** field, select **ACME Books**.

5. Enter the following in the **Descriptive Elements** field:

   ❑ **A5 - 210 x 148 mm** as the value for the **Size** field

   ❑ The **Color** as **White**

   ❑ The **Weight** as **80gsm**

6. Select the **Update Description** button to change the Item description.

7. Save the record.

Searching for Items using catalog attributes

Let's search for Items using the catalog attributes:

1. Navigate to **Items | Items Search**.

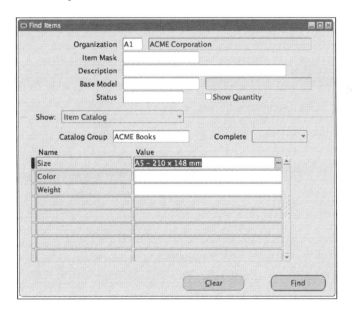

2. In the **Show** region, select **Item Catalog.**

3. In the **Catalog Group** field, select **ACME Books**.

4. In the **Size** field, select **A5 - 210 x 148 mm.**

5. Click on the **Find** button.

6. The **Item Search** form displays the record based on the catalog attributes.

2

Purchasing Items in Procurement

In this chapter, we will cover:

- ▶ Raising Requisitions for Items
- ▶ Approving Requisitions
- ▶ Creating Suppliers
- ▶ Creating Purchase Orders
- ▶ Receiving Items
- ▶ Reviewing Procurement Accounting Transactions

Introduction

Items that are sold in an organization are manufactured or purchased. In this chapter, we will look at how to purchase Items in procurement. Let's start by looking at the procurement process.

The following diagram details the procurement process:

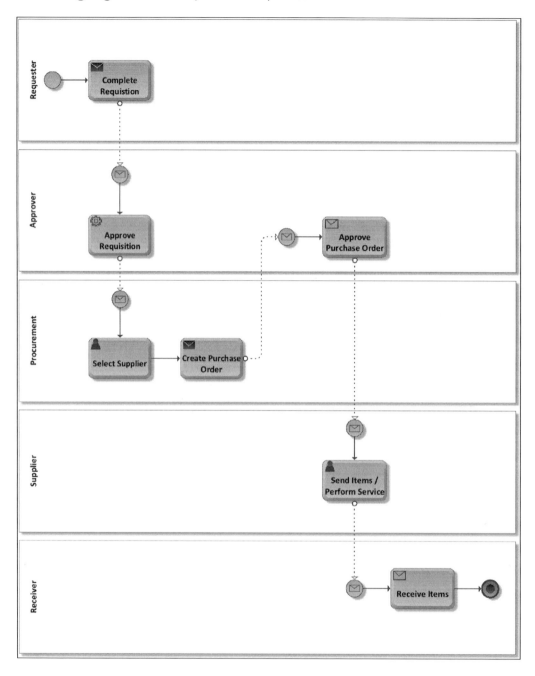

1. **Requester** completes the requisition based on demand. Requisition creation can be automated through the Requisition Import program, based on demand from various sources. For example, drop shipments in Order Management and min-max planning in Inventory.

2. The **Approver** approves the requisition.

3. The **Supplier** is selected based on business sourcing rules, including **Request for Quotations** (**RFQ**). If the supplier does not exist, a new supplier is created.

4. The **Procurement** team (buyers) creates the purchase order.

5. The **Approver** approves the purchase order. The purchase order is created and sent to the **Supplier**.

6. The **Supplier** receives the purchase order, and fulfils the order by sending the Items. If the purchase order is for a service, the service is provided to the organization.

7. The **Receiver** receives the Items and enters the receipts on the system.

Let's look at how requisitions are raised for Items.

Raising requisitions for Items

Oracle iProcurement provides us with the functionality to create requisitions. Requisitions can be manually created from the purchasing or iProcurement modules. Requisitions can be imported from external systems and also generated from other modules including Order Management, Work in Process, and Inventory.

In this recipe, we will raise a requisition with two lines:

1. Catalog Requisition: 100 Items of PRD20001 Paper Widgets

2. Non-Catalog Requisition: Consulting services relating to the Widgets for a fixed amount of $150

We can raise a requisition for a catalog and a non-catalog Item in an iProcurement.

Getting ready

Log in to Oracle E-Business Suite R12 with the username and password assigned to you by the system administrator. If you are working on the Vision demonstration database, you can use OPERATIONS/WELCOME as the USERNAME/PASSWORD.

How to do it...

Let's list the steps required to create a requisition:

1. Navigate to the **iProcurement** responsibility.

2. Select the **Main Store**.

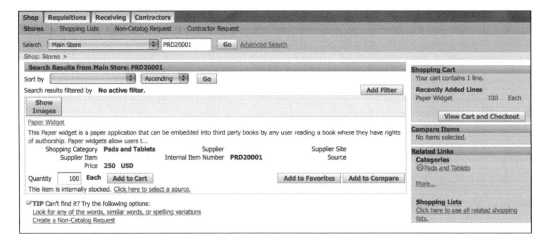

3. Search for the **PRD20001** Item and click on the **Go** button.

4. If the Item can be sourced internally, a link will be enabled that will allow the user to select the source. It is also possible to have a blanket agreement with a supplier to supply the goods at a specific price.

5. Enter the **Quantity** of **100** and click on the **Add to Cart** button.

6. Let's create the requisition line for the consulting services. We will create a non-catalog request for services billed by amount.

7. Select the **Non-Catalog Request** link to enter the details of fitting the Item at a fixed price.

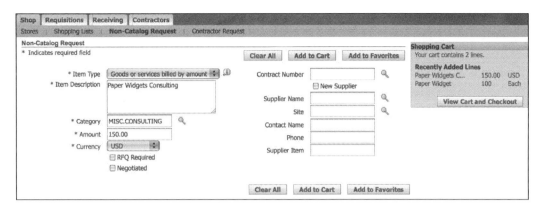

8. The following are the three Item types used for non-catalog requisitions:

    ❑ Goods billed by quantity, for example, 10 widgets at 250 USD each

    ❑ Services billed by quantity; for example, 10 hours of service at a rate of 50 USD an hour

    ❑ Goods or services billed by amount, for example, for a fixed amount of 500 USD for services rendered

9. In the **Item Type** field, select **Goods or services billed by amount** in the drop-down list, because our request is for a fixed amount for service.

10. In the **Item Description** field, enter the description of the service. For example, **Paper Widgets Consulting**.

11. Enter the **Category**, for example, **MISC.CONSULTING**.

12. Enter the **Amount**, for example, **150.00**.

13. If the details of the supplier are known, the supplier details can be added to the requisition. It is also possible to have a Contract Agreement with a supplier that can be attached to the details of the Non-Catalog requisition.

14. Click on the **View Cart and Checkout** button.

15. Click on the **Checkout** button.

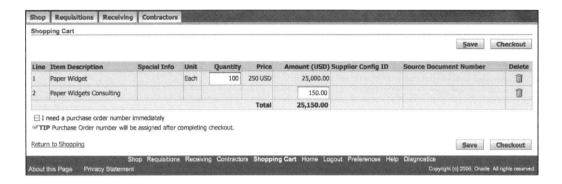

16. In the **Requisition Description** field, for example, enter **100 Paper Widgets**.

17. Review the **Need-by-Date**, **Requester**, and the **Deliver-To Location**.

18. Click on the **Edit Lines** button to review the line details.

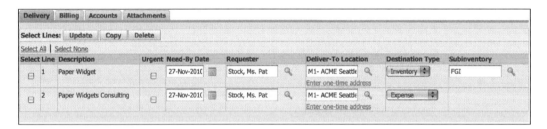

19. In the **Delivery Tab**, details of the **Destination Type** of **Inventory** and **Expense** with the **Subinventory** of **FGI** are displayed for the delivery of the Items.

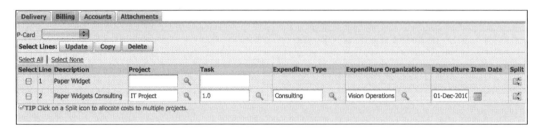

20. Click on the **Billing Tab** to view the allocation to **Project** details.

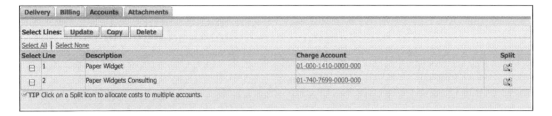

21. Click on the **Accounts Tab** to view the **Charge Account** allocated to the transaction.

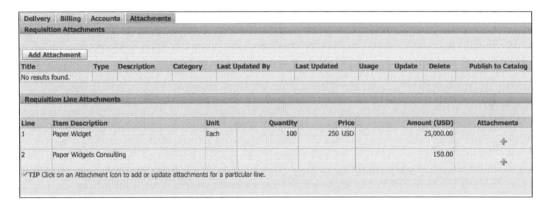

22. In the **Attachments** tab, we can add attachments at the line level.

23. Click on the **Next** button.

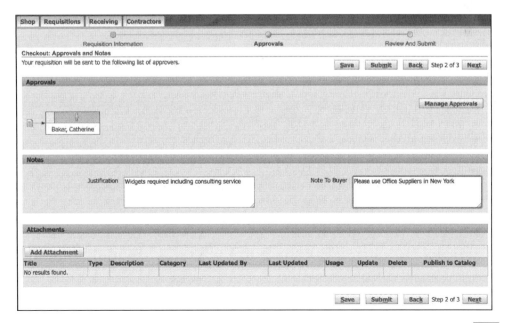

24. In the **Approvals** section, the approval details are shown. The requisition needs to be approved by **Baker, Catherine**.

25. In the **Notes** section, enter the **Justification**, for example, **Widgets required including consulting service**.

26. Enter the **Note To Buyer**, for example, **Please use Office Suppliers in New York**.

27. Click on the **Next** button.

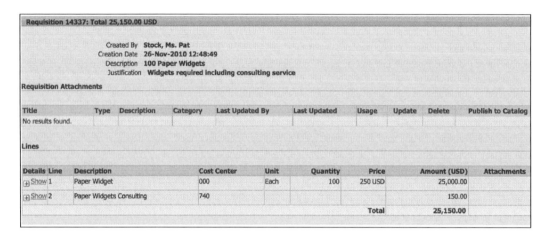

28. Review the **Requisition** details.

29. Click on the **Submit** button.

30. **Confirmation** of the **Requisition** is displayed. This includes the **Requisition** number **14337** and the submission to **Baker, Catherine** as the approver.

31. Click on the **Continue Shopping** button to proceed.

How it works...

Requisitions can be created for catalog and non-catalog Items. A catalog Item can be loaded directly from an XML file, CSV file, or by punchout (a link to an external source for automatic updates to the catalogs) to the supplier's site. We can also create a catalog requisition for Expense Items, Assets, and Items held in Inventory. If an Item is not found in a catalog, a non-catalog requisition may be created.

There's more...

Now let's explore the following relevant tasks concerning the creation of requisitions:

- ▶ The use of smart forms to create requisitions
- ▶ Review of the account generator to create the charge account codes
- ▶ The management of requisitions including copying, correcting, and canceling requisitions

Let's start by looking at smart forms.

Smart forms

Smart forms are templates for non-catalog requisitions that are pre-populated with values for a type of purchase. For example, smart forms for travel expenses, legal services, and so on. The requester only enters some information to complete the line entry. Additional information can also be entered into smart forms through information templates.

Let's assume that our company has a contract with **Jones, Gray, and Associates**, for the supply of legal services. A contract agreement No **4514** is already in place for these services. We are going to enter a requisition for legal services for **3** hours of work at $**150** per hour. We also require **Alan Johnson**, a consultant from the **United Kingdom**, to supply these services. A smart form has already been created for this type of service.

1. Navigate to the **iProcurement** responsibility.

Legal Services
* Indicates required field

| Clear All | Add to Cart | Add to Favorites |

Request Type	Legal Consulting
Item Type	**Services billed by quantity**
* Item Description	Requisition for Tax Consulting
* Category	SERVICES.LEGAL
* Quantity	3
* Unit of Measure	Hour
* Rate per Unit	150
Currency	**USD**
	☐ RFQ Required
	☐ Negotiated

Contract Number	4514
	☐ New Supplier
Supplier Name	**Jones, Gray, and Associates**
Site	**JGA MAIN**
Contact Name	Gray,Randy
Phone	212 435-5435
Supplier Item	

Applicant Information

* Name	Alan Johnson
* Country of Birth	United Kingdom
* Gender	Male

| * Date of Birth | 02-Jan-1980 |
| * Phone Number | +44987230081 |

Legal Consultation

| * Description of Issues | Filing of Tax Accounts |
| * Type of Consultation | Taxes |

| Clear All | Add to Cart | Add to Favorites |

2. In the **Main Store** field, select the **Legal Services** link.

3. Select the **Legal Consulting** link.

4. Review the pre-populated values in the main area of the smart form. The **Supplier Name** and **Site** details are automatically populated and cannot be changed.

5. Enter **3** in the **Quantity** field.

6. Change the **Rate per Unit** to **150**.

7. Review the additional information section. This includes the **Applicant Information** and the **Legal Consultation** section.

8. In the **Name** field, enter **Alan Johnson**.

9. In the **Country of Birth** field, enter **United Kingdom**.

10. In the **Gender** field, select **Male**.

11. In the **Date of Birth** field, enter **02-Jan-1980**.

12. In the **Phone Number** field, enter **+44987230081**.

13. In the **Description of Issues** field, enter **Filing of Tax Accounts**.

14. In the **Type of Consultation** field, select **Taxes**.

15. Click the **Add to Cart** button.

16. Click on the **View Cart and Checkout** button.

17. Click on the **Submit** button.

18. The **Confirmation** page is displayed with the requisition number **14340**; click on **Continue Shopping** to return to the main store.

Accounting codes

When requisitions are created, accounting codes are automatically generated based on the rules in the Account Generator workflow engine. The default values for Inventory and Asset Items are based on the Item and Subinventory.

The Account Generator does not use the Inventory and Asset account rules if the Item is an expense Item. The rules for generating expense Items are based on the Expense Accounts Rules, Employee Default Charge Account, and Favorite Charge Account.

Let's look at how the expense accounts are determined:

1. Navigate to the **Purchasing** responsibility.

2. Navigate to **Setup | Financials | Accounting | Expense Account Rules**.

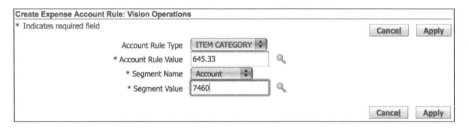

3. Click on the **Create** button.

4. In the **Account Rule Type** field, select **ITEM CATEGORY**.

5. In the **Account Rule Value** field, enter **645.33**.

6. In the **Segment Name** field, select **Account**.

7. In the **Segment Value** field, enter **7460**.

8. Click on **Apply**.

Let's create a non-catalog requisition to see the default account that is used:

1. Navigate to the **iProcurement** responsibility.

2. Select the main store.

3. Select **Non-Catalog Request**.

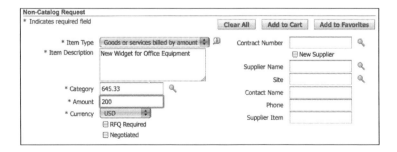

4. In the **Item Type** field, select **Goods or services billed by amount.**

5. In the **Item Description** field, enter **New Widget for Office Equipment**.

6. In the **Category** field, enter **645.33**.

7. In the **Amount** field, enter **200**.

8. Click on the **Add to Cart** button.

9. Click on the **View Cart and Checkout** button.

10. In the **Shopping Cart** screen, click on the **Checkout** button.

11. In the **Checkout** screen, click on **Edit Lines**.

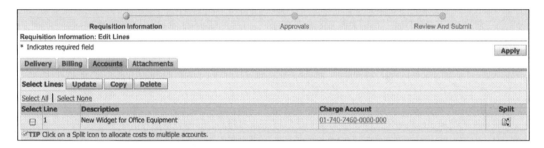

12. Select the **Accounts** tab.

13. The **Charge Account** uses **01-740-7460-0000-000** for the account segment.

The Cost centre segment defaults from the Purchase Order Information in the employee record.

We will now navigate to the employee record and change the expense account:

1. Select the **Human Resources** responsibility.

2. Navigate to **People | Enter and Maintain**.

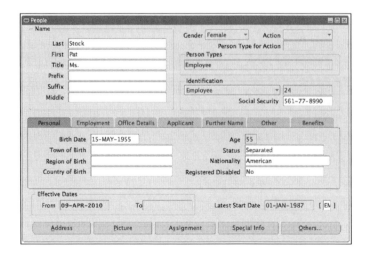

3. In the find **People** form, search for the details of **Pat Stock.**

4. Select the **Assignment** button.

5. Select the **Purchase Order Information** tab.

6. The **Default Expense Account** is **01-740-7699-0000-000**.

7. The account generator uses the department segment **740** to determine the value of the cost center segment.

8. Change the value to **01-730-7699-0000-000**.

9. Click on the **Update** button.

10. Save the record.

Let's create a non-catalog requisition to see the default account:

1. Navigate to the **iProcurement** responsibility.

2. Select the main store.

3. Select **Non-Catalog Request**.

4. In the **Item Type** field, select **Goods or services billed by amount**.

5. In the **Description** field, enter **New Widget for Finance**.

6. In the **Category** field, enter **645.33**.

7. In the **amount** field, enter **200**.

8. Click on the **Add to Cart** button.

9. Click on the **View Cart and Checkout** button.

10. In the **Shopping Cart** screen, click on the **Checkout** button.

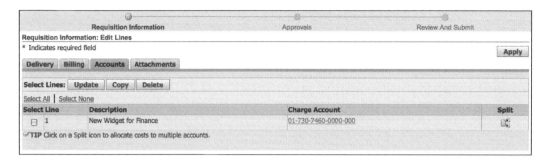

11. In the **Checkout** screen, click on **Edit Lines**.

12. Select the **Accounts** tab.

13. The **Charge Account** uses **730** for the department segment.

If no rules are specified for any of the segments, the account generator uses the primary account in the user preferences to generate the default account:

1. Navigate to the **iProcurement** responsibility.

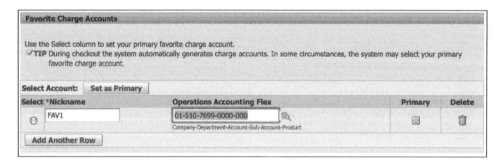

2. Select the **Preferences** link on the homepage.

3. Select **iProcurement Preferences** in the side navigation.

4. Review the **01-510-7699-0000-000** account in the **Favorite Charge Accounts** region.

Let's now look at how to manage requisitions.

Copying a requisition

We need to create another requisition for Legal Consulting. Let's copy an existing requisition number, 14340:

1. Search for requisition number **14340**.

2. Navigate to the **iProcurement** responsibility.

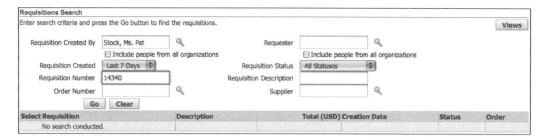

3. In the **Requisitions** tab, select the **Search** button.

4. In the **Requisitions Search** form, enter **14340** in the **Requisition Number** field.

5. Click on the **Go** button.

6. Copy the requisition to the **Shopping Cart**.

7. Select the requisition and click on the **Copy To Cart** button.

8. The requisition is added to the shopping cart.

9. Click on the **Checkout** button in the **Shopping Cart** form.

10. Click on the **Submit** button.

11. The new **Requisition 14343** is created.

Correcting a requisition

We need to correct the requisition number **14343** for Legal Consulting. Let's amend the rate to $1000 per hour:

1. Navigate to the **iProcurement** responsibility.

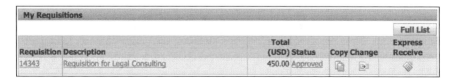

2. In the **My Requisitions** region, click on the **Change** icon.

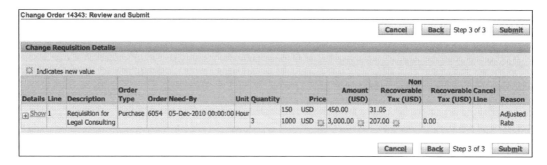

3. In the **Change Requisition Details** form, change the **Price** to **1000** and enter a **Reason**, for example, **Adjusted Rate**.

4. Click on the **Next** button.

5. Click on **Next** in the **Mange Approvals** screen.

6. Review the **Change Order**.

7. Click on the **Submit** button.

8. The requisition is amended.

Canceling a requisition

We need to cancel the requisition number **14343** for legal consulting. A requisition can be canceled before it is placed on a purchase order. If a requisition is placed on a purchase order, we can only cancel the requisition lines.

1. Navigate to the **iProcurement** responsibility.

2. In the **My Requisitions** region, click on the **14343 Requisition** link.

3. Click on the **Cancel Requisition** button.

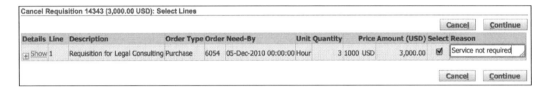

4. In the **Cancel Requisition** form, click the **Select** checkbox, and enter a **Reason**, for example, **Service not required.**

5. Click on the **Continue** button.

6. Click on the **Submit** button.

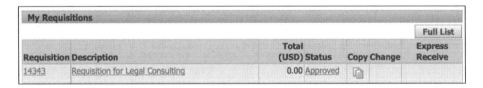

7. The requisition is canceled with the total amount of USD **0.00 ,** as shown on the requisition.

See also

Creating Items recipe in this chapter

Creating Purchase Orders recipe in Chapter 2, Purchasing Items in Procurement

Approving requisitions

Requisitions are approved based on the approval rules. In this recipe, we will look at how to approve requisitions.

The requisition number 14337 needs to be approved by Catherine Baker.

Getting ready

We need to log in as the approver to approve the requisition. If you are using the VISION demonstration database, log in with CBAKER/WELCOME as the USERNAME/PASSWORD.

How to do it...

Let's list the steps required to complete the task:

1. Select the **iProcurement** responsibility.

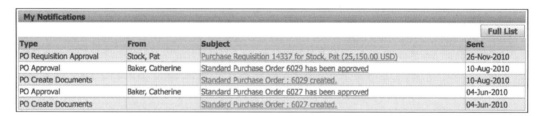

My Notifications			
			Full List
Type	**From**	**Subject**	**Sent**
PO Requisition Approval	Stock, Pat	Purchase Requisition 14337 for Stock, Pat (25,150.00 USD)	26-Nov-2010
PO Approval	Baker, Catherine	Standard Purchase Order 6029 has been approved	10-Aug-2010
PO Create Documents		Standard Purchase Order : 6029 created.	10-Aug-2010
PO Approval	Baker, Catherine	Standard Purchase Order 6027 has been approved	04-Jun-2010
PO Create Documents		Standard Purchase Order : 6027 created.	04-Jun-2010

2. In the **My Notifications** region, select the link to the requisition **Purchase Requisition 14337 for Stock, Pat (25,150.00 USD)**.

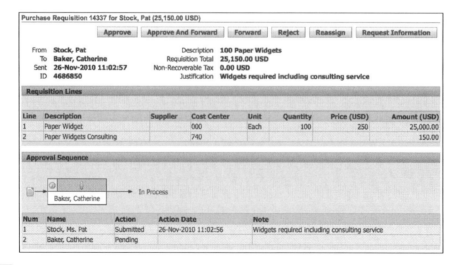

3. We now have the option to **Approve, Approve And Forward, Forward, Reject, Reassign**, or **Request Information**.

4. Review the requisition and click on the **Approve** button to approve the requisition.

Type	From	Subject	Sent
PO Requisition Approval	Baker, Catherine	Purchase Requisition 14337 has been approved	27-Nov-2010

5. A notification is sent to the requester of the approval of the requisition.

How it works...

Purchase requisition approvals are based on a hierarchy, which determines how the documents flow, based on approval limits and controls. Approvals can be routed based on employee/supervisor relationship or positions. Approval rules can also be defined using the Oracle Approvals Management Engine for purchase requisitions.

When a document is created, depending on the approval routing and the controls, the document will be routed for approval. Once the document is approved, the requisition is available to be used in the creation of a purchase order.

There's more...

Let's explore how the Position Hierarchy was set up.

The approvers are employees of the organization. Let's start by reviewing the employee setup for Pat Stock.

Reviewing the employee setup

1. Select the **Human Resources** responsibility.

2. Navigate to **People | Enter and Maintain**.

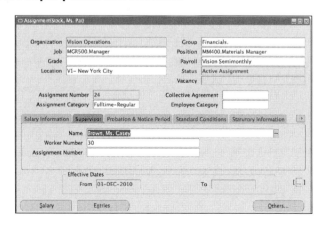

3. In the find **Person**, search for **Pat Stock.**

4. Select the **Assignment** button.

5. Pat Stock's **Position** is **MM400.Materials Manager**.

6. Select the **Supervisor** tab.

7. The supervisor's **Name** is **Ms Casey Brown**. This is used for employee / supervisor-based approvals.

The employee needs to be placed in a Position Hierarchy called Materials. Let's review the Position Hierarchy setup.

Reviewing the Position Hierarchy

1. Select the **Purchasing** responsibility.

2. Navigate to **Setup | Personnel | Position Hierarchy**.

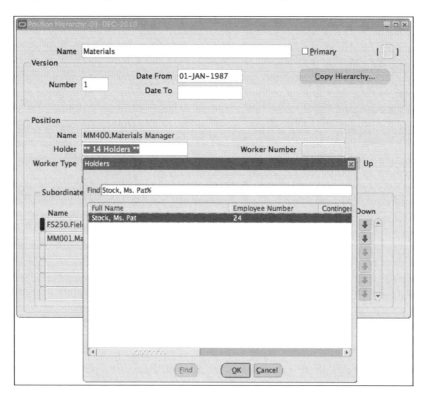

3. Search for the **Materials** in the **Name** field.

4. Search for **MM400.Materials Manager** in the **Name** field, in the **Position** region.

5. There are **14 Holders** of the position.

6. Search for **Stock%** in the field. **Stock, Ms. Pat** is retrieved as one of the holders.

Let's review the Purchase Requisition document type.

Reviewing the document types

1. Navigate to **Setup | Purchasing | Document Types**.

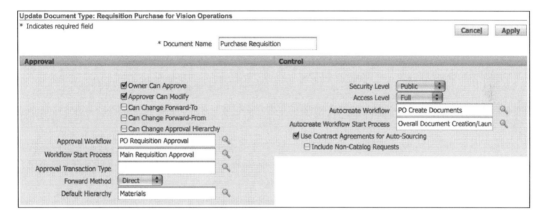

2. In the **Update Document Type** form, select the update icon for Purchase Requisition.

3. Review the details in the **Approvals** section.

4. The **Default Hierarchy** is **Materials**.

Reviewing the approval groups

This is where the authorization rules are set up. They can be set up for the following object types: Document Total, Account Range, Item Range, Item Category Range, and Location.

1. Navigate to **Setup | Approvals | Approval Groups**.

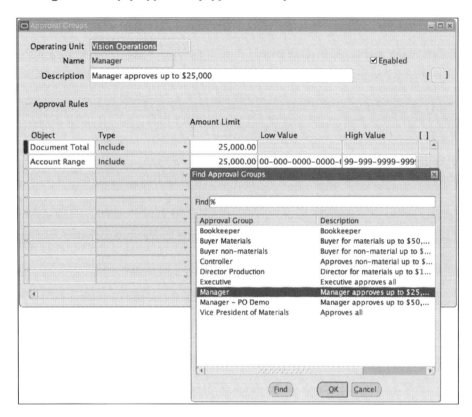

2. Click on the **Find** icon and select the **Approval Group** of **Manager.**

3. The **Amount Limit** of **25,000** in the **Document Total** field and **The Account Range** includes all account ranges.

Reviewing the approvals assignment

1. Navigate to **Setup | Approvals | Approvals Assignment**.

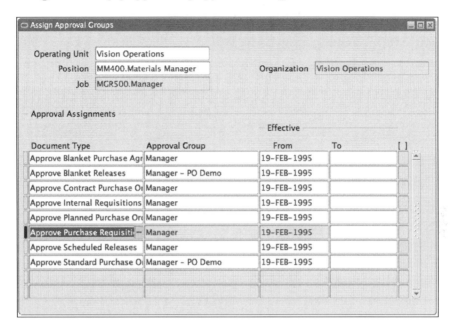

2. In the **Operating Unit** field, select **Vision Operations**.

3. In the **Position** field, select **MM400.Materials Manager**.

4. The **Document Type**, **Approve Purchase Requisitions** has the **Approval Group** of **Manger** assigned to it.

Creating suppliers

Suppliers are required for the creation of a purchase order. In this recipe, we will create a supplier called Office Widgets Suppliers, Inc.

Getting ready

Suppliers can be created from the purchasing or payables responsibilities. Before the supplier is created, we need to establish that the supplier does not exist on the system, and the necessary payables, purchasing, and financials options have been set.

How to do it...

Let's list the steps required to create a supplier:

1. Navigate to the **Purchasing** responsibility.

2. Navigate to **Supply Base | Suppliers**.

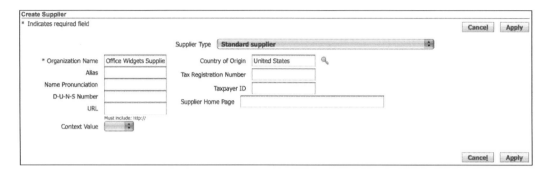

3. Click on **Create Supplier**.

4. In the **Supplier Type** field, select **Standard Supplier** from the drop-down list.

5. In the **Organization Name** field, enter a unique name for the supplier name. For example, **Office Widgets Suppliers, Inc**. Organizations should have a naming convention for suppliers to avoid duplicate entries. The **Organization Name** is case sensitive.

6. In the **Country of Origin** field, enter **United States**.

7. Click on the **Apply** button.

Let's create the address for the supplier's site:

1. Click on the **Address Book** link on the left navigation bar.

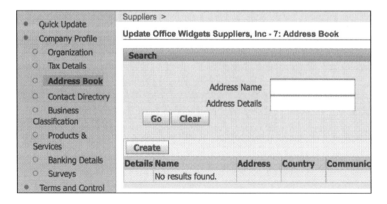

2. Click on the **Create** button to enter the site details.

3. Enter the **Address Details**.

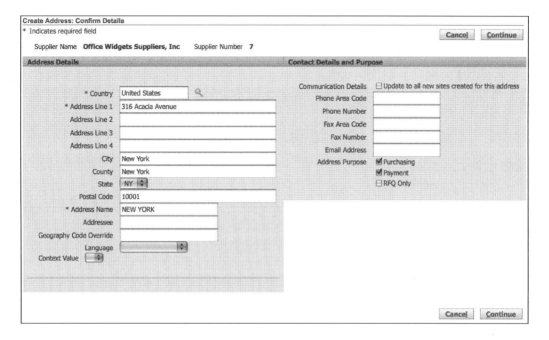

4. In the **Address Line 1** field, enter **316 Acacia Avenue**.

5. In the **City** field, enter **New York**.

6. In the **County** field, enter **New York**.

7. In the **State** field, select **NY** from the drop-down list.

8. In the **Postal Code** field, enter **10001**.

9. In the **Address Name** field, enter **NEW YORK**.

10. In the **Address Purpose** field, select **Purchasing** and **Payment**.

11. Click on the **Continue** button.

12. Assign the site name to the operating unit.

13. Click on the **Apply** button.

14. The new supplier and the supplier site is created.

How it works...

Supplier data consists of two main sections:

1. The header: This contains the core supplier's details, for example, the name, tax registration details, DUNS number, supplier's URL, type of supplier, and so on.

2. The site: This contains the supplier's address specific information, for example, the purpose of the site, contact information, operating unit assignment, an address of the supplier, and so on.

Let's add some additional information to the supplier's details.

There's more...

Now let's look at additional data that can be set up for the supplier.

Creating a contact

Contacts for a supplier can be created and associated with supplier sites. Let's create a contact:

1. Select the **Contact Directory** link from the left navigation bar.

2. Click on the **Create** button.

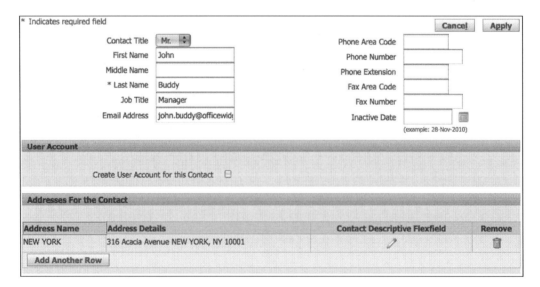

3. Enter the following details:

- ❑ Enter the **First Name**, for example, **John**
- ❑ Enter the **Last Name**, for example, **Buddy**. The **Last Name** field is mandatory.
- ❑ Enter the **Email Address**, for example, **john.buddy@officewidgets.com**.

Let's associate an address with the contact:

1. Click on **Add Another Row**.
2. Enter **NEW YORK** in the **Address Name** field.
3. Click on the **Apply** button.

Creating a bank account

Suppliers require a bank account to be paid by electronic transfers. Let's create a bank account for the supplier:

1. Select the **Banking Details** link from the left navigation bar.
2. In the **Bank Accounts** region, click on the **Create** button.

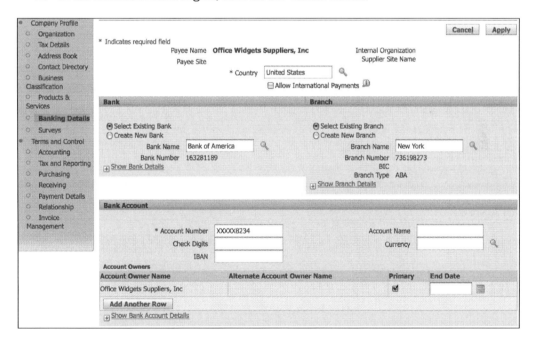

3. In the **Country** field, enter **United States**.
4. In the **Bank** region, enter **Bank of America** in the **Bank Name** field.
5. In the **Branch** region, enter **New York** in the **Branch Name** field.

6. In the **Account Number** field, enter the account number.

7. Click on the **Apply** button.

8. Click on the **Save** button.

Reviewing the accounting details

Let's review the accounting details.

1. Select the **Accounting** link from the left navigation bar.

2. Review the **Ledger** in the **Ledger** field.

3. In the **Liability** tab, review the **Liability Account** details (**01-000-2210-0000-000**).

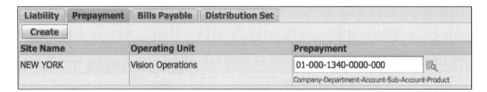

4. In the **Prepayment** tab, review the **Prepayment** account details (**01-000-1340-0000-000**).

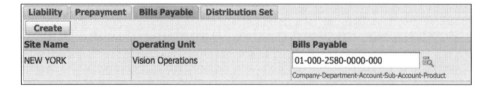

5. In the **Bills Payable** tab, review the bill payables account details (**01-000-2580-0000-000**).

Reviewing the purchasing options

Let's review the purchasing options:

1. Select the **Purchasing** link from the left navigation bar.

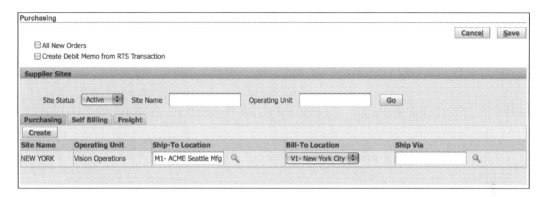

2. Review the default **Ship-To Location** and **Bill-To Location** for the site in the **Purchasing** section.

Setting the receiving options

Let's enter the receiving options. The values can be overridden when entering a purchase order:

1. Select the **Receiving** link from the left navigation bar.

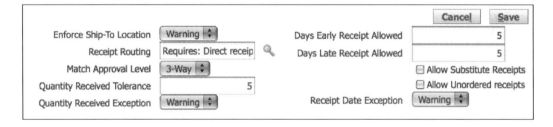

2. In the **Enforce Ship-To Location** field, select **Warning** in the drop-down list. This field determines whether the receiving location must be the same as the ship-to location.

3. In the **Receipt Routing** field, enter **Requires: Direct receipt**. This is the receiving routing assigned to the Items.

4. In the **Match Approval Level** field, select **3-Way** in the drop-down list. Invoices from the supplier can be matched to the purchase order in payables, based on the **Match Approval Level**.

5. The invoice price should not be more than the purchase order price. If the invoice price is more, it should be within the tolerance set. The match approvals are based on the quantity invoiced, including the invoice price check. There are three levels, listed as follows:

❑ 2-Way Match: Quantity invoiced, not more than the quantity ordered.

❑ 3-Way Match: 2-Way match and quantity invoiced, not more than the quantity received.

❑ 4-Way Match: 3-Way match and quantity invoiced, not more than the quantity accepted.

6. In the **Quantity Received Tolerance** field, enter **5**. This represents the maximum over receipt tolerance of five percent.

7. In the **Quantity Received Exception** field, select **Warning** from the drop-down list.

8. In the **Days Early Receipt Allowed** field, enter **5**. We can accept receipts from the supplier 5 days early.

9. In the **Days Late Receipt Allowed** field, enter **5**. We can accept receipts from the supplier 5 days late.

10. Leave the **Allow Substitute Receipts** field unchecked.

11. Leave the **Allow Unordered Receipts** field unchecked.

12. In the **Receipt Date Exception** field, select **Warning** from the drop-down list.

Setting the payment details

Let's set the payment details:

1. Select the **Payment Details** link from the left navigation bar.

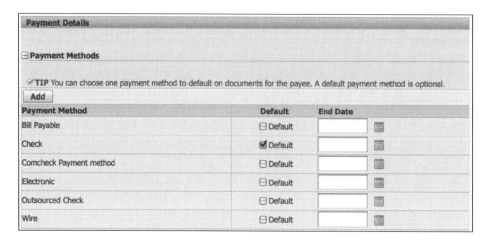

2. In the **Payments Method** region, select **Check** as the **Default** method.

3. Click on the **Save** button.

Creating purchase orders

Purchase orders are created from requisitions, or created separately without a requisition. Once the purchase order is created and approved, it can be sent to the supplier for fulfillment of the order. In this recipe, we will create a standard purchase order for the requisition 14337, and use the Office Widget Suppliers, Inc. as the supplier.

Getting ready

We need to be set up as buyers to create purchase orders. Let's review the buyer setup details for Pat Stock:

1. Log in to the **Purchasing** responsibility.

2. Navigate to **Setup | Personnel | Buyers.**

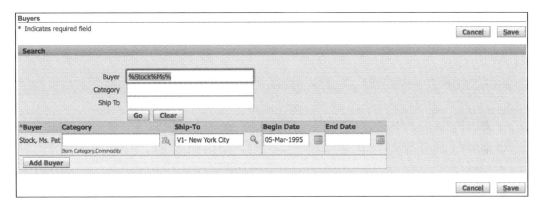

3. Search for the buyer attached to the user.

4. In the **Buyer** field, enter **%Stock%Ms%,** and click on the **Go** button.

5. The buyers details are displayed.

How to do it...

Let's list the steps required to complete the task:

1. Navigate to **Buyer Work Center | Requisitions.**

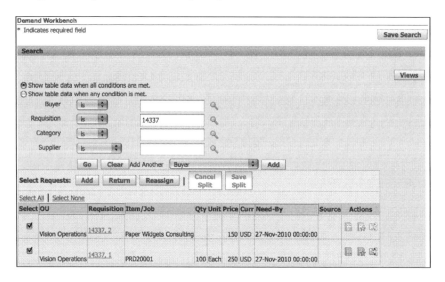

2. In the **Demand Workbench,** click on the **Search** button.

3. Click on the **Clear** button.

4. Enter the **Requisition** number **14337** in the **Requisition** field.

5. Click on the **Go** button to display the lines of the requisition.

6. Click on the **Select All** link and click on the **Add** button.

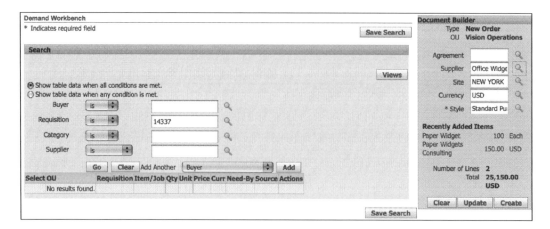

7. In the **Document Builder** section, enter **Office Widgets** and press the *Tab* key; the **Supplier** details and the **site** details will be automatically entered.

8. Click on the **Create** button to create the **Standard Purchase Order**.

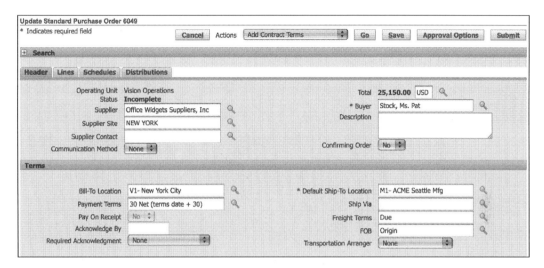

9. Review the purchase order **Header** details.

10. Review details from the supplier setup. For example, the **Bill-To Location**.

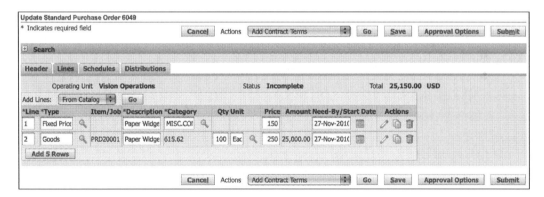

11. Select the **Lines** tab to review the lines details. Review the **Price**, the **Quantity**, and other details obtained from the requisition.

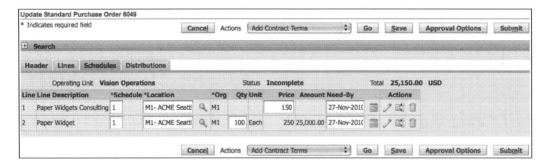

12. In the **Schedules** tab, review the **Delivery Location** details and the **Need-By** date.

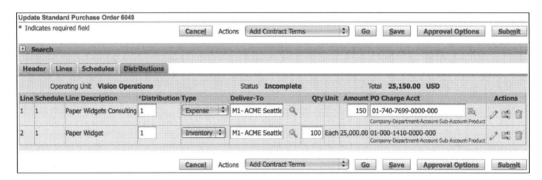

13. In the **Distributions** tab, review the **Distribution Type** and the **PO Charge Acct.**

14. Click on the **Save** button.

DRAFT   Standard Purchase Order 6049, 0

Vision Operations
475 Park Avenue
New York, NY 10022
United States

Type	**Standard Purchase Order**
Order	**6049**
Revision	**0**
Order Date	**28-NOV-2010**
Created By	**Stock, MS. Pat**
Revision Date	
Current Buyer	

Supplier: **Office Widgets Suppliers, Inc**
            316 Acacia Avenue
            New York, NY 10001
            United States

Ship To: **3455 108th Avenue**
            Seattle, WA 98101
            United States

Bill To: **90 Fifth Avenue**
            New York, NY 10022-3422
            United States

Customer Account No	Supplier No	Payment Terms	Freight Terms	FOB	Transportation	Ship Via
	7	30 Net (terms date + 30)	Due	Origin		

Confirm To/Telephone	Requester/Deliver To
	Stock, MS. Pat

Notes: All dates referenced in this document are in GMT-6 America/Chicago
           All prices and amounts on this order are expressed in USD

Line	Part Number / Description	Delivery Date/Time	Quantity	UOM	Unit Price (USD)	Tax	Amount (USD)
1	Paper Widgets Consulting	Needed: 27-NOV-2010 00:00:00				Y	150.00
	Ship To: Use the ship-to address at the top of page 1						
	Deliver To: Stock, MS. Pat nobody@localhost						
2	PRD20001	Needed: 27-NOV-2010 00:00:00	100	Each	250	Y	25,000.00
	Paper Widget						
	Ship To: Use the ship-to address at the top of page 1						
	Deliver To: Stock, MS. Pat (100) nobody@localhost						

Total: **25,150.00 (USD)**

15. Review the **Draft** PDF of the purchase order.

16. Select **View PDF** in the **Actions** field.

17. Click on the **Go** button.

18. View the PDF file.

19. Click on the **Submit** button to send the Purchase Order for **Approval**.

20. The purchase order should be automatically approved.

There's more...

We can also create **Blanket Purchase Agreements** (**BPA**) and **Contract Purchase Agreement** (**CPA**). Blanket Purchase Agreements are used with catalog requisitions. Contract Purchase Agreements are mainly used with non-catalog requisitions. Let's explore the use of CPA and BPA. We will also look at some of the purchasing options and approvals.

Using Blanket Purchase Agreements (BPA)

1. Prepare the upload CSV file in Excel.
2. From the **Purchasing** responsibility, navigate to **Buyer Work Center | Agreements**.

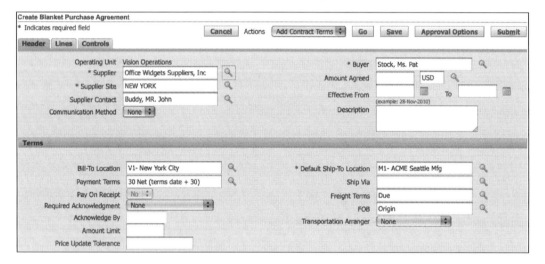

3. In the **Create** field, select **Blanket Purchase Agreement** in the drop-down list, and click on the **Go** button.
4. Enter **Office Widgets, Inc** as the **Supplier**.
5. Enter **NEW YORK** as the **Supplier Site**.
6. Click on the **Save** button to save our work.

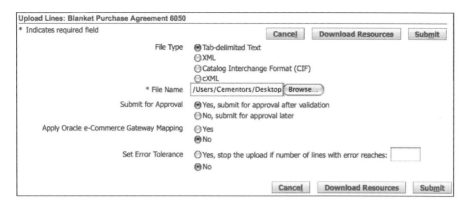

7. Click on the **Lines** tab.

8. In the **Add Lines** field, select **Via Upload** and click on the **Go** button.

9. In the **File Name** field, select the upload file.

10. Click on the **Submit** button.

11. A job confirmation is received for the **Blanket Purchase Agreement 6050**.

12. Search for the **Status** of the agreement.

13. Select the **Agreement** tab.

14. Enter **6050** in the **Agreement** field.

15. Click on the **Go** button.

16. The agreement is retrieved with the status of **Approved**.

17. Click on **6050** in the **Agreement** link.

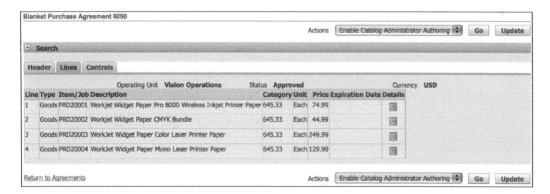

18. Click on the **Lines** tab to review the uploaded lines.

Viewing the agreement in iProcurement

Let's view the Items in an iProcurement catalog:

1. Switch to the **iProcurement** responsibility.

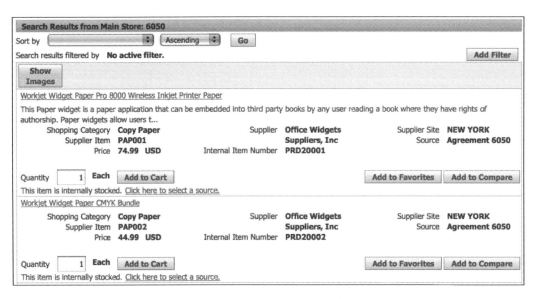

2. In the **Main Store** field, enter the Blanket Purchase Agreement number **6050**.

3. Click on the **Go** button.

4. The catalog Items are displayed in iProcurement.

Using Contract Purchase Agreements (CPAs)

Let's create a CPA:

1. Navigate to **Buyer Work Center | Agreements**.

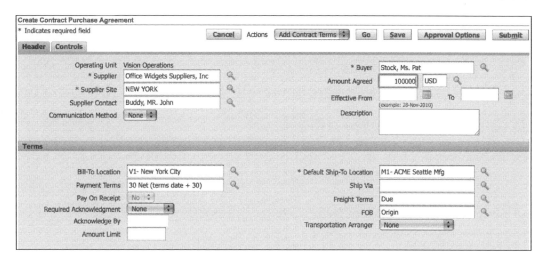

2. In the **Create** field, select **Contract Purchase Agreement** in the drop-down list and click on the **Go** button.

3. Enter **Office Widgets Suppliers, Inc** as the **Supplier**.

4. Enter **NEW YORK** as the **Supplier Site**.

5. Enter an **Amount Agreed** of **100,000**.

6. Click on the **Save** button to save our work.

7. Click on the **Controls** tab and review the details.

8. Click on the **Submit** button.

9. A confirmation of the submission of the Contract Purchase Agreement **6051** for approval is displayed.

10. Search for the status of the agreement.

11. Select the **Agreement** tab.

12. Enter **6051** in the **Agreement** field.

13. Click on the **Go** button.

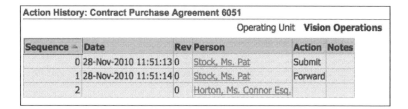

14. The **Agreement** is retrieved with the status of **In-Process**.

15. Click on **In Process** in the **Status**.

16. The approval **Action History** is displayed.

17. The next approver is **Horton, Ms. Connor Esq**.

Using the contract in iProcurement

Let's use the CPA in iProcurement:

1. Switch to the **iProcurement** responsibility.

2. In the **Main Store** field, select the **Non-Catalog Request** link to enter the details of the non-catalog request.

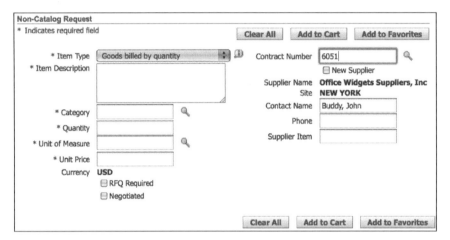

3. Enter **6051** in the **Contract Number** field.

4. The supplier details are entered automatically.

Reviewing the purchasing options

Let's review some of the default values used in purchasing:

1. Navigate to **Setup | Organizations | Purchasing Options**.

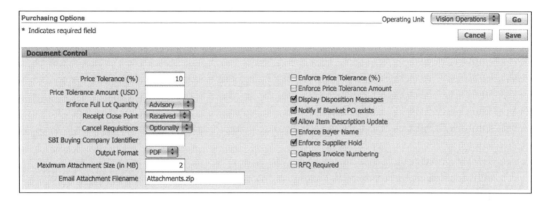

2. Review the **Document Control** region. We have various options to control the purchase order, for example, **Allow Item Description Update**, **Enforce Buyer Name**, and so on.

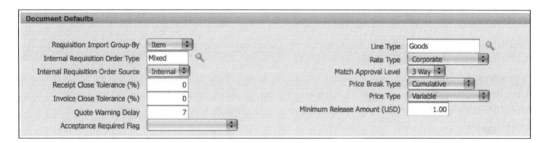

3. Review the **Document Defaults** region. We have various options to determine the default values on the purchase order, for example, **Match Approval Level**, **Rate Type**, and so on.

4. Review the **Receipt Accounting** region. We have the **Receipt Accounting** options to determine the accrual methods for Expense and Inventory Items and the default **AP Accrual Account**.

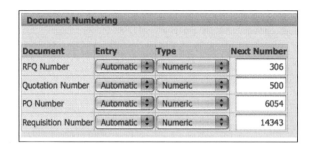

5. Review the **Document Numbering** region. We have the options to set the **Document Numbering** format (**Numeric** or **Alphanumeric**) for **RFQ Number**, **Quotation Number**, **PO Number**, and **Requisition Number**. We can also set the numbering to **Automatic** or **Manual**.

Approving purchase orders and agreements

Log in as the approver:

1. Select the **iProcurement** responsibility.

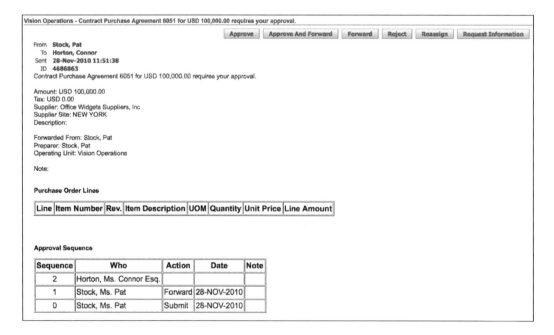

2. In the **My Notifications** region, select the link to the **Contract Purchase Agreement Vision Operations - Contract Purchase Agreement 6051 for USD 100,000.00 requires your approval**.

3. We now have the option to **Approve, Approve And Forward, Forward, Reject, Reassign**, or **Request Information**.

4. Review the Document and click on the **Approve** button to approve the requisition.

5. A notification is sent to the requester of the approval of the requisition.

See also

Creating Suppliers recipe in this chapter

Raising Requisitions for Items recipe in this chapter

Approving Requisitions recipe in this chapter

Receiving Items

Receiving Items consists of two main parts: receiving into a receiving bay, and then delivery into a Subinventory or Expense location. In this recipe, we will look at direct delivery into a Subinventory location. Receiving can occur in purchasing or iProcurement; we will use iProcurement to receive in this recipe.

We are going to receive 45 of the 100 paper widgets from Office Widget Suppliers, Inc.

Getting ready

We need an approved purchase order before we can receive the Items in iProcurement.

How to do it...

1. Select the **iProcurement** responsibility.

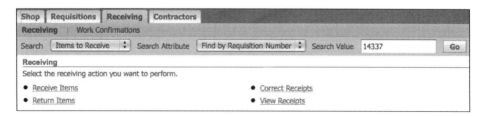

2. Click on the **Receiving** tab and enter the requisition number **14337** in the **Search Value** field.

3. Click on the **Go** button.

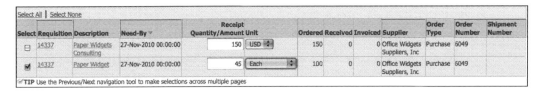

Select	Requisition	Description	Need-By	Receipt Quantity/Amount Unit		Ordered	Received	Invoiced	Supplier	Order Type	Order Number	Shipment Number
☐	14337	Paper Widgets Consulting	27-Nov-2010 00:00:00	150	USD	150	0	0	Office Widgets Suppliers, Inc	Purchase	6049	
☑	14337	Paper Widget	27-Nov-2010 00:00:00	45	Each	100	0	0	Office Widgets Suppliers, Inc	Purchase	6049	

TIP Use the Previous/Next navigation tool to make selections across multiple pages

4. Select the line for the **Paper Widget** and enter **45** in the **Receipt Quantity / Amount** field. We need to ensure that that the correct unit of measure is selected.

5. Click on the **Next** button.

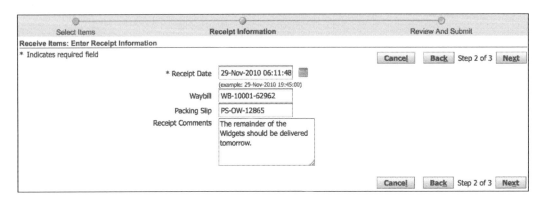

6. Enter the **Receipt Date**.

7. Enter the **Waybill** number, for example, **WB-10001-62962**. This is the consignment note issued by the delivery carrier.

8. Enter the **Packing Slip** number, for example, **PS-OW-12865**. This is the delivery note issued by the supplier.

9. Enter any receipts comments, for example, **The remainder of the Widgets should be delivered tomorrow**.

10. Click on the **Next** button.

11. Review the **Receipt** and click on the **Submit** button.

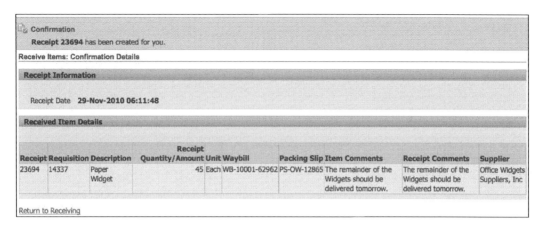

Confirmation

Receipt **23694** has been created for you.

Receive Items: Confirmation Details

Receipt Information

Receipt Date **29-Nov-2010 06:11:48**

Received Item Details

Receipt	Requisition	Description	Receipt Quantity/Amount	Unit	Waybill	Packing Slip	Item Comments	Receipt Comments	Supplier
23694	14337	Paper Widget	45	Each	WB-10001-62962	PS-OW-12865	The remainder of the Widgets should be delivered tomorrow.	The remainder of the Widgets should be delivered tomorrow.	Office Widgets Suppliers, Inc

Return to Receiving

12. A **Confirmation** page is displayed with the receipt number **23694**.

13. Click on the **Return to Receiving** link.

Let's view the Items in Inventory:

1. Log in to the **Inventory** responsibility.

2. Navigate to **On-Hand, Availability | On-Hand Quantity**.

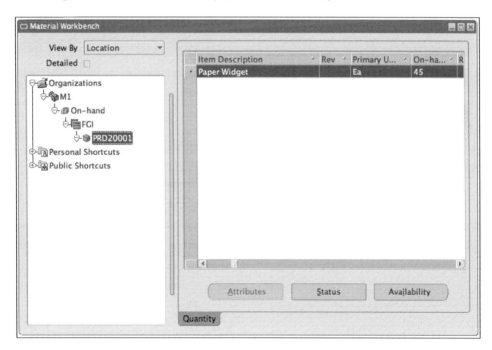

3. In the **Query Material** form, enter **PRD20001** in the **Item / Revision** field.

4. Click on the **Find** button.

5. In the **Material Workbench** form, expand the tree.

6. The **On-Hand** availability displays the quantity as **45** in the **FGI** Subinventory.

There's more...

Let's explore how Express Receiving works and how receipts are managed.

Express Receiving

The second consignment has now arrived and we need to receive the remainder of the Items on the requisition (55 Items). We also need to receive the consultancy services, as the work has been done.

With Express Receiving, we can receive all the Items in a requisition in one step. We accept the order quantity as the receipt quantity.

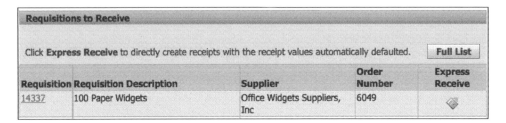

Requisition	Requisition Description	Supplier	Order Number	Express Receive
14337	100 Paper Widgets	Office Widgets Suppliers, Inc	6049	

1. Select the **iProcurement** responsibility.

2. Select the **Receiving** tab.

3. Click on the **Express Receive** icon.

4. Review the **Receipt** and click on the **Submit** button.

5. A **Confirmation** page is displayed with the Receipt number **23695**.

6. Click on the **Return to Receiving** link.

Returning Items

We need to return the whole of the second consignment and five Items of the first consignment back to the supplier, a total of 60 Items. This is due to damages to the packaging on some of the first consignment, and the wrong Items being delivered in the second consignment

1. Select the **iProcurement** responsibility.

2. Select the **Receiving** tab.

3. Click on the **Return Items** link.

4. Enter the **Requisition** number **14337**.

5. Click on the **Go** button.

Receipt	Requisition	Description	Return Quantity Unit		Quantity Received	Supplier	Order Number
23694	14337	Paper Widget	5	Each	45	Office Widgets Suppliers, Inc	6049
23695	14337	Paper Widget	55	Each	55	Office Widgets Suppliers, Inc	6049

6. Enter **5** and **55** in the **Return Quantity Unit** fields.

7. Click on the **Next** button.

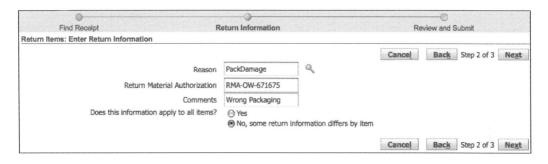

8. Enter the **Return Information**.

9. Enter **PackDamage** in the **Reason** field.

10. Enter the **Return Material Authorization** (RMA) number **RMA-OW-671675**. The supplier provides the RMA number.

11. Enter comments in the **Comments** field, for example, **Wrong Packaging**.

12. In the field, **Does this information apply to all Items?**, select **No, some return information differs by Item**.

13. Click on the **Next** button.

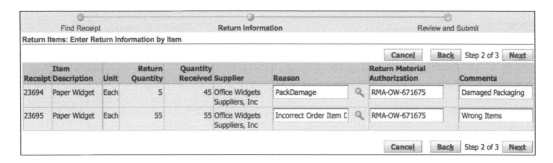

14. In the receipt line for the first consignment, enter **Damaged Packaging** in the **Comments** field.

15. In the receipt line for the second consignment, enter **Incorrect Order Item Delivered** in the **Reason** field and **Wrong Items** in the **Comments** field.

16. Click on the **Next** button.

17. Review the **Return Items**.

18. Click on the **Submit** button.

19. A **Confirmation** page is displayed.

20. Click on the **Return to Receiving** link.

Correcting receipts

The widgets are counted in the stores and we discover that 38 widgets were received in total and not 40 Items. We need to adjust the receipt:

1. Select the **iProcurement** responsibility.

2. Select the **Receiving** tab.

3. Click on the **Correct Receipts** link.

4. In the **Item Received** field, select **Today**.

5. Click on the **Go** button.

Receipt	Requisition	Description	Correct Quantity/Amount	Unit	Received	Supplier	Order Number
23694	14337	Paper Widget	38	Each	40	Office Widgets Suppliers, Inc	6049
23695	14337	Paper Widget		Each	0	Office Widgets Suppliers, Inc	6049
23695	14337	Paper Widgets Consulting		USD	150	Office Widgets Suppliers, Inc	6049

6. Enter **38** in the **Correct Quantity / Amount Unit** field.

7. Click on the **Continue** button.

8. Review the correction. The change in quantity is **-2** in the **Change** field.

9. Click on the **Submit** button.

10. A correction confirmation is received.

11. Click on the **Return to Receiving** link.

Viewing receipts

We can view the receipts transactions:

1. Select the **iProcurement** responsibility.

2. Select the **Receiving** tab.

3. Click on the **View Receipts** link.

4. In the **Item Received** field, select **Today**.

5. Click on the **Go** button.

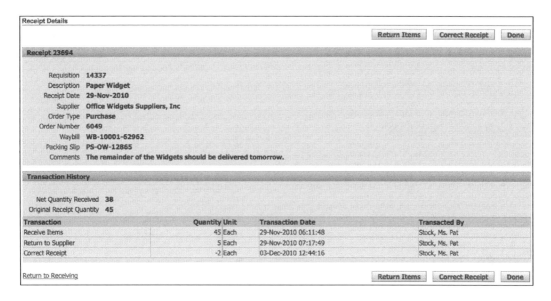

6. Select the link on the **Received** amount of **38**.

7. Review the transactions.

8. Click on the **Done** button.

9. Click on the **Return to Receiving** link.

Reviewing receiving options

1. Select the **Purchasing** responsibility.

2. Navigate to **Setup | Organizations | Receiving Options**.

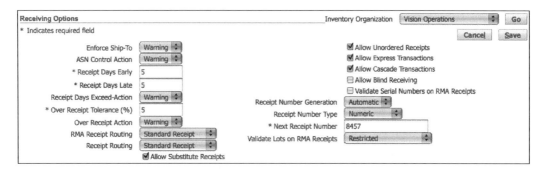

3. Review the options, for example, **Next Receipt Number**, **Receipt Days Early**, **Receipt Days Late**, **Over Receipt Tolerance** (%), and so on.

Reviewing procurement accounting transactions

Oracle purchasing supports cash and accruals accounting. In this recipe, let's review the accounting transactions for accruing on receipt for direct delivery.

How to do it...

Let's list the steps required to review the accounting transactions:

1. Select the **Purchasing** responsibility.

2. Navigate to **Receiving | Receiving Transactions Summary**.

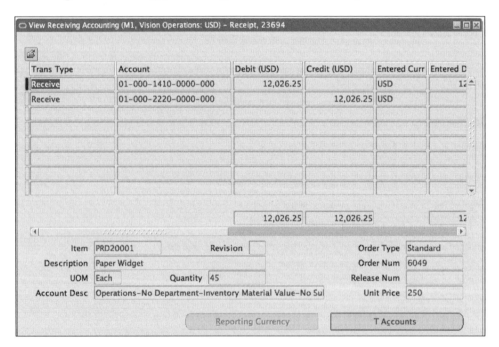

3. In the **Find Receiving Transactions** form, select the **Supplier and Internal** tab.

4. Enter **Office Widgets Suppliers, Inc** in the **Supplier** field.

5. Click on the **Find** button.

6. In the **Receipts Headers Summary** form, click on the **Transactions** button.

7. From the **Tools** menu, select **View Accounting**.

8. Review the **Accounting Transactions**.

How it works...

Accounting distributions stored in the purchase orders are used to determine the accounting transactions sent to the General Ledger. Once the Items are receipted, a receipt accrual is sent to the General Ledger. The accounting transactions are displayed in the following table:

Account	Dr	Cr
PO Distribution Charge Expense Account /	XX	
Receiving Inventory Account (Quantity x PO line unit price)		
Expense / Inventory AP Accrual account		XX
(Uninvoiced receipts account)		

There's more...

Now let's look at the setup of the accounts that are used in procurement.

The Receiving Inventory Account

The Receiving Inventory Account is used for receipt accruals. The account is set up in the Receiving options and can also be set up in the organization parameters in Inventory. The account is debited when a receipt is entered. After the transfer to GL is run, the account is cleared and the Material account is credited:

1. Select the **Inventory** responsibility.

2. Navigate to **Setup | Organizations | Organizations**.

3. In the **Find Organization** form, enter **ACME Seattle Manufacturing** in the name field and click on **Find** button.

4. In the **Organizations Classifications** section, select **Inventory Organization** and click on the **Others** button.

5. Select **Receiving Information** in the **Additional Organization Information**.

6. The **Receiving Options** form is displayed.

7. Review the **01-000-1410-0000-000 Receiving Inventory Account.**

8. Select the Purchasing responsibility.

9. Navigate to **Setup | Organizations | Receiving Options**

10. The **Receiving Options** form is displayed.

11. Review the **01-000-1410-0000-000 Receiving Inventory Account**.

Inventory AP Accrual Account

The Inventory AP Accrual Account is used by Purchasing to accrue payable liabilities for inventory Items. This account represents the uninvoiced receipt liability account. The account is cleared when the invoice is matched and validated in Payables:

1. Select the **Inventory** responsibility.

2. Navigate to **Setup | Organizations | Organizations**.

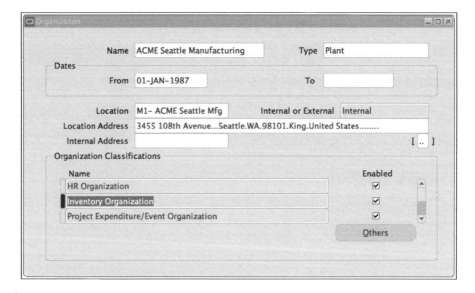

3. In the **Find Organization** form, enter **ACME Seattle Manufacturing** in the **Name** field and click on **Find** button.

4. In the **Organizations Classifications** section, select **Inventory Organization** and click on the **Others** button.

5. Select **Inventory Information** in the **Additional Organization Information.**

6. The **Organization Parameters** form is displayed.

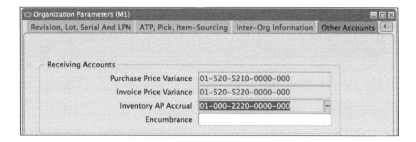

7. Select the **Other Accounts** tab.

8. Review the **01-000-2220-0000-000 Inventory AP Accrual** account.

Expense AP Accrual Account

The Expense AP Accrual Account is used by Purchasing to accrue liabilities for expense Items. This account represents the uninvoiced receipt liability account. The account is cleared when the invoice is matched and validated in Payables:

1. Select the **Purchasing** responsibility.

2. Navigate to **Setup | Organizations | Purchasing Options**.

3. Review the **01-000-2220-0000-000 Expense AP Accrual Account**.

Material Cost Account

The Material Cost Account is an asset account that tracks material cost. The account is credited after the transfer to GL program is run.

Specify this account when you define inventory information for your inventory organizations in the **Valuation Accounts** region for the **Costing Information** tab:

1. Select the **Inventory** responsibility.

2. Navigate to **Setup | Organizations | Organizations**.

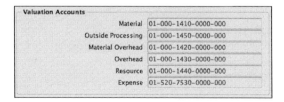

3. In the **Find Organization** form, enter **ACME Seattle Manufacturing** in the **Name** field and click on **Find** button.

4. In the **Organizations Classifications** section, select **Inventory Organization** and click on the **Others** button.

5. Select **Inventory Information** in the **Additional Organization Information**.

6. The **Organization Parameters** form is displayed.

7. Select the **Costing Information** tab.

8. Review the **01-000-1410-0000-000 Material** account.

PO Distribution Charge Account

During the creation of a Requisition, a charge account is generated. This account is transferred to the Purchase Order and will ultimately be transferred to the balance sheet or income statement.

Items with a destination type of expense can either be an asset clearing account or an expense account. Items with a destination type of inventory will use the Material account.

Financial options

1. Select the **Purchasing** responsibility.

2. Navigate to **Setup | Organizations | Receiving Options**.

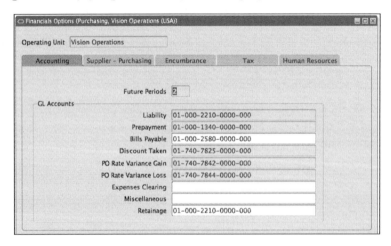

3. Select the **Accounting** tab.

4. Review the **GL Accounts.**

See also

Defining Subledger Accounting recipe in Chapter 8, Defining Transactions for the General Ledger

3
Paying Supplier Invoices in Payables

In this chapter, we will cover:

- ▶ Entering invoices
- ▶ Entering a prepayment
- ▶ Entering credit memos
- ▶ Applying holds to an invoice
- ▶ Canceling an invoice
- ▶ Paying invoices
- ▶ Creating a payment process template
- ▶ Voiding a payment
- ▶ Reviewing payables accounting transactions

Invoices for goods and services that are purchased in an organization are sent from the supplier, and payments are made to the suppliers based on the amount on the invoice. In this chapter, we will look at how to enter and pay supplier invoices in payables. Let's start by looking at the payables process.

The following diagram summarizes an example of the payables process:

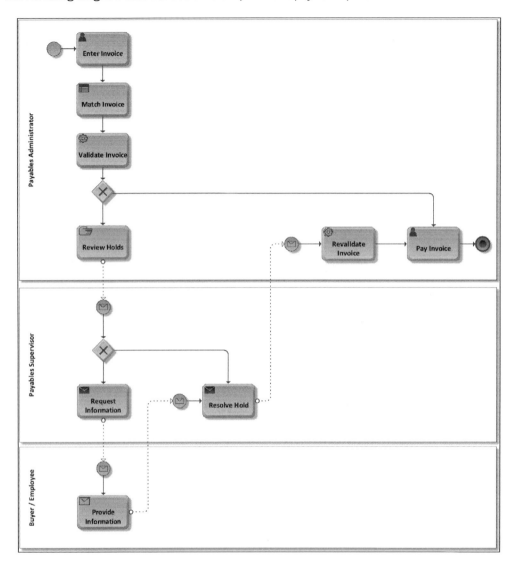

1. The **Payables Administrator** enters the invoice in Oracle Payables. Invoices can also be automatically generated by other sources, for example, through the invoice open interface, from XML files, self-billing programs, and scanned images.

2. The entered invoices are matched to the purchase order or receipt details.

3. The invoice is validated. If no holds are placed on the invoice, the invoice is validated and paid. If holds are placed on the invoice, the administrator reviews the holds and the supervisor is notified.

4. The supervisor reviews the holds and either resolves the holds or requests additional information from the buyer or employee.

5. The buyer or employee sends the required information to the supervisor, who resolves the holds. The invoice is revalidated and then the invoice becomes eligible for payment.

Let's start by looking at how invoices from suppliers are entered.

Entering invoices

Oracle Payables provides us with the functionality to enter invoices from suppliers. An invoice contains the description of the goods supplied and/or service provided to the organization.

In this recipe, we will create a standard invoice and match it to a purchase order. We will also add an additional line for freight charges and tax. The main tasks are as follows:

▶ Match to purchase order 6059-2 Paper Widgets at $50 each

▶ Enter Freight Charges for $20 (includes tax)

▶ Calculate the tax added to the invoice

The total invoice value is $128.60.

 Invoices can also be matched to multiple Purchase Orders.

Getting ready

Log in to Oracle E-Business Suite R12 with the username and password assigned to you by the system administrator. If you are working on the Vision demonstration database, you can use OPERATIONS/WELCOME as the USERNAME/PASSWORD.

We also need an approved **Purchase Order** (**PO**) with some Items receipted on the system.

How to do it...

Let's look at the steps required to enter an invoice:

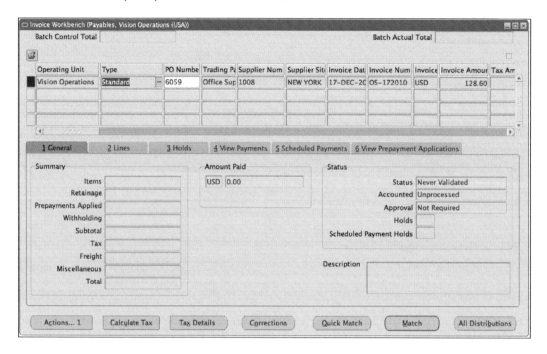

1. Select the **Payables** responsibility.

2. Navigate to **Invoices | Entry | Invoices**.

3. In the invoice type field, select **Standard**. The different types of invoices are listed as follows:

   ❏ **Standard**: Amounts due for goods or services purchased. They can be matched to a purchase order.

   ❏ **Credit Memo**: A document from the supplier representing a credit amount towards goods or services.

   ❏ **Debit Memo**: An entry to record a credit for a supplier where a credit memo does not exist.

   ❏ **Expense Report**: Amount due to an employee for expense reimbursement.

   ❏ **Prepayment**: An advance payment to a supplier or employee.

❑ **Withholding Tax**: Entry of remittance of taxes withheld to the appropriate tax authority.

❑ **Mixed**: Entry of positive or negative amounts to purchase orders and invoices.

4. Enter **6059** in the **PO Number** field. The **Trading Partner**, **Supplier Number**, and the **Supplier Site** are populated automatically.

5. Enter the invoice date, for example, **17-DEC-2010**.

6. Enter the unique **Invoice Number** from the supplier, for example, **OS-172010**.

7. Enter the **Invoice Amount** of **$128.60**.

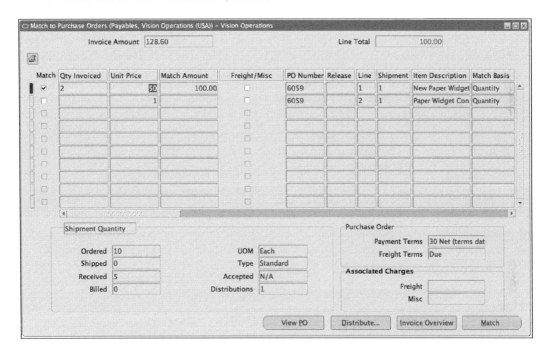

8. Click on the **Match** button to match the invoice to the **Purchase Order**.

9. Click on the **Find** button to find the **Purchase Order**. The **Purchase Order** number is automatically defaulted in from the Invoice **Workbench** screen.

10. Select the line on the purchase order to match to the invoice.

11. Enter the **Quantity Invoiced** of **2**.

12. Click on the **Match** button to match the invoice to the **Purchase Order**.

13. Let's enter the freight charges.

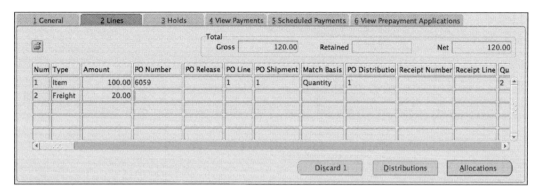

14. Select the **Lines** tab.

15. Select **Freight** as the **Type** in line **2**.

16. Enter **20** in the **Amount** field.

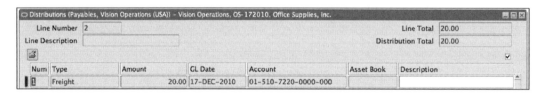

17. Click on the **Distributions** button.

18. Enter **20.00** in the **Amount** field. The **Freight** can also be allocated to more than one account.

19. Enter the distribution account of **01-510-7220-0000-000**.

20. Save your work.

21. Let's calculate the tax.

22. Click on the **Calculate tax** button.

23. The tax values are calculated.

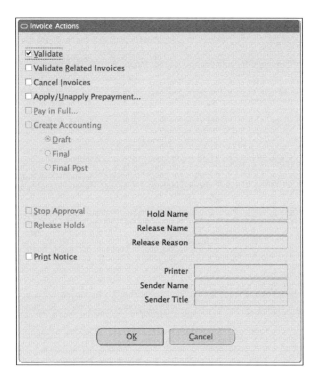

24. Click on the **Actions...1** button.
25. Click on the **Validate** checkbox.
26. Click on the **OK** button to validate the invoice.
27. The invoice **Status** changes to validated.

How it works...

The supplier sends the invoice to the organization after the goods and services are supplied. The receiver of the goods enters the receipts on the system, if the invoice needs to be matched to a receipt.

An invoice consists of two main parts:

1. The header: This contains common invoice data such as **Invoice Type**, **Date**, **Number**, **Supplier Name**, **Site**, **Payment Terms**, and **Payment Information**.

2. The lines: This contains the details of the Items, Freight, Miscellaneous, or Tax charges. An invoice can contain multiple lines. Invoice lines also contain accounting distributions. An invoice line can contain multiple distributions.

The tax lines are added based on the E-Business tax setup.

See also

Defining subledger accounting recipe in Chapter 8, Defining Transactions for the General Ledger

Defining E-Business tax accounting recipe in Chapter 8, Defining Transactions for the General Ledger

Creating purchase orders recipe in this Chapter

Entering a prepayment

A prepayment is an advance payment made to a supplier. A prepayment can be **Temporary** (can be applied to invoices) or **Permanent** (cannot be applied to invoices). In this recipe, we will create a prepayment to **Office Supplies, Inc** for cleaning services.

Getting ready

Log in to Oracle E-Business Suite R12 with the username and password assigned to you by the system administrator. If you are working on the vision demonstration database, you can use OPERATIONS/WELCOME as the USERNAME/PASSWORD.

How to do it...

Let's list the steps required to enter a prepayment:

1. Select the **Payables** responsibility.

2. Navigate to **Invoices | Entry | Invoices**.

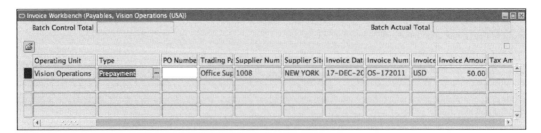

3. In the invoice **Type** field, select **Prepayment**.

4. Enter **Office Supplies, Inc** in the **Trading Partner** field.

5. Select **NEW YORK** as the **Supplier Site**.

6. Enter the **Invoice Date**, for example, **17-DEC-2010**.

7. Enter the unique **Invoice Number** from the **Supplier**, for example, **OS-172011**.

8. Enter the **Invoice Amount** of **50**.

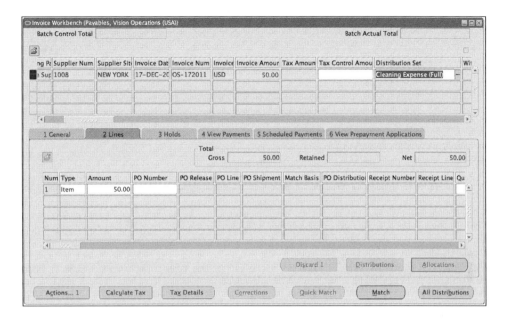

9. Scroll to the right using the horizontal scrollbar.

10. In the **Distribution Set**, select **Cleaning Expense (Full)**.

11. In the **Lines** tab, enter **50.00** as the **Amount**.

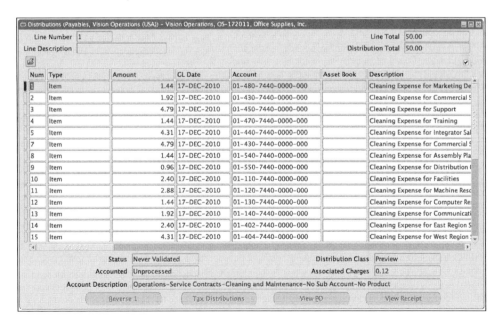

12. Click on the **Distributions** button to see the allocation based on the distribution set.

13. The **Tax** is automatically calculated.

14. Adjust the invoice amount to include the tax amount by changing the invoice amount to **52.04**.

15. Save the record.

16. Invoices needs to be validated before they are paid.

17. Click on the **Actions...1** button.

18. Click on the **Validate** checkbox.

19. Click on the **OK** button to validate the invoice.

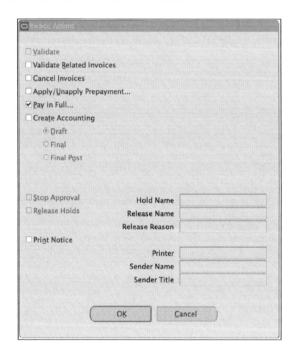

20. We need to pay the invoice before we can apply it.

21. Click on the **Actions...1** button.

22. Click on the **Pay in Full** checkbox.

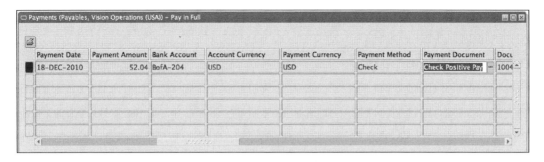

23. Click on the **OK** button to open the **Pay in Full** window.

24. In the **Payment Date** field, enter **18-DEC-2010**.

25. In the **Bank Account** field, enter **BofA-204**.

26. In the **Payment Document** field, enter **Check Positive Pay**.

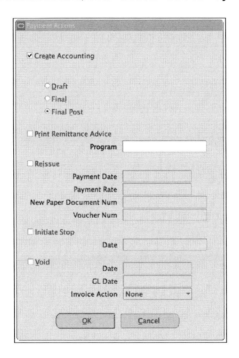

27. Click on the **Actions...1** button.

28. Click on the **Create Accounting** checkbox.

29. Select the **Final Post** option.

30. Click on the **OK** button to run the Payment program and create the accounting for the payment.

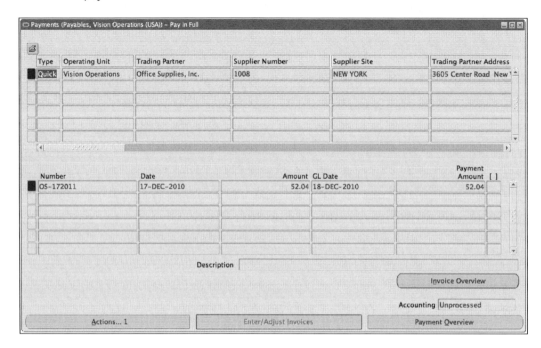

31. The Payment run completes.

There's more...

Let's enter a quick invoice and apply the prepayment to the invoice.

Entering a quick invoice for a prepayment

Invoices can be entered quickly using Quick Invoice. It is used mainly for manually entering a large number of invoices:

1. Let's enter a quick invoice for the prepayment.

2. Navigate to **Invoices | Entry | Quick Invoices**.

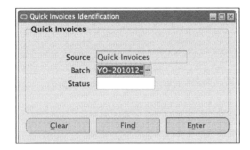

3. Select **Quick Invoices** as the **Source**.

4. Enter a **Batch**, for example, **YO-201012-1**.

5. Click on the **Enter** button.

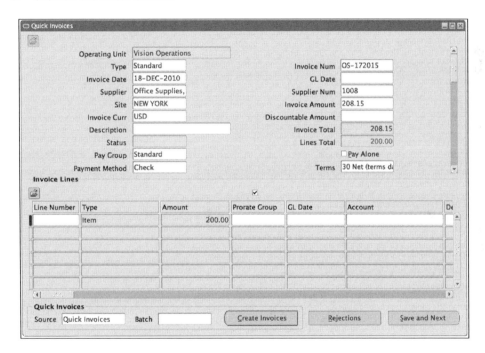

6. In the **Type** field, select **Standard**.

7. Enter **OS-172015** as the **Invoice Num**.

8. Enter **18-DEC-2010** as the **Invoice Date**.

9. Select **Office Supplies, Inc** as the **Supplier**; the **Supplier Num** will be entered automatically.

10. Select **NEW YORK** as the site.

11. Enter **208.15** for the **Invoice Amount**.

12. In the lines region, select **Type** as **Item**.

13. Enter **200.00** in the amount.

14. Scroll horizontally, and select **Cleaning Expense (Full)** as the distribution set.

15. Click on the **Create Invoices** button.

16. In the **Create Invoices** window, click on the **OK** button.

17. A concurrent program will run in the background to transfer the invoice details to the open interface tables.

Applying a prepayment to an invoice

A prepayment can be applied to an invoice:

1. Navigate to **Invoices | Entry | Invoices**.

2. Search for the quick invoice using the **Find** icon.

3. Enter the **OS-172015** in the **Invoice Num** field.

4. Click on the **Find** button.

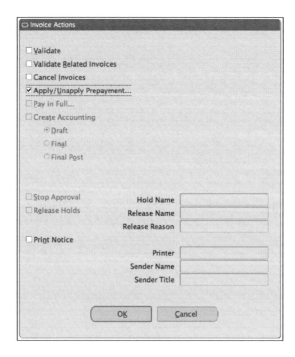

5. All the details of the invoice are displayed.

6. Click on the **Actions...1** button.

7. Click on the **Apply/Unapply Prepayment...** checkbox.

8. Click on the **OK** button.

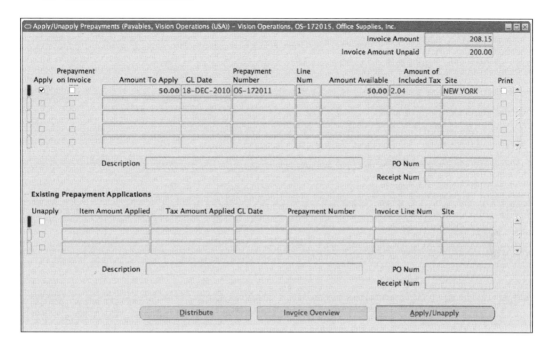

9. In the **Apply/Unapply** form, select the **Apply** checkbox.

10. Click on the **Apply/Unapply** button.

11. Close the form.

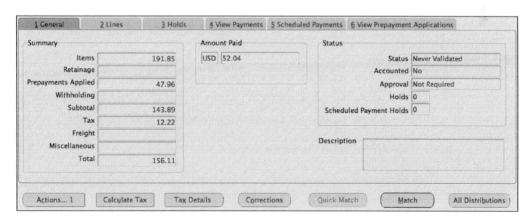

12. The prepayments are now applied to the invoice.

13. Click on the **Actions...1** button.

14. Click on the **Validate** checkbox.

15. Click on the **OK** button.

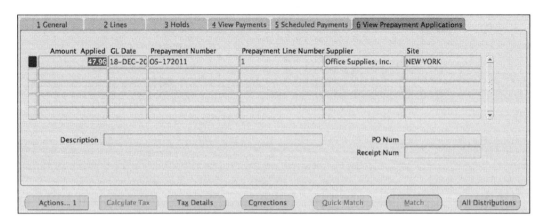

16. Click on the **View Prepayment Applications** tab to view the allocation of the prepayments.

Entering credit memos

Credit memos are credit invoices from a supplier representing a credit toward goods or services. Credit memos are also called **credit notes**.

Debit memos are invoices entered to record a credit for a supplier, where a credit memo is not received from the supplier. They can be netted with an invoice, when the invoice is paid. The steps for creating a debit memo are similar to creating a credit memo. We will look at how to enter a credit memo in this recipe.

Getting ready

Log in to Oracle E-Business Suite R12 with the username and password assigned to you by the system administrator. If you are working on the Vision demonstration database, you can use OPERATIONS/WELCOME as the USERNAME/PASSWORD.

How to do it...

Let's list the steps required to enter a credit memo:

1. Select the **Payables** responsibility.

2. Navigate to **Invoices | Entry | Invoices**.

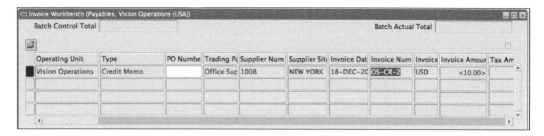

3. In the invoice **Type** field, select **Credit Memo**.

4. Enter **Office Supplies, Inc** in the **Trading Partner** field.

5. Select **NEW YORK** as the **Supplier Site**.

6. Enter the **Invoice Date**, for example, **18-DEC-2010**.

7. Enter the unique **Invoice Number** from the supplier, for example, **OS-CR-2**.

8. Enter the **Invoice Amount** of **10.00**.

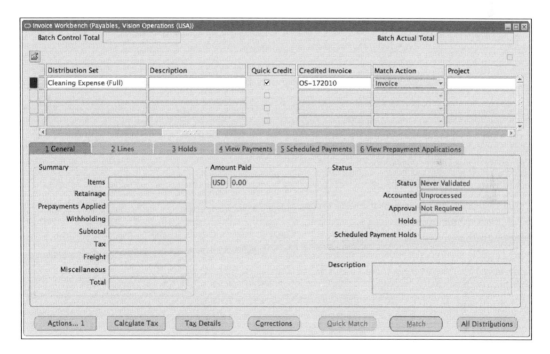

9. Click on the horizontal scrollbar and select the **Distribution Set** field.

10. Select **Cleaning Expense (Full)** from the list of values.

11. Click on the **Quick Credit** checkbox.

12. Select the **OS-172010** from the list of values in the **Credited Invoice** field.

13. Select **Invoice** as the **Match Action**.

14. In the **Lines** tab, enter **-10** in the **Amount** field.

15. Click on the **Actions...1** button.

16. Click on the **Validate** checkbox.

17. Click on **OK**.

18. The **Credit Note** is validated.

Applying holds to an invoice

In this recipe, we will assume that the supplier has sent in an invoice for four paper widgets at $75 each for purchase order number 6059. We have only received five paper widgets and we have previously been billed for two paper widgets. This should generate two system holds when we try to validate the invoice:

► Qty Rec: Quantity billed exceeds quantity received

► Price: Invoice price exceeds purchase order price

Let's also assume that the supplier has not submitted all the documents required, for example, insurance certificates and so on. We will place a manual hold on the invoice to reflect this. We will also look at how to resolve the holds.

Let's create a standard invoice and match it to the purchase order.

Getting ready

Log in to Oracle E-Business Suite R12 with the username and password assigned to you by the system administrator. If you are working on the Vision demonstration database, you can use OPERATIONS/WELCOME as the USERNAME/PASSWORD.

How to do it...

Let's list the steps required to apply holds to an invoice:

1. Select the **Payables** responsibility.

2. Navigate to **Invoices | Entry | Invoices**.

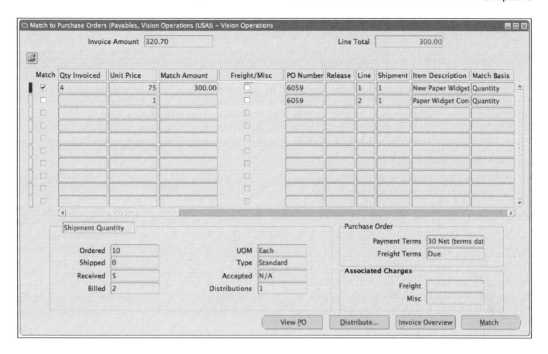

3. In the invoice **Type** field select **Standard**.

4. Enter **6059** in the **PO Number** field. The **Trading Partner**, **Supplier Number**, and the **Supplier Site** are populated automatically.

5. Enter the **Invoice Date**, for example, **18-DEC-2010**.

6. Enter the unique **Invoice Number** from the supplier, for example, **OS-172018**.

7. Enter the **Invoice Amount** of **$320.70**.

8. Click on the **Match** button to match the invoice to the **Purchase Order**.

9. Click on the **Find** button to find the **Purchase Order**.

10. Select the **Line** on the purchase order to match to the invoice.

11. Enter the **Qty Invoiced** of **4**.

12. Change the **Unit Price** to **75**. The match amount should change to **300.00**.

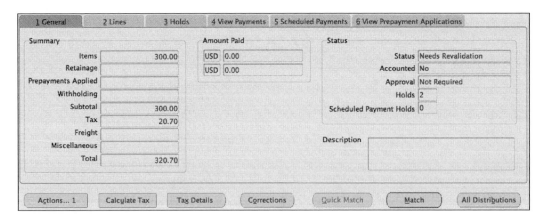

13. Click on the **Match** button to match the invoice to the **Purchase Order**.

14. Click on the **Calculate tax** button.

15. The **Tax** values are calculated.

16. Click on the **Actions...1** button.

17. Click on the **Validate** checkbox.

18. Click on the **OK** button.

19. The **Status** of the Invoice is **Needs Revalidation**, and **2** holds have been placed on the Invoice.

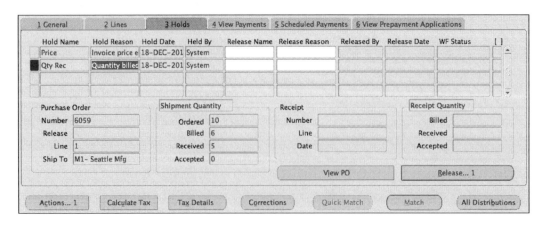

20. Select the **Holds** tab.

21. Review the holds placed:

- ❑ **Hold Name** is **Price**, with a **Hold Reason** of **Invoice price exceeds purchase order price**. The invoice line on the purchase order is $50, and the invoice line is $75. We may have agreed the price with the supplier, as the price difference is out of the tolerance. The system will automatically place a hold on the invoice. The hold can be manually released.

- ❑ **Hold Name** is **Qty Rec**, with a **Hold Reason** of **Quantity billed exceeds quantity received**. The supplier has billed us for **6** paper widgets, but only **5** have been received. The hold can be released by receiving the Item in inventory, purchasing, or iProcurement. We then need to revalidate to automatically release the hold.

22. Place a manual hold on the invoice to reflect the **PO deliverable**.

23. Select the **Holds** tab.

24. In the **Hold Name** field, select **PO Deliverable**. The **Hold Reason** is automatically populated as PO deliverables are not submitted by the subcontractor.

25. Save the record.

Resolving the holds:

1. Let's receive the Item in Inventory.

2. Select the **Inventory** responsibility.

3. Navigate to **Transactions | Receiving | Receipts**.

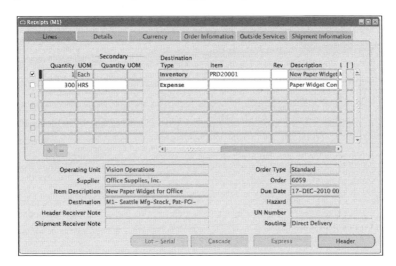

4. Select the **M1** inventory organization.

5. In the **Purchase Order** field, enter **6059**.

6. Click on the **Find** button.

7. Select the **Receipts line tab.**

8. Enter the **Quantity** of **1**.

9. Save the record.

Revalidating the invoice:

1. Select the **Payables** responsibility.

2. Navigate to **Invoices | Entry | Invoices**.

1 General		2 Lines		3 Holds		4 View Payments	5 Scheduled Payments		6 View Prepayment Applications	

Hold Name	Hold Reason	Hold Date	Held By	Release Name	Release Reason	Released By	Release Date	WF Status	[ ]
PO Deliverable	PO deliverable	18-DEC-201	MFG	Validated	Hold Released				
Price	Invoice price e	18-DEC-201	System	Match Override	Matching hold rel	MFG	18-DEC-2010		

3. Find the invoice based on **Invoice Number OS-172018**.

4. Select the **Holds** tab.

5. Select the **Release Name** field. For the **Price Hold**, select **Match Override** to release the price hold.

6. In the **Release Name** field, for the **PO Deliverable** hold, select **Validated** to release the **PO Deliverable** hold.

7. Save the form.

8. The invoice is validated.

How it works...

Holds can be placed on an invoice, either manually or by the system. Holds can prevent the invoice from being paid. System holds are automatically placed on an invoice if an invoice fails the validation process. Manual holds must be manually released.

Hold and release names are defined in the **Invoice Hold and Release Names** form. The definition can also be used to determine if accounting entries can be created before the hold is released.

Invoice holds and release form:

1. Select the **Payables** responsibility.

2. Navigate to **Setup | Invoice | Hold and Release Names**.

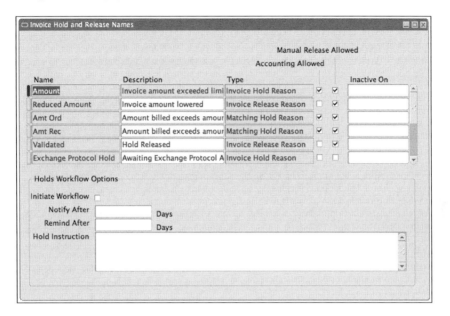

3. Search for all records by pressing _Ctrl+F11_.

4. View the **Invoice Hold and Release Names**.

There's more...

Now let's look at some other ways that holds can be applied to an invoice.

Reviewing invoice management holds

Holds can also be automatically applied to a supplier and supplier site by entering invoice controls. Default values can be entered at the supplier level. The values are automatically defaulted to all sites. Any values set at the site level will override the supplier level:

1. Select the **Payables** responsibility.

2. Navigate to **Suppliers | Entry**.

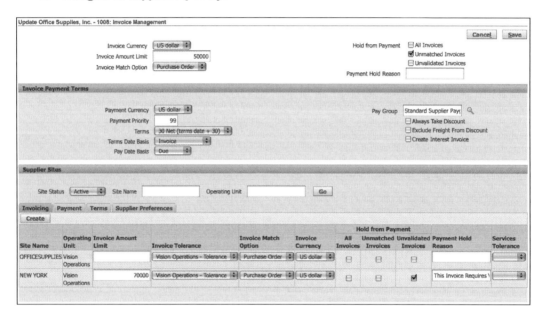

3. Search for the supplier **Office Supplies, Inc**.

4. Select the **Invoice Management** link form the side navigation bar.

5. In the **Invoice Amount Limit** field, enter **50000**. This places a hold on the supplier's invoice if the invoice amount exceeds $50,000.

6. Enable the **Unmatched Invoices** checkbox.

7. In the **Supplier Sites** section, enter **70000** in the **Invoice Amount Limit** field.

8. Enable the **Unvalidated Invoices** checkbox at the **Supplier sites** and enter a **Payment Hold Reason**, for example, **This Invoice Required Validation**.

9. Save the record.

10. Enter an invoice for **Office Supplies, Inc** from the **NEW YORK** site for **$90,000**.

11. The system will issue a warning when creating the invoice and will apply two system holds to the invoice.

See also

Creating suppliers recipe in Chapter 2, Purchasing Items in Procurement

Canceling an invoice

It is possible to enter an invoice in error, and we need to cancel the invoice. In this recipe, we will cancel invoice number OS-172018. An audit trail is maintained on the system for the canceled invoice.

Getting ready

Log in to Oracle E-Business Suite R12 with the username and password assigned to you by the System Administrator. If you are working on the Vision demonstration database, you can use OPERATIONS/WELCOME as the USERNAME/PASSWORD.

How to do it...

Let's list the steps required to cancel an invoice:

1. Select the **Payables** responsibility.

2. Navigate to **Invoices | Entry | Invoices**.

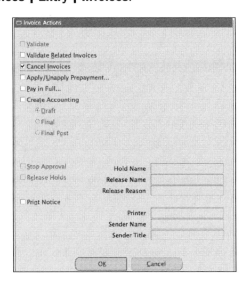

3. Find the invoice based on **Invoice Number OS-172018**.

4. Click on the **Actions...1** button.

5. Click on the **Cancel Invoices** checkbox.

6. Click on the **OK** button.

7. Click on the **OK** button on the displayed note.

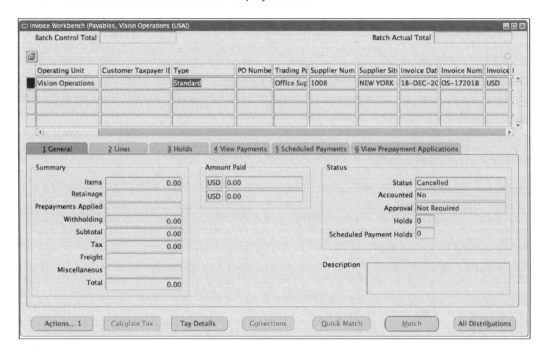

8. The invoice is now canceled.

Paying invoices

Once invoices are due, the amounts due are paid to the supplier. In this recipe, we will pay invoices due to ACME General Electric.

Getting ready

Log in to Oracle E-Business Suite R12 with the username and password assigned to you by the system administrator. If you are working on the Vision demonstration database, you can use OPERATIONS/WELCOME as the USERNAME/PASSWORD.

We need validated invoices that are due for payment. For this recipe, we have a payment due to ACME General Electric for $220.

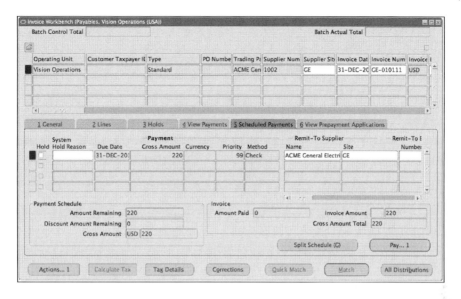

How to do it...

Let's list the steps required to pay invoices:

1. Select the **Payables** responsibility.

2. Navigate to **Payments | Entry | Payments Manager**.

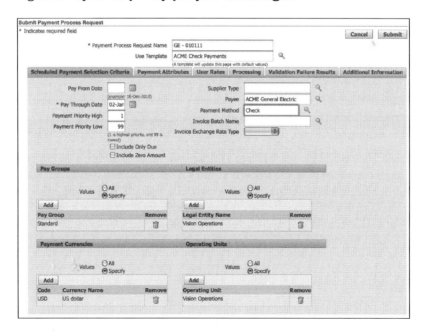

3. Select the **Payment Process Request** tab. The page is used to view, submit, and schedule requests.

4. Click on the **Submit Payment Process Request** button. This is used to submit a single request for payment.

5. To schedule a payment process to run periodically, use the **Schedule Repeating Request** button.

6. In the **Payment Process Request Name** field, enter a unique name, for example, **GE – 0101111**.

7. In the **Use Template** field, select **ACME Check Payments**. The template will enable us to automatically enter the data based on pre-specified values.

8. In the **Payee** field, select **ACME General Electric**.

9. In the **Payment Method** field, select **Check**.

10. Click on the **Submit** button.

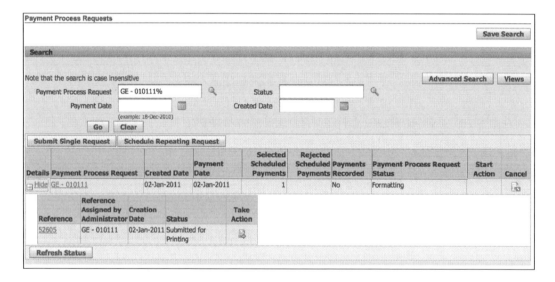

11. Search for the **Payment Process Request GE – 0101111**. The request is retrieved with the current **Payment Process Request Status** as **Formatting**.

12. Expand the details and a reference is displayed; the current **Status** is set to **Submitted for Printing**, and the **Take Action** icon is enabled.

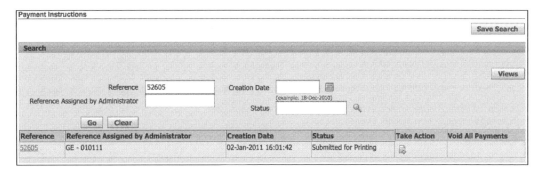

13. Select the **Payment Instructions** tab and search for reference **52605**.

14. Click on the **Take Action** icon. Specific invoices can also be excluded from the payment run.

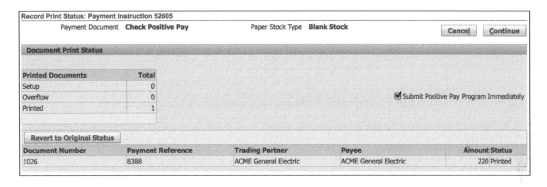

15. In the **Document Print Status** region, enable the **Submit Positive Pay Program Immediately** checkbox.

16. Click on the **Continue** button, and then the **Apply** button.

17. The payment is processed in the background.

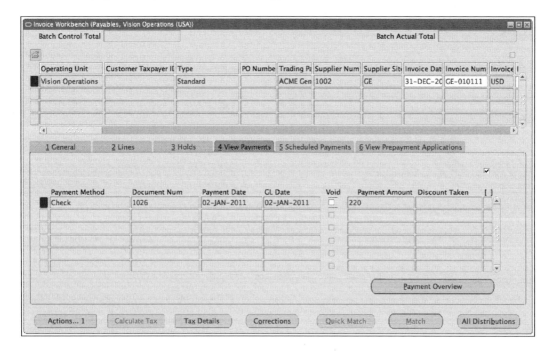

18. Navigate to **Invoices | Entry | Invoices**.

19. Find the invoice based on invoice number **GE-010111**

How it works...

Oracle payments are used to configure the setup for payments in Payables. The core of the payment process is defined in the Payment Process profile:

1. Select the **Oracle Payments Payment Administrator** responsibility.

2. Navigate to **Oracle Payments Setup | Payments Setup | Funds Disbursement Setup | Payment Process Profiles**.

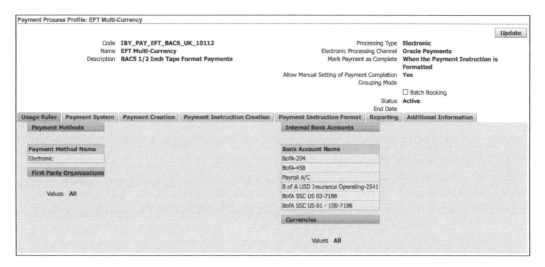

Payment Process Profile: EFT Multi-Currency

Update

Code **IBY_PAY_EFT_BACS_UK_10112**
Name **EFT Multi-Currency**
Description **BACS 1/2 Inch Tape Format Payments**

Processing Type **Electronic**
Electronic Processing Channel **Oracle Payments**
Mark Payment as Complete **When the Payment Instruction is Formatted**
Allow Manual Setting of Payment Completion **Yes**
Grouping Mode

☐ Batch Booking
Status **Active**
End Date

Usage Rules | Payment System | Payment Creation | Payment Instruction Creation | Payment Instruction Format | Reporting | Additional Information

Payment Methods

Internal Bank Accounts

Payment Method Name
Electronic

First Party Organizations

Values **All**

Bank Account Name
BofA-204
BofA-458
Payroll A/C
B of A USD Insurance Operating-2541
BofA SSC US 02-7188
BofA SSC US 01 - 100-7186

Currencies

Values **All**

3. Click on the **Go To Task** icon.

4. In the **Name** field, enter **EFT Multi-Currency**.

5. In the **Processing Type** drop-down box select **Electronic**, and click on the **Go** button.

6. Click on the **EFT Multi-Currency** link.

7. The **Usage Rules** are displayed. The rules determine when the payment profiles can be used when processing documents for payments.

Creating a payment process template

The Payments Manager uses payment process request templates to simplify a payment run. The template includes information such as invoice selection criteria, payment attributes, processing instructions, and also defines how validation failures should be handled. It is useful for automatically selecting invoices to pay during a payment run. In this recipe, we will create a Payment Process template.

Getting ready

Log in to Oracle E-Business Suite R12 with the username and password assigned to you by the system administrator. If you are working on the Vision demonstration database, you can use OPERATIONS/WELCOME as the USERNAME/PASSWORD.

How to do it...

Let's list the steps required to create the template:

1. Select the **Payables** responsibility.

2. Navigate to **Payments | Entry | Payments Manager**.

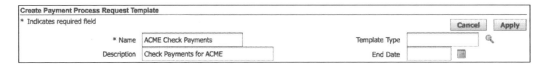

3. Select the **Templates** tab.

4. Click on the **Create** button.

5. Enter the unique **Name** of the template, for example, **ACME Check Payments**.

6. Enter a **Description,** for example, **Check Payments for ACME**.

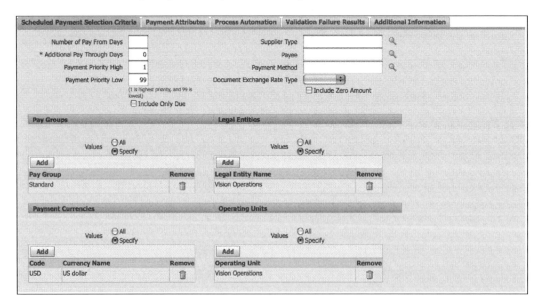

7. Select the **Scheduled Payment Selection Criteria** tab.

8. Enter **0** as the **Additional Pay Through Days**. This is used to determine the **Pay Through Date** when you initiate a payment process request.

9. In the **Pay Groups** region, click on the **Specify** option, and add **Standard** as the **Pay Group**.

10. In the **Legal Entities** region, click on the **Specify** option, and add **Vision Operations** as the **Legal Entity**.

11. In the **Payment Currencies** region, click on the **Specify** option and add **USD** as the **Currency**.

12. In the **Operating Units** region, click on the **Specify** option and add **Vision Operations** as the **Operating Unit**.

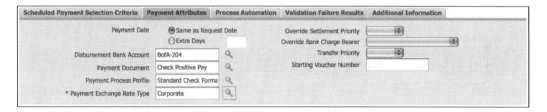

13. Select the **Payment Attributes** tab.

14. Select **BofA-204** as the **Disbursement Bank Account**.

15. Select **Check Positive Pay** as the **Payment Document**.

16. Select **Standard Check Format** as the **Payment Process Profile**.

17. Select **Corporate** as the **Payment Exchange Rate Type**.

18. Leave the defaults for the rest of the tabs.

19. Click on the **Apply** button to save the template.

There's more...

Now let's look at how to use the template to create a scheduled payment.

Creating a scheduled payment

Let's use the template to create a scheduled payment run:

1. Select the **Payables** responsibility.

2. Navigate to **Payments | Entry | Payments Manager**.

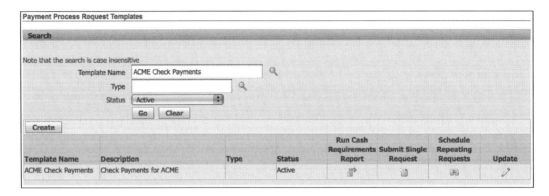

3. Select the **Templates** tab.

4. Search for the **ACME Check Payments** templates.

5. Select the **Schedule Repeating Requests** icon.

6. In the **Schedule Request: Name** form, accept the defaults and click on the **Next** button.

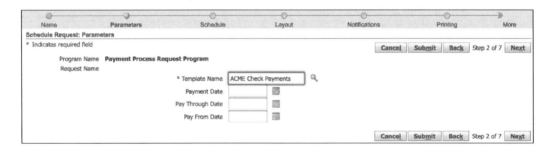

7. In the **Schedule Request: Parameters** form, enter **ACME Check Payments** in the **Template Name** field.

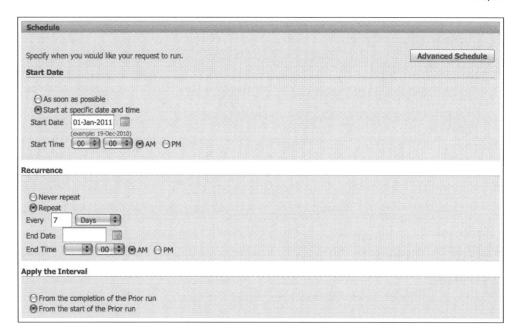

8. In the **Schedule Request: Schedule** form, enter the **Start Date** to start at a specific date and time, for example **01-Jan-2011** and **00:00 am**.

9. In the **Recurrence** region, select repeat every **7** days.

10. In the **Apply the Interval** region, select **From the start of the Prior run**.

11. Click on the **Next** button.

12. In the **Notifications** form, click on the **Next** button.

13. In the **Printing** form, click on the **Next** button.

14. Review the details.

15. Click on the **Submit** button to schedule the payment run to commence from the settings defined.

Voiding a payment

A payment may need to be canceled or voided. Let's look at how to void a payment.

Getting ready

Log in to Oracle E-Business Suite R12 with the username and password assigned to you by the system administrator. If you are working on the Vision demonstration database, you can use OPERATIONS/WELCOME as the USERNAME/PASSWORD.

How to do it...

Let's list the steps required to void a payment:

1. Select the **Payables** responsibility.

2. Navigate to **Payments | Entry | Payments Manager**.

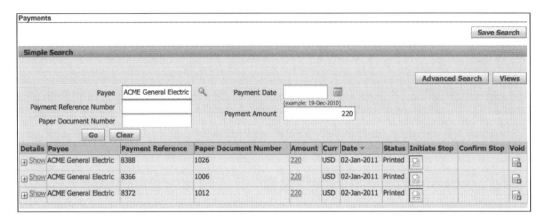

3. Select the **Payments** tab.

4. Enter **ACME General Electric** in the **Payee** field and **220** in the **Payment Amount**.

5. Click on the **Go** button.

6. Click on the **Void** icon for the **8388 Payment Reference**.

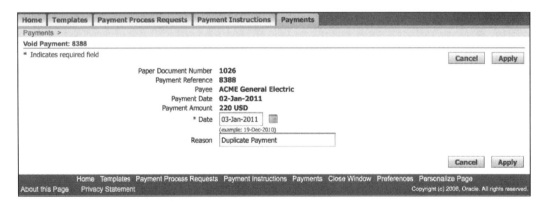

7. Enter a reason, for example, **Duplicate payment**.

8. Click on the **Apply** button.

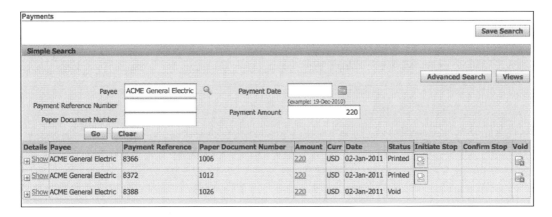

9. A warning message is displayed. Click on the **Yes** button to accept the action to void the payment.

10. The payment **Status** is now **Void**.

There's more...

Now let's look at how to stop a payment.

Stopping a payment

A stop payment needs to be initiated if the payment has been sent to the bank and the payment needs to be canceled. The payment is voided after the stop is issued:

1. Select the **Payables** responsibility.

2. Navigate to **Payments | Entry | Payments Manager**.

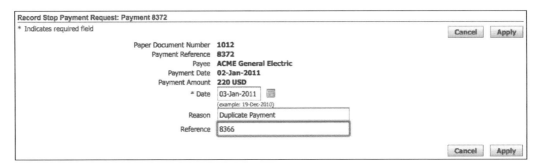

3. Select the **Payments** tab.

4. Enter **ACME General Electric** in the **Payee** field and the **220 USD** in the **Payment Amount**.

5. Click on the **Go** button.

6. Click on the **Initiate Stop** icon for the **8372 Payment Reference**.

7. Enter **03-Jan-2011** in the **Date** field.

8. Enter **Duplicate Payment** in the **Reason** field.

9. Enter **8366** in the **Reference** field.

10. Click on the **Apply** button.

11. Click on the **Confirm Stop** icon to stop the payment.

12. Enter **Duplicate Payment** in the **Reason** field.

13. Enter **8366** in the **Reference** field.

14. Click on the **Apply** button.

15. A warning message is displayed; click on the **Yes** button to accept the action to void the payment.

16. The stop is now placed on the payment, and it is voided.

Reviewing payables accounting transactions

In this recipe, we will transfer transactions to the General Ledger and review the accounting transactions generated.

Getting ready

Log in to Oracle E-Business Suite R12 with the username and password assigned to you by the System Administrator. If you are working on the Vision demonstration database, you can use OPERATIONS/WELCOME as the USERNAME/PASSWORD.

We need validated invoices for this recipe.

How to do it...

Let's list the steps required to transfer accounting transactions to the General Ledger from the Invoice Workbench:

1. Select the **Payables** responsibility.

2. Navigate to **Invoices | Entry | Invoices**.

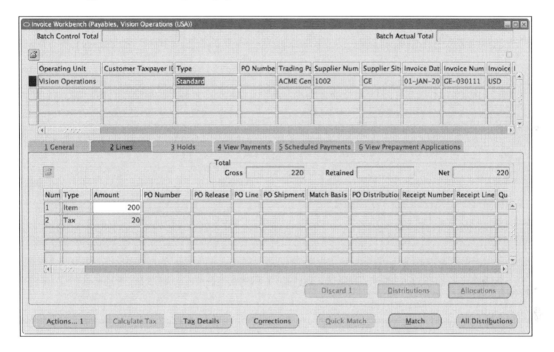

3. Search the **Invoice Number GE-030111** for **$220** from **ACME General Electric** on **01-JAN-2011** in the **Invoice Workbench**.

4. Click on the **Actions...1** button.

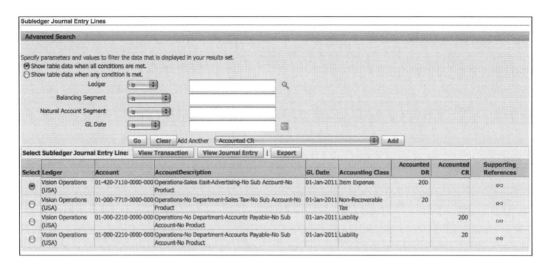

5. Click on the **Create Accounting** checkbox and select **Final Post** option.

6. Click on the **OK** button. A note will be displayed to confirm that the accounting transactions have been generated.

7. View the **Accounting** transactions by selecting **View Accounting** from **Reports** on the menu.

Let's view the transactions from General Ledger:

1. Switch responsibilities by selecting **File | Switch Responsibility**.

2. Select the **General Ledger** responsibility.

3. Navigate to **Journals | Enter**.

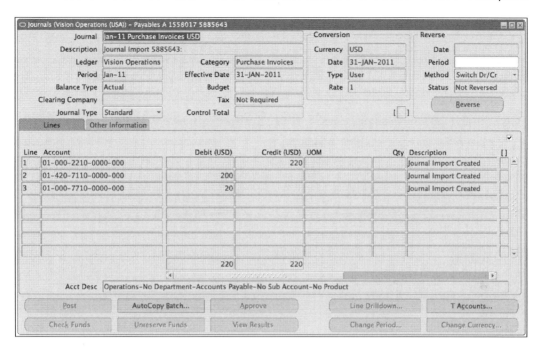

4. Search for the journal by selecting the **Source** as **Payables**, **Category** as **Purchase Invoices**, and the **Period** as **Jan-11**.

5. Click on the **Review Journal** button to review the journal.

6. We need to pay the invoice to reverse the liability.

7. Switch responsibilities by selecting **File | Switch Responsibility**.

8. Select the **Payables** responsibility.

9. Navigate to **Invoices | Entry | Invoices**.

10. Search for **Invoice Number GE-030111** for **$220**, from **ACME General Electric** on **01-JAN-2011** in the **Invoice Workbench**.

11. Click on the **Actions...1** button.

12. Click on the **Pay in Full** checkbox.

13. Click on the **OK** button to open the **Pay in Full** window.

14. In the **Payment Date** field, enter **03-JAN-2011**.

15. In the **Bank Account** field, enter **BofA-204**.

16. In the **Payment Document** field, enter **Check Positive Pay**.

17. Click on the **Actions...1** button.

18. Click on the **Create Accounting** checkbox.

19. Select the **Final Post** option.

20. Click on the **Ok** button to run the Payment program and create the accounting for the payment.

Let's view the transactions from General Ledger:

1. Switch responsibilities by selecting **File | Switch Responsibility**.

2. Select the **General Ledger** responsibility.

3. Navigate to **Journals | Enter**.

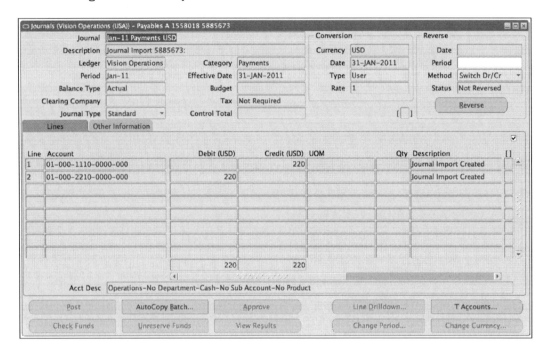

4. Search for the journal by selecting the **Source** as **Payables, Category** as **Purchase Invoices**, and the **Period** as **Jan-11**

5. Click on the **Review Journal** button to review the journal.

How it works...

Payables use the accounting event model defined in Subledger Accounting to determine the transactions that generate accounting transactions.

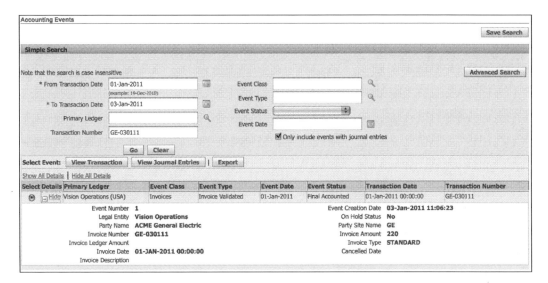

Let's review the structure of the Event Model, which consists of entities, classes, types, and events:

1. Select the **Payables** responsibility.

2. Navigate to **Setup | Accounting Setups | Subledger Accounting Setup | Accounting Methods Builder | Events | Event Model**.

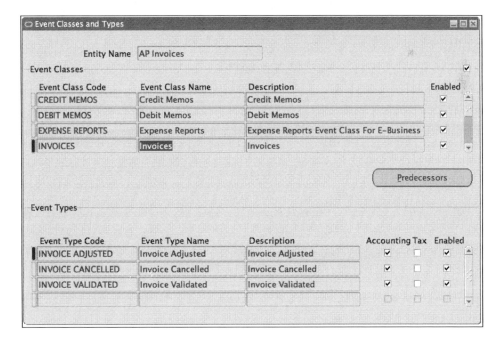

3. The event model consists of the **AP Invoices** and AP Payments Entities.

4. Click on the **Event Classes** button.

5. Each event class also has its associated **Event Types**. The events are categorized into event types.

There's more...

Now let's look at how to create accounting transactions for multiple invoices.

Creating accounting transactions for multiple invoices

To create the accounting transactions for multiple transactions, use the Create Accounting program. Let's look at how this is done:

1. Select the **Payables** responsibility.

2. Navigate to **Other | Requests | Run** or select **View | Requests** from the menu.

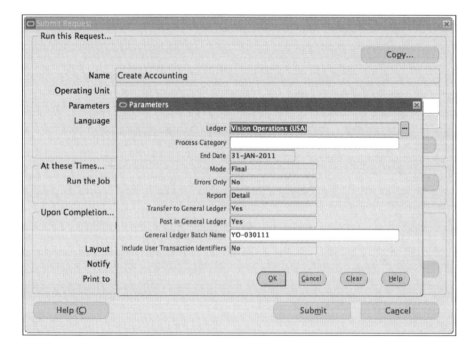

3. Click on the **Submit a New Request** button.

4. Select **Single Request** from the **Options**.

5. Click on the **OK** button.

6. In the **Submit Request** form, select **Create Accounting** from the list of values.

7. Select the **Parameters** field and select **Vision Operations (USA)** as the **Ledger**. Enter **31-JAN-2011** as the **End Date**. Select **Yes** as the parameter for **Post in General Ledger** and enter **YO-030111** as the **General Ledger Batch Name**.

8. Accept the default values for the remaining fields.

9. Click on the **OK** button.

10. We can schedule the program to run periodically, for example, every month.

11. Click on the **Submit** button to submit the request.

12. Review the requests.

13. Navigate to **View | Requests** from the menu.

14. Click on the **find** button.

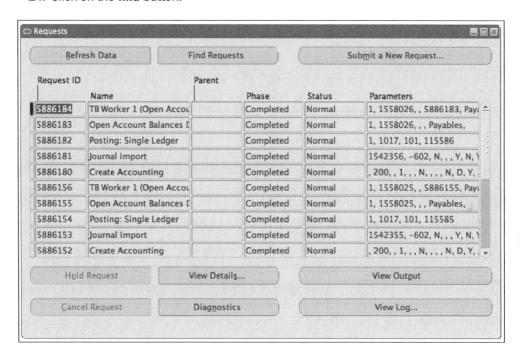

15. The **Create Accounting** program also spawns other programs to complete the transfer and posting of the journal in General Ledger.

See also

Defining subledger accounting recipe in Chapter 8, Defining Transactions for the General Ledger

4
Managing Assets

In this chapter, we will cover:

- ▶ Adding assets
- ▶ Adjusting assets
- ▶ Depreciating assets
- ▶ Retiring assets
- ▶ Reviewing asset accounting transactions

Introduction

Assets used in an organization need to be maintained and accounted for. Assets can be loaded from payables, projects, or from spreadsheets using **Web Application Desktop Integrator** (**ADI**). In this chapter, we will look at how to maintain assets by adding, adjusting, transferring, depreciating, and retiring assets. We will also review asset accounting transactions. Let's start by looking at the asset management process.

The following diagram summarizes the asset management process:

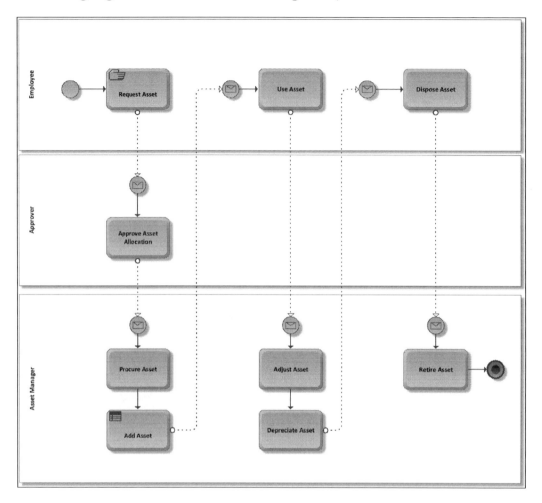

1.   The **Employee** requests the asset.

2.   An **Approver** authorizes that the asset can be used by the employee.

3.   The **Asset Manager** procures the asset or issues the asset out of inventory. The asset is added to Oracle assets.

4.   The **Employee** uses the asset.

5.   Any adjustment that needs to be made to the asset including costs, reallocations, and so on is managed by the **Asset Manager**.

6.   The **Asset Manager** depreciates the asset over its useful economic life, if the asset is capitalized.

7.   After the asset is used, it is disposed of, and the **Asset Manager** retires the asset.

Adding assets

Before assets can be managed, they need to be added to Oracle assets. Assets are mainly purchased, leased, or built by organizations. Purchased assets can be added from Oracle payables.

Assets can be added from the Subledger, entered manually, or loaded from an external source through the **ADI**. In this recipe, we will look at how to enter assets. Let's start by entering assets that have been entered from Oracle payables.

Getting ready

Log in to Oracle E-Business Suite R12 with the username and password assigned to you by the system administrator. If you are working on the Vision demonstration database, you can use OPERATIONS/WELCOME as the USERNAME/PASSWORD.

Run the **Mass Additions Create** program in payables to transfer the assets into the interface tables in readiness for the preparation of mass additions:

1. Select the **Payables** responsibility.

2. Navigate to **Other | Requests | Run**.

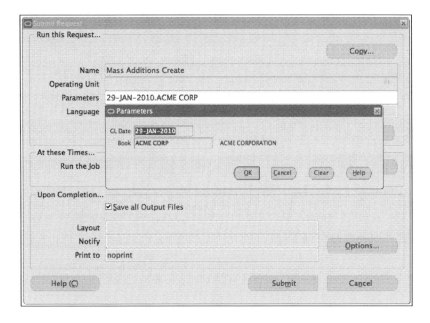

3. Select **Single Request** and click on the **OK** button.

4. In the **Submit Request** form, enter **Mass Additions Create** in the **Name** field.

5. In the **Parameters** field, enter **29-JAN-2010** in the **GL Date** and **ACME CORP** in the **Book** field.

6. Click on the **OK** button.

7. Click on the **Submit** button to submit the request.

8. In the **Submit Another Request Decision** box, select the **Yes** button to review the **Mass Additions**.

9. In the **Submit Request** form, enter **Mass Additions Create Report** in the **Name** field.

10. In the **Parameters** field, enter **ACME CORP** in the **Book** field.

11. Click on the **Submit** button to submit the request.

12. In the **Submit Another Request Decision** box, select the **Yes** button.

How to do it...

Let's list the steps required to complete the task:

1. Run the **Prepare Mass Additions** program.

2. Select the **Assets** responsibility.

3. Navigate to **Other | Requests | Run**.

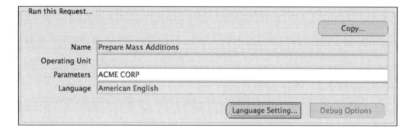

4. Select **Single Request** and click on the **OK** button.

5. In the **Submit Request** form, enter **Prepare Mass Additions** in the **Name** field.

6. In the **Parameters** field, enter **ACME CORP** in the **Book** field.

7. Click on the **Submit** button to submit the request.

8. In the **Submit Another Request Decision** box, select the **No** button.

Let's review the Mass Additions.

1. Navigate to **Mass Additions | Prepare Mass Additions**.

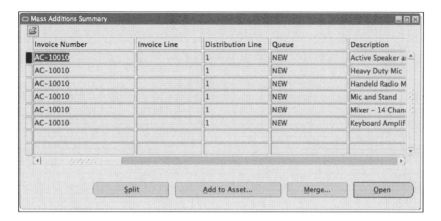

2. Select **ACME CORP** in the **Book** field.

3. Select **NEW** in the **Queue** field.

4. Click on the **Find** button.

5. A list of assets ready to be added is displayed, as shown in the following screenshot:

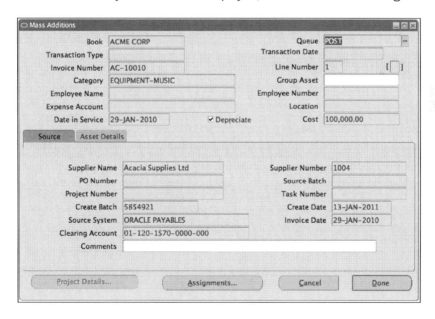

6. Click on the **Open** button to review the asset.

7. Open the **Assets Details** tab and review the information:

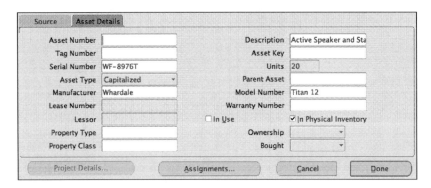

8. In the **Units** field, change the number of units to **20**.

9. Click on the **Assignments...** button.

10. In the **Units** field enter **20**.

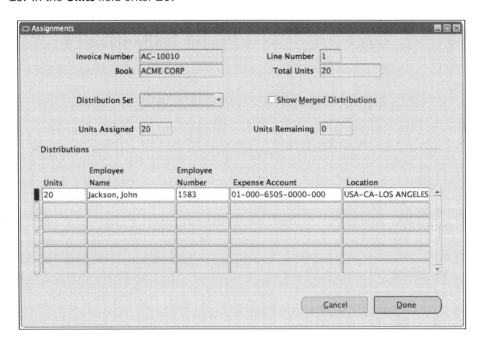

11. In the **Employee Name** field, select **Jackson, John**.

12. In the **Location** field, select **USA-CA-LOS ANGELES-1**.

13. Click on the **Done** button to close the window.

14. Change the **Queue** to **POST**.

Let's post the Mass Additions.

1. Navigate to **Mass Additions | Post Mass Additions**.

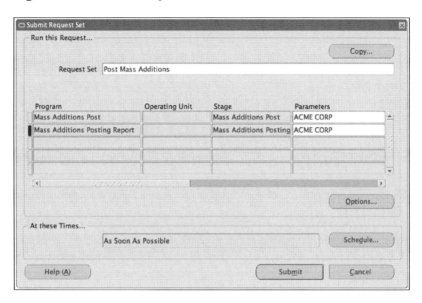

2. Enter **ACME CORP** in the **Parameters** field for the **Mass Additions Post**.

3 Enter **ACME CORP** in the **Parameters** field for the **Mass Additions Posting Report**.

4. View your requests by navigating to **Other | Concurrent**.

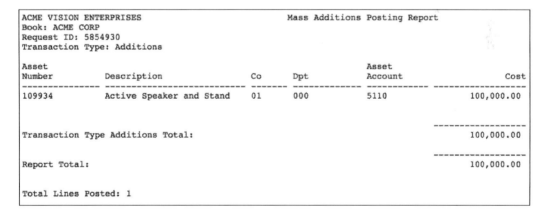

5. Click on the **View Output** button to view the details of the posting.

6. Note the **Asset Number 109934**.

Let's view the asset in the Asset Workbench.

1. Navigate to **Assets | Assets Workbench**.

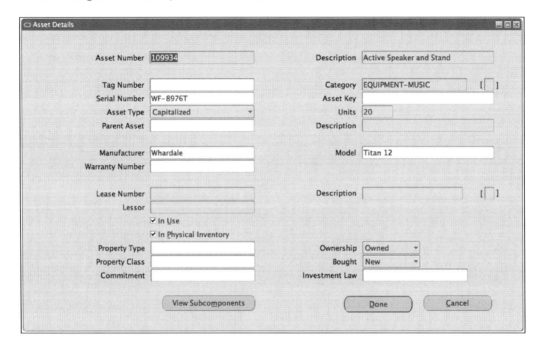

2. Enter the **Asset Number** as **109934** and enter **ACME CORP** in the **Book** field.
3. Review the asset in the workbench.

How it works...

The core steps were as follows:

▶ **Create mass additions**: The **Mass Additions Create** program transfers mass addition data from Payables to the **FA_MASS_ADDITIONS** table. At this stage, the assets are not yet assets in Oracle Assets. You can also send transactions to Oracle Assets by running the PRC: Interface Assets to Oracle Assets program from Oracle Projects.

▶ **Prepare mass additions**: This is used to enter additional data for the mass addition, including assigning the asset to an employee and location. The form is also used for adjustments before the asset is posted.

▶ **Post mass additions**: This is used to transfer the asset information from the **FA_MASS_ADDITIONS** table to the other assets tables. This is used for creating the assets for asset management, for example depreciating the asset.

When the invoice was created in Oracle payables, the Asset Clearing account associated with the Asset book was used. Let's look at the invoice details in payables:

1. Select the **Payables** responsibility.

2. Navigate to **Invoices | Entry | Invoices**.

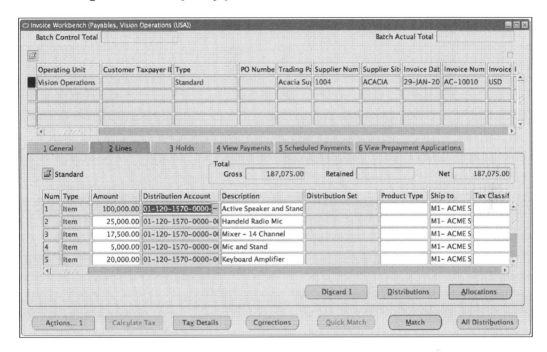

3. Search for the Supplier's invoice number **AC-10010** for **Acacia Suppliers**.

4. Select the **Lines** tab.

5. Review the lines and note that the distribution account is **01-120-1570-0000-000**. The natural accounts segment is **1570**. This is the Asset clearing account.

6. Close the form.

Let's review the **ACME CORPS** Asset books:

1. Select the **Assets** responsibility.

2. Navigate to **Setup | Asset System | Book Controls**:

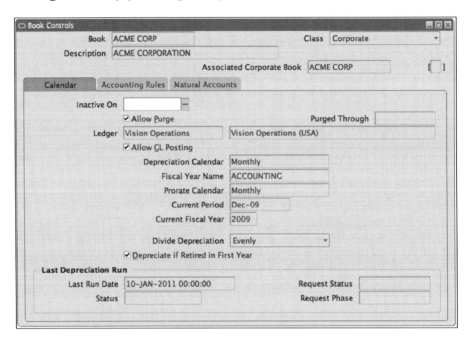

3. Search for **ACME CORP** in the **Book** field.

4. Note the following:

   ❑ **Ledger** assigned to the book is **Vision Operations**

   ❑ The **Depreciation Calendar** is **Monthly**

   ❑ The **Prorate Calendar** is **Monthly**

5. Note that the **Class** of the Asset book is **Corporate**. Assets can also be managed in tax books.

All assets are required to have a category. The category is used to classify the asset based on similar characteristics; this will enable us to apply similar accounting rules to the transactions:

1. Select the **Assets** responsibility.

2. Navigate to **Setup | Asset System | Asset Categories**:

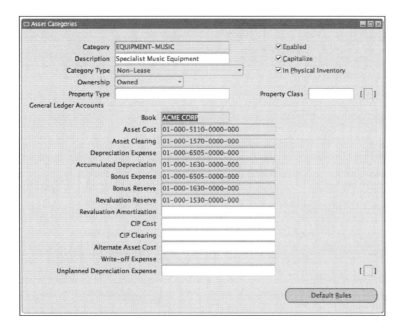

3. Navigate to **View | Query By Example | Enter** or press the *F11* key on the keyboard to enter the query mode.

4. Search for the **EQUIPMENT-MUSIC** category.

5. Review the **General Ledger Accounts** used for the category.

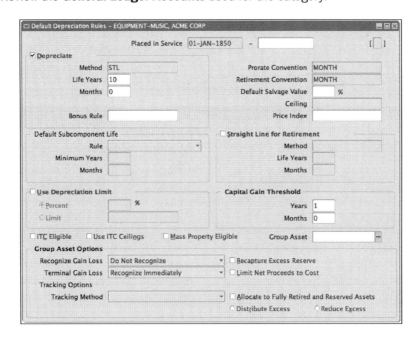

6. Click on the **Default Rules** button.

7. Review the **Depreciation Rules** for the category.

There's more...

Now let's look at some other methods of entering assets.

Manually entering assets

Let's look at how to enter a CIP (Construction in Progress) asset manually.

1. Select the **Assets** responsibility.

2. Navigate to **Assets | Assets Workbench**.

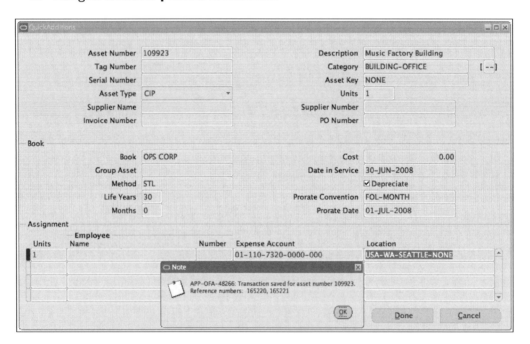

3. Select the **QuickAdditions** button.

4. Enter **Music Factory Building** as the **Description**.

5. In the **Category** field, enter **BUILDING-OFFICE**.

6. Select **CIP** as the **Asset Type**.

7. Select **OPS CORP** as the **Book**.

8. The values for **Date in Service, Depreciation Method,** and the **Prorate Convention** should be defaulted in the relevant fields.

9. Enter the **Expense Account** of **01-110-7320-0000-000**.

10. Enter the location **USA-WA-SEATTLE-NONE**.

11. Click on the **Done** button.

12. Note the **Asset Number 109923** generated by the system.

13. Click on the **OK** button.

Adding assets to the CIP asset

Let's add an asset to the CIP asset:

1. Navigate to **Mass Additions | Prepare Mass Additions**.

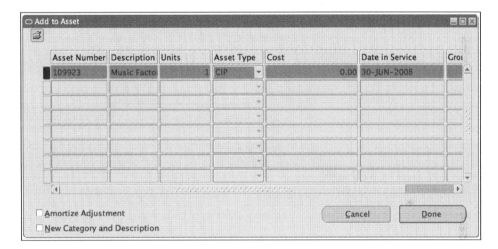

2. Select **OPS CORP** in the **Book** field.

3. Select **NEW** in the **Queue** field.

4. Enter **CP-10002** in the **Invoice** field.

5. Click on the **Find** button.

6. Click on the **Add to Asset** button.

7. Enter **109923** as the **Asset number**.

8. Click on the **Find** button.

9. Click on the **Done** button to add the asset.

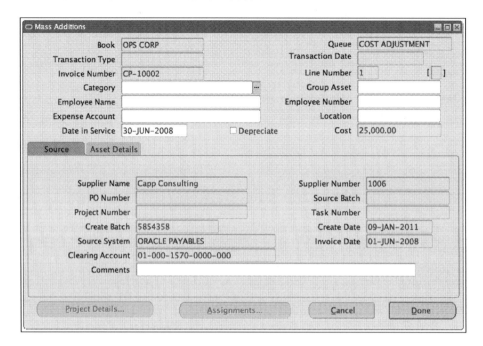

10. Click on the **Open** button to review the asset.

11. Change the **Queue** to **Post**, the system changes the queue to **COST ADJUSTMENT** automatically.

12. Click on the **Done** button.

Let's post the asset to the books:

1. Navigate to **Mass Additions | Post Mass Additions**.

2. Enter **OPS CORP** in the **Parameters** field for the **Mass Additions Post**.

3. Enter **OPS CORP** in the **Parameters** field for the **Mass Additions Posting Report**.

4. View the **Asset** in the **Asset Workbench**.

5. Navigate to **Assets | Assets Workbench**.

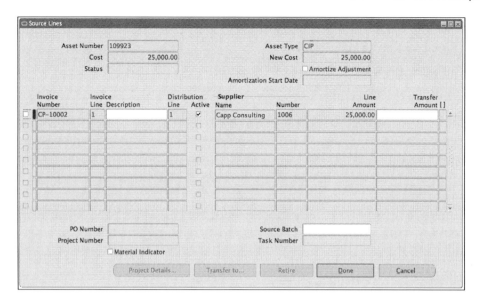

6. Enter the **Asset Number 109923** and enter **OPS CORP** in the **Book** field.

7. Click on the **Source Lines** button.

8. Note that the **Asset** is now added to the **CIP Asset**.

Mass posting of assets

We can set the aueue for a number of assets at the same time, rather than setting them individually:

1. Select the **Assets** responsibility.

2. Navigate to **Mass Additions | Prepare Mass Additions**.

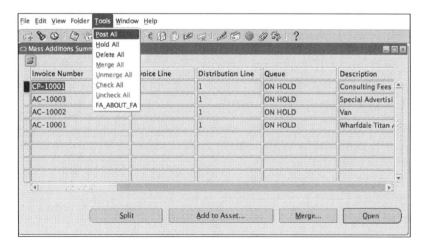

3. Search for all assets in the queue for the **01-JUN-2008**.

4. Select **OPS CORP** in the **Book** field.

5. Enter **01-JUN-2008** in the **Invoice Date** field.

6. Click on the **Find** button.

7. From the **Tools** menu, select **Post All**.

8. In the displayed caution box, select the **OK** button.

9. The **Queue** for all the assets is now changed to **Post**.

Merging assets

We can also merge, unmerge, split, and add to assets. Let's look at an example, where we have just leased a van and our supplier has added a delivery charge to the invoice number AC-10002. The cost of the van needs to be allocated to various sales departments.

We need to merge the delivery charge to the van as part of the cost of the van. We also need to distribute the costs. Let's also assume that we need to distribute the costs to the sales department, based on the OPS Sales Distribution Set:

1. Select the **Assets** responsibility.

2. Navigate to **Mass Additions | Prepare Mass Additions**.

3. Select **OPS CORP** in the **Book** field.

4. Enter **Acacia Supplies Ltd** in the **Supplier** field.

5. Enter **AC-10002** in the **Invoice Number** field.

6. Click on the **Find** button.

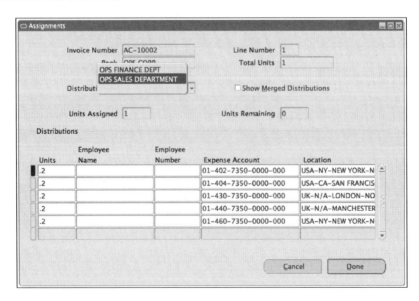

7. Select the **Van** line.

8. In the **Mass Additions** form, click on the **Assignment** button.

9. In the **Assignments Form**, select **OPS Sales Department** in the **Distribution Set**. The costs are re-allocated to the various **Sales** departments.

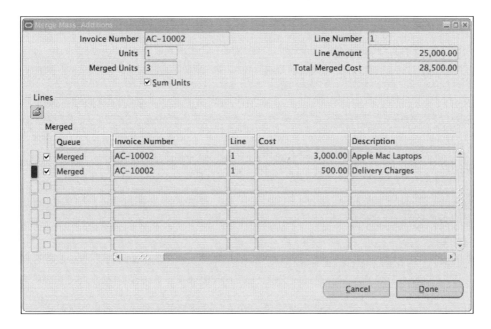

10. Let's merge the laptop and the delivery charge to the van.

11. Click on the **Merge** button.

12. In the **Mass Additions** form, select the **Sum Units** checkbox.

13. Click on the **Merged** checkbox for the **Delivery Charges** and the **Apple Mac Laptops**.

14. The **Queue** name should change to **Merged** and the **Total Merged Cost** should change to **$28,500.00**.

15. Click on the **Done** button.

16. In the **Mass Additions** form, change the **Queue** to **POST**.

See also

Entering Invoices recipe in Chapter 3, Paying Supplier Invoices in Payables

Adjusting assets

Assets may need to be adjusted for a number of reasons, for example:

- ▸ The wrong category may be applied to an asset
- ▸ An asset may change location
- ▸ An asset may need to be reallocated to an employee
- ▸ The number of units of an asset may need to readjusted
- ▸ The value of an asset may change due to economic reasons

When assets are added from Oracle Payables, the default number of units per line is 1 unit. You can change the number of units in Oracle Assets. Once we change the number of units, we need to change the assignments to the assets.

In this recipe, we will adjust the number of units from 1 to 5 units for asset number 109924.

Getting ready

Log in to Oracle E-Business Suite R12 with the username and password assigned to you by the System Administrator. If you are working on the Vision demonstration database, you can use OPERATIONS/WELCOME as the USERNAME/PASSWORD.

We also need to have assets already created in the Assets Workbench.

How to do it...

Let's list the steps required to adjust the units:

1. Select the **Assets** responsibility.
2. Navigate to **Assets | Assets Workbench**.

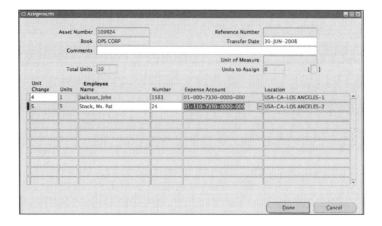

3. Enter **109924** in the **Asset Number** field.

4. Select **OPS CORP** in the **Book** field.

5. Click on the **Find** button.

6. In the **Assets Form**, click on the **Open** button.

7. Change the **Units** from **1** to **10**.

8. Click on the **Done** button.

9. In the **Assignments** form, allocate the **5** units to the employee **John Jackson**, and **5** units to **Pat Stock**, at the **USA-CA-LOS ANGELES-2** location.

10. In the **Unit Change** field, enter **4**.

11. Select the second line and enter **5** in the **Unit Change** field.

12. In the **Employee Name** field, enter **Stock** and press the *Tab* key. The full **Employee Name** should be populated.

13. Enter **01-110-7330-0000-000** as the **Expense Account** number.

14. Enter **USA-CA-LOS ANGELES-2** as the location.

15. Click on the **Done** button to save the changes to your transaction.

There's more...

Now let's look at some other types of adjustments to assets.

Adjusting Expense Accounts and Locations

You can use the assignments window to adjust and transfer assets between expense accounts and locations. Let's transfer 2 units to another employee in another location.

1. Navigate to **Assets | Assets Workbench**.

2. Enter **109924** in the **Asset Number** field.

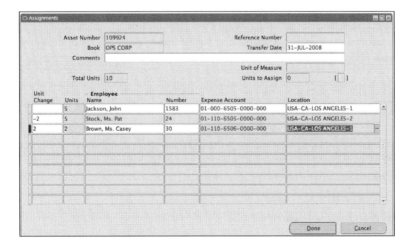

3. Select **OPS CORP** in the **Book** field.

4. Click on the **Find** button.

5. Select the **Assignments** button.

6. Enter **-2** in the **Unit Change** field for the employee **Pat Stock**.

7. Select the line below and enter **2** in the **Unit Change** field.

8. Enter **Casey Brown** as the **Employee**.

9. Enter **01-110-6506-0000-000** as the **Expense Account** number.

10. Enter **USA-CA-LOS ANGELES-1** as the location.

11. Click on the **Done** button.

Adjusting assets categories

The **Keyboard Amplifier** needs to be reclassified from **EQUIPMENT-MOVABLE** to **EQUIPMENT-MUSIC**.

1. Select the **Assets** responsibility.

2. Navigate to **Assets | Assets Workbench**:

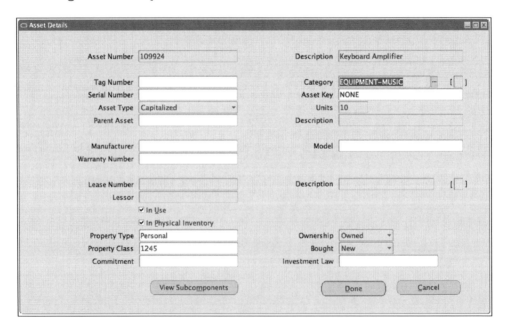

3. Enter **109924** in the **Asset Number** field.

4. Select **OPS CORP** in the **Book** field.

5. Click on the **Find** button.

6. In the **Assets** form, click on the **Open** button.

7. In the **Category** field, change the **Category** to **EQUIPMENT-MUSIC**.

8. Click on the **Done** button to save the changes to your transaction.

Adjusting asset values

The financial information may need to be adjusted due to a revaluation of the asset based on current costs. We need to adjust the current cost to $20,000 from $25,000:

1. Select the **Assets** responsibility.

2. Navigate to **Assets | Assets Workbench**.

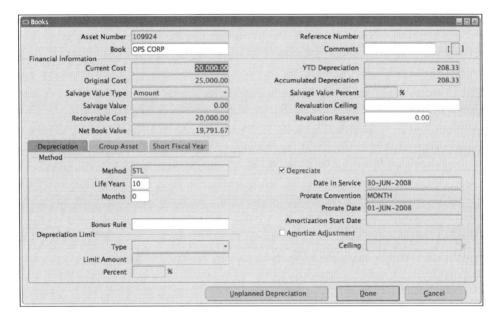

3. Enter **109924** in the **Asset Number** field.

4. Select **OPS CORP** in the **Book** field.

5. Click on the **Find** button.

6. In the **Assets** form, click on the **Books** button.

7. In the **Book** field, enter **OPS CORP**.

8. Click on the **Current Cost** field. The data in the financial information region is then prepopulated.

9. Change the **Current Cost** to **20000**.

10. Click on the **Done** button to save the record.

Transferring costs

You can also transfer costs from an asset to another. Let's now transfer some of the costs from asset 109923 to asset 109922:

1. Navigate to **Assets | Assets Workbench**.

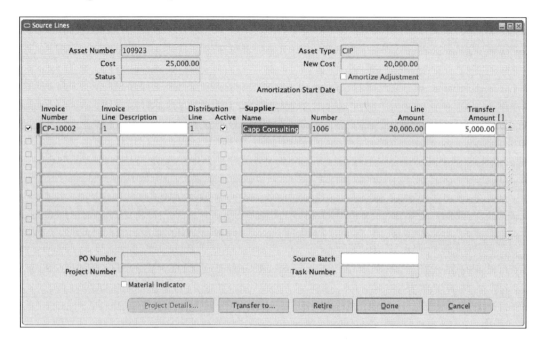

2. Enter the **Asset** number **109923**, and enter **OPS CORP** in the **Book** field.

3. Click on the **Source Lines** button.

4. In the **Transfer Amount** field, enter **5000** and press the *Tab* key. The **Transfer To** button is now enabled.

5. Click on the **Transfer To** button:

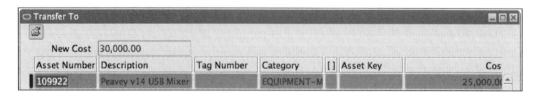

6. Search for the **Asset** by pressing *F11*, entering **109922** in the **Asset Number** field, and pressing *Ctrl+F11* to execute the query.

7. Click on the **Done** button.

8. Click on the **Source Lines** button:

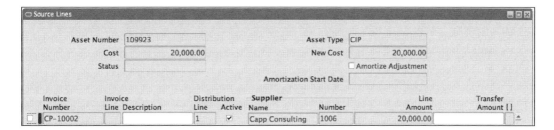

9. The value of asset source line is now reduced by **5000** to **20000**.
10. Click on **cancel** to exit the form.

Depreciating assets

Assets need to be depreciated based on defined depreciation methods. In this recipe, we will look at how to run depreciation and close a period.

Getting ready

Log in to Oracle E-Business Suite R12 with the username and password assigned to you by the System Administrator. If you are working on the Vision demonstration database, you can use OPERATIONS/WELCOME as the USERNAME/PASSWORD.

Run the following reports to check if all assets are assigned to the correct expense accounts and books:

▶ Assets Not Assigned to Any Cost Centers Listing
▶ Assets Not Assigned to Any Books Listing

How to do it...

Let's list the steps required to run depreciation:

1. Select the **Assets** responsibility.
2. Navigate to **Depreciation | Run Depreciation**.

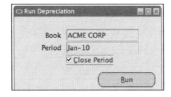

3. In the **Book** field, select **ACME CORP**.

4. The **Period** is automatically entered.

5. Select the **Close Period** checkbox to close the period. Once a period is closed, it cannot be reopened.

6. Click on the **Run** button.

7. In the **Caution** dialog box, select the **OK** button.

8. The system submits a concurrent request.

9. Click on the **OK** button.

How it works...

Let's look at how these steps allow us to depreciate the assets in the period.

The depreciation process starts and runs a number of concurrent programs including the following:

▶ **Generate Accounts**: This builds the accounting combinations using Oracle Workflow

▶ **Calculate Gains** and **Losses**: This calculates the gains and losses resulting from retirements

▶ **Depreciation Run**: This calculates the depreciation expense

▶ **Reserve Ledger Reports**: Runs the Journal Entry Reserve Ledger Report

The transactions are generated based on the depreciation methods and the prorate conventions.

There's more...

Now let's look at some other options or possibly some pieces of general information that are relevant to this task.

Reviewing depreciation methods

Let's review the Straight Line (STL) depreciation method:

1. Select the **Assets** responsibility.

2. Navigate to **Setup | Depreciation | Methods**:

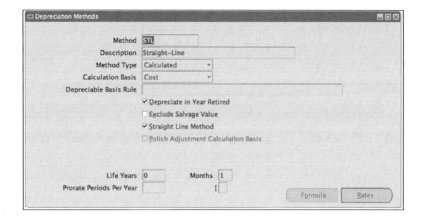

3. In the **Depreciation Methods** form, search for the **STL** method.

4. Depreciation can also be based on a table, based on units of production, flat, or based on a formula.

5. The **Calculation Basis** could also be based on **Cost** or **Net Book** value.

Reviewing prorate conventions

Prorate conventions are used to determine the apportionment of the depreciation expense in the first and last year of the life of the asset:

1. Select the **Assets** responsibility.

2. Navigate to **Setup | Asset System | Prorate Conventions**:

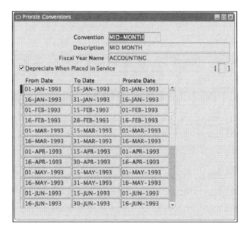

3. In the **Prorate Conventions** form, search for **MID-MONTH Convention**.

4. The **Prorate Date** determines when the proration of the depreciation expense will start and end.

Chapter 9, End of Period Processing

Retiring assets

Assets are retired once they are no longer in use by an organization. In this recipe, we will look at how to retire assets.

Getting ready

Log in to Oracle E-Business Suite R12 with the username and password assigned to you by the system administrator. If you are working on the Vision demonstration database, you can use OPERATIONS/WELCOME as the USERNAME/PASSWORD.

How to do it...

A Genesis–1.0 Speaker, asset number 109931, has been sold for $37,000 on the 31st of March 2010. Let's retire the asset in the ACME CORP asset book:

1. Select the **Assets** responsibility.

2. Navigate to **Assets | Assets Workbench**.

3. In the **Category** field, enter **EQUIPMENT-MOVABLE**.

4. Select **ACME CORP** in the **Book** field.

5. Click on the **Find** button.

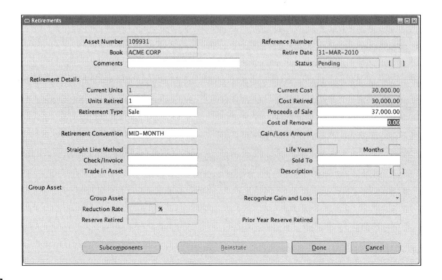

6. In the **Assets** form, find the asset number **109931**.

7. Click on the **Retirements** button.

8. In the **Retirements** form, enter the **ACME CORP** in the **Book** field.

9. Accept the default date of **31-MAR-2010** as the **Retire Date**.

10. Enter the **Units Retired** as **1**.

11. Select the **Retirement Type** as **Sale**.

12. Enter the **Proceeds of Sale** as **37000**.

13. Save the record.

14. Click on the **Done** button.

There's more...

Now let's look at some other options related to the retirement of assets.

Partial retirement

One of the 20 Active Speakers and Stand (**Asset Number 109934**) was lost during asset verification check. Let's partially retire the asset in the ACME CORP books:

1. Select the **Assets** responsibility.

2. Navigate to **Assets | Asset Workbench**.

3. In the **Assets** form, find asset number **109934**.

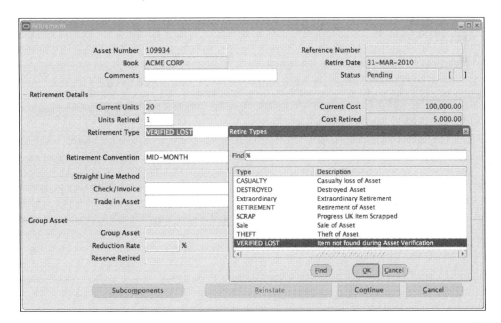

4. Select the **Retirements** button.

5. In the **Retirements** form, enter the **ACME CORP** in the **Book** field.

6. Accept the default date of **31-MAR-2010** as the **Retire Date**.

7. In the **Units Retired** field, enter **1**.

8. In the **Retirement Type** field, select **VERIFIED LOST** from the list of values.

9. Click on the **Continue** button.

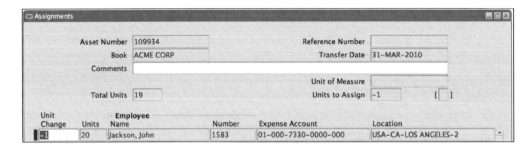

10. In the **Assignments** form, enter **–1** in the **Units to Assign** field.

11. Save your work.

12. Click on the **Done** button.

Calculating gains and losses

Let's run the **Calculate Gains and Losses** program to calculate the gains and losses resulting from retirements. The depreciation program also automatically processes retirements:

1. Select the **Assets** responsibility.

2. Navigate to **Depreciation | Calculate Gains and Losses**:

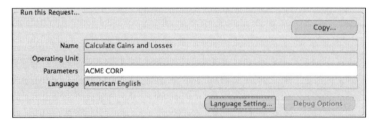

3. In the **Parameters** window, select **ACME CORP** in the **Book** field.

4. Click on the **OK** button.

5. Click on the **Submit** button.

6. In the **Request Submitted** note, click on the **OK** button.

7. Navigate to **Asset | Asset Workbench**.

8. In the **Assets** form, find **Asset Number 109934**.

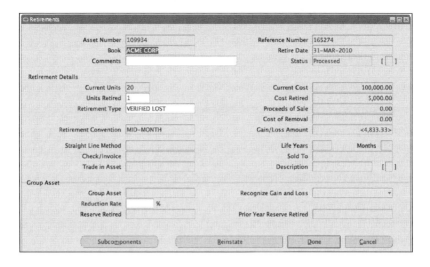

9. Click on the **Retirements** button.
10. Press the *Ctrl+F11* keys to query the retirement.
11. The **Gain/Loss Amount** is now displayed as **<4,833.33>**.
12. Click on the **Cancel** button to close the window.

Mass retirements

All the assets in Los Angeles building 2 (USA-CA-LOS ANGELES-2) are sold for $250,000, with a $500 removal fee. Let's look at how to retire a group of assets:

1. Select the **Assets** responsibility.
2. Navigate to **Mass Transactions | Retirements | Create and Reinstate**.

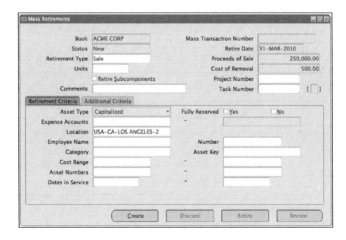

3. In the **Mass Retirements** form, select **ACME CORP** as the **Book**.

4. Enter **31-MAR-2010** in the **Retire Date** field.

5. Select **Sale** as the **Retirement Type**.

6. In the **Proceeds of Sale** field, enter **250,000.00**.

7. In the **Cost of Removal** field, enter **500.00**.

8. In the **Location** field, enter **USA-CA-LOS ANGELES-2**.

9. Click on the **Create** button.

10. Click on **OK** in the concurrent request note form.

11. Note the **Mass Transaction Number** of **294**.

12. Requery the form, press *F11* on the **Mass Transfer** form, enter **294** in the **Mass Transaction Number** field, and press *Ctrl+F11*.

13. The form is now populated.

14. The **Discard** and **Retire** buttons are now enabled.

15. Click on the **Retire** button.

16. Click on **OK** in the concurrent request note form.

```
ACME VISION ENTERPRISES                      Mass Retirements Report              Report Date:  17-JAN-2011 21:11
Book:  ACME CORP                          Mass Retirement Number: 294                  Page:      1   of       1
Company:  01
Asset Type:  Capitalized
Account:  1530
Department:  000

Asset Number -                Date Placed Date                       Proceeds of                  Parent Asset       Trans
Description                   in Service  Retired     Cost Retired           Sale   Removal Cost         Number      Number
---------------------------   ----------- ----------- ------------   ------------   ------------   ---------------   --------
109932 - YG ACOUSTICS - Kipod - 15-DEC-2009 31-MAR-2010    40,000.00     74,074.07         148.14                     165276
109934 - Active Speaker and Sta 29-JAN-2010 31-MAR-2010    95,000.00    175,925.93         351.86                     165277

                                                      ------------   ------------   ------------
Department 000 Totals:                                   135,000.00     250,000.00         500.00

                                                      ------------   ------------   ------------
Account 1530 Totals:                                     135,000.00     250,000.00         500.00

                                                      ------------   ------------   ------------
Asset Type Capitalized Totals:                           135,000.00     250,000.00         500.00

                                                      ------------   ------------   ------------
Company 01 Totals:                                       135,000.00     250,000.00         500.00

                                                      ------------   ------------   ------------
Report Totals:                                           135,000.00     250,000.00         500.00
                                                      ============   ============   ============
```

17. Requery the form, press *F11* on the **Mass Transfer** form, enter **294** in the **Mass Transaction Number** field, and press *Ctrl+F11*.

18. Click on the **Review** button.

19. Navigate to **View | Request** on the menu, and select the **Find** button.

20. Click on the **View Output** button to view the details of the posting.

21. Note that the proceeds of sale are apportioned to the assets.

Reviewing asset accounting

In this recipe, we will review some of the accounting transactions created in Oracle Assets.

How to do it...

The **Create Accounting** program generates Subledger accounting entries for accounting events. An accounting event is created for asset transactions that have an impact on accounting:

1. Select the **Assets** responsibility.

2. Navigate to **Create Accounting**.

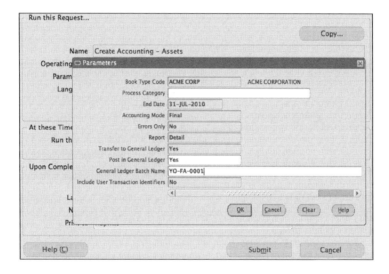

3. Enter the following details in the request form:

    ☐ **Book Type Code** field select **ACME CORP**

    ☐ Enter **31-JUL-2010** as the **End Date**

    ☐ **Accounting Mode** field select **Final** from the list of values

    ☐ **Errors Only** field select **No**

    ☐ **Report** field select **Detail**

    ☐ **Transfer to General Ledger** select **Yes**

    ☐ **Post in General Ledger** select **Yes**

    ☐ **General Ledger Batch Name** field enter **YO-FA-0001**

    ☐ **Include User Transaction Identifiers** field select **No**

4. Click on the **OK** button.

5. Click on the **Submit** button.

Let's view some of the transactions from the General Ledger:

1. Switch responsibilities by selecting **File | Switch Responsibility**.

2. Select the **General Ledger** responsibility.

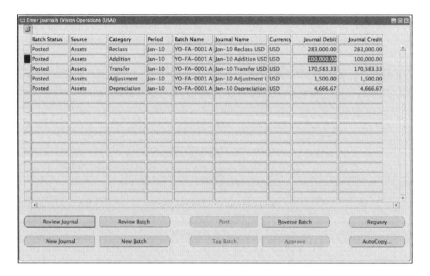

3. Navigate to **Journals | Enter**.

4. Search for the journal by selecting the **Source** as **Assets**, **Batch** as **YO-FA-0001%**, and the **Period** as **Jan-10**.

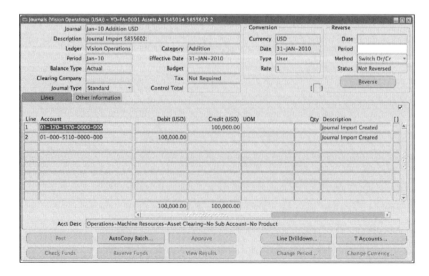

5. Click on the **Journal** with a **Category** of **Addition**.

6. Select the **Review Journal** button.

7. Note that the **Asset Cost Account** (5110) for the **Category** is debited and the **Asset** clearing account is **Credited**.

8. Close the form.

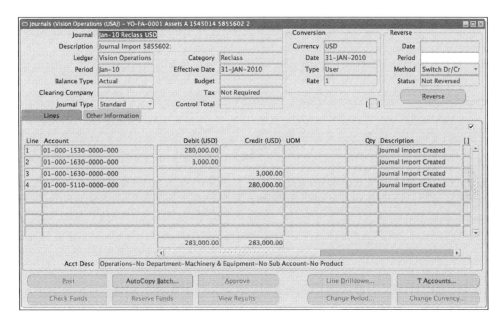

9. Click on the **Journal** with a **Category** of **Reclass**.

10. Select the **Review Journal** button.

11. Note that the **Asset Cost Account** for the new category (**1530**) is debited and the old **Asset Cost** account (**5110**) is credited.

12. Close the form.

How it works...

Oracle Assets uses the accounting event model defined in Subledger Accounting to determine the transactions that generate accounting transactions. Oracle Assets groups all the accounting events classes into four main event model entities:

1. Deferred depreciation

2. Depreciation

3. Inter assets transactions

4. Transactions

These are further classified into event classes and event types:

1. Select the **Assets** responsibility.

2. Navigate to **Setup | Financials | Subledger Accounting | Accounting Methods Builder | Events | Event Model**.

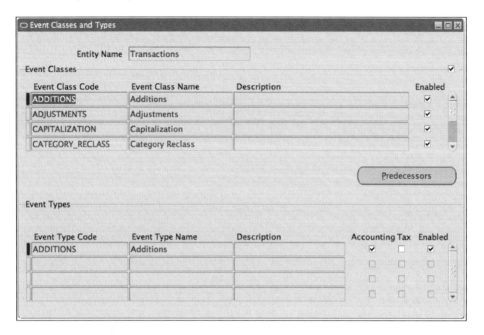

3. Select the **Transactions Entity Name**.

4. Click on the **Event Classes** to view the **Event Classes** and the **Event Types**.

There's more...

Let's review the **Accounting Events** for a transaction:

1. Select the **Assets** responsibility.

2. Navigate to **Inquiry | Subledger Accounting | Accounting Events**:

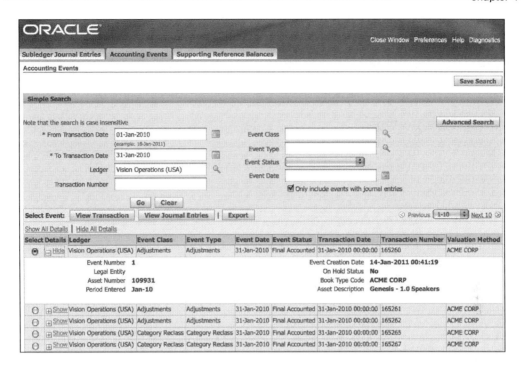

3. In the **Accounting Events** tab, enter **01-JAN-2010** in the **From Transaction Date** field.

4. Enter **31-JAN-2010** in the **To Transaction Date** field.

5. Select **Vision Operations (USA)** in the **Ledger** field.

6. Click on the **Go** button.

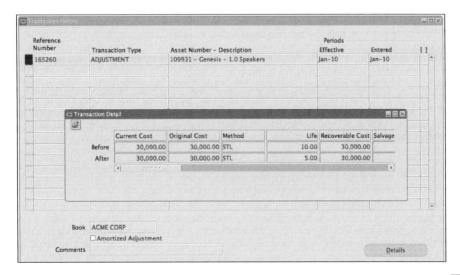

7. In the list of the accounting events, select the transaction.

8. Click on the **View Transaction** button.

9. Click on the **Details** button. Details of the accounting event are displayed.

10. Close the **Transaction History** window.

See also

Defining subledger accounting recipe in Chapter 8, Defining Transactions for the General Ledger

5
Selling Items to Customers in Order Management

In this chapter, we will cover:

- ▶ Creating customers
- ▶ Entering sales orders
- ▶ Adding Items to Price List
- ▶ Reviewing Order Management workflow
- ▶ Creating Drop Ship orders
- ▶ Creating Back-to-Back orders
- ▶ Creating a return
- ▶ Applying holds
- ▶ Releasing orders
- ▶ Shipping orders
- ▶ Creating an invoice

Introduction

Oracle Order Management is used to capture and fulfill orders from different sources. These include entering orders manually, importing orders from XML Gateway, CRM, online orders through EDI, Oracle iStore, and Oracle Quoting. Fulfillment of the order can be through making, buying, or selling through stock in inventory. Oracle Order Management uses workflow, which can be customized to drive the process.

The following diagram summarizes a typical Order Management process:

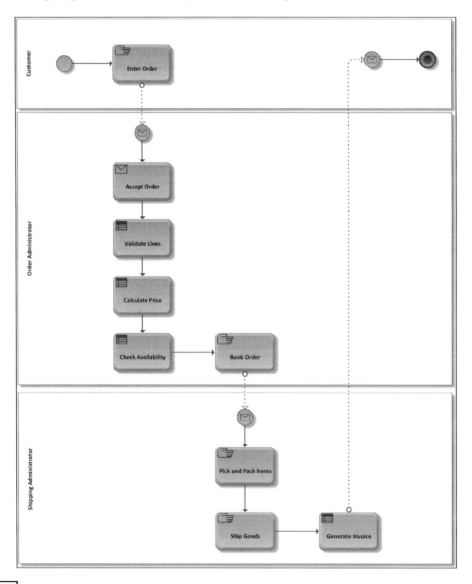

1. The **Customer** enters the order from an external source. An order entry clerk can also enter the order.

2. The order is imported into Order Management and checked for validity.

3. The order is accepted, after it is checked.

4. The Items on the lines are validated in inventory and a price is calculated for the line.

5. The availability of the Items are checked and may be reserved, purchased, or manufactured.

6. The order is booked ready to be picked and shipped to the **Customer**.

7. The Items are picked, packed, and shipped to the customer. The invoice is also generated and sent to the **Customer**.

This chapter assumes that you to have access to a Vision demonstration database, and you are using the standard seeded workflows. Log in to Oracle E-Business Suite R12 with the username and password assigned to you by the system administrator. If you are working on the Vision demonstration database, you can use OPERATIONS/WELCOME as the USERNAME/PASSWORD.

Creating customers

Before we can sell Items, we need customers. In this recipe, we will look at how to create customers. We will create a customer called **Sheepwall Inc** with an address called a site. The site can be used as a bill to, ship to, and deliver to address.

Getting ready

Log in to Oracle E-Business Suite R12 with the username and password assigned to you by the system administrator. If you are working on the Vision demonstration database, you can use OPERATIONS/WELCOME as the USERNAME/PASSWORD.

How to do it...

Let's create a customer:

1. Select the **Order Management** responsibility.

2. Navigate to **Customers | Standard**.

3. Click on the **Create** button.

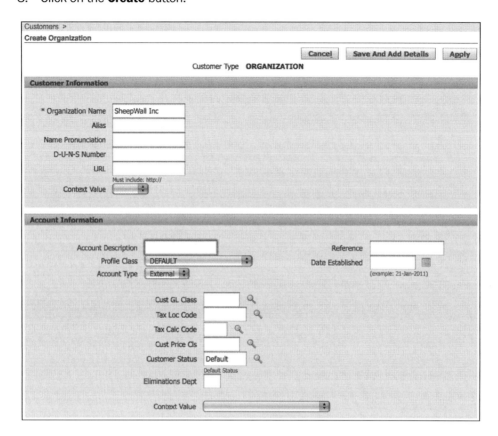

4. In the **Customer Information** region, enter **SheepWall Inc** in the **Organization Name**.

5. In the **Account Information** region:

    ❑   Select **DEFAULT** as the **Profile Class**

    ❑   Select **External** as the **Account Type**

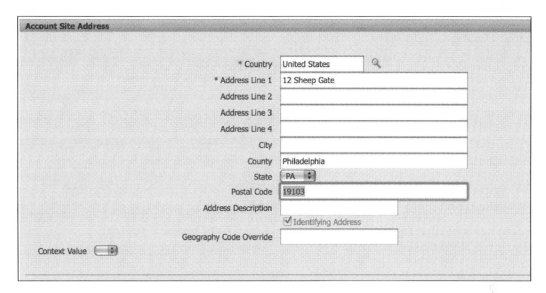

6. In the **Account Site Address** region:

    ❏   Enter **United States** in the **Country** field

    ❏   Enter **12 Sheep Gate** in **Address Line 1**

    ❏   Enter **Philadelphia** in the **County** field

    ❏   Select **PA** in the **State** field

    ❏   Enter **19103** as the **Postal Code**

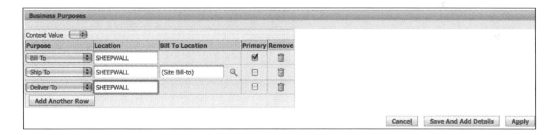

7. In the **Business Purposes** region:

    ❏   Select the **Bill To** as the **Purpose** and check the **Primary** checkbox

    ❏   Click on the **Add Another Row** button

    ❏   Select **Ship To** in the **Purpose** field and assign the **(Site Bill-to)** site as the **Bill To Location**

    ❏   Select **Deliver To** in the **Purpose** field

8. Click on the **Apply** button.

How it works...

Customers are set up in the **Trading Community Architecture** (**TCA**) as a party. The main purpose of the TCA is to hold master data information relating to an entity in a central repository. The information can then be used by more than one module as a "single source of truth" throughout the lifecycle of the party. For example, a customer can start as a prospect in CRM and can later in its lifecycle become a customer in receivables. A party can be an organization or a person. A party has information about itself, for example, a customer has a name—the name of the customer created in the previous section, that is, Sheepwall Inc.

Oracle uses party relationships to link the details of the parties to each other. For example, a person as a party can be a contact in an Organization.

A party has a site that links a party with its location and it defines the purpose of the site. For example, a site can be used as a Ship To site for shipping of goods.

Profile classes are used to manage customer accounts based on groups. The groups contain information about the similar characteristics of the customers. Examples are credit and collection, payment terms, receipts, statements, and invoicing requirements. Every customer must be assigned a profile class.

Customers have information held at the customer header, for example, organization profiles, communication, party relationships, and tax profiles. Customers also have information held at the site level, for example, site address, business purposes, communication, payment details, site profiles, profile amounts, and details of late charges settings.

There's more...

Now let's look at some other options, and general information that is relevant to this task.

Adding a customer site

Let's add a new site to the customer. The site will also be used as a Ship-To site:

1. Select the **Order Management** responsibility.
2. Navigate to **Customers | Standard**.

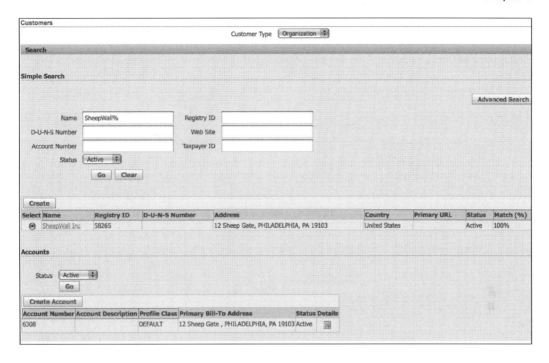

3. Enter **SheepWall%** in the **Name** field and click on the **Go** button.

4. Click on the **SheepWall Inc** link.

5. Click on the **Create Site** button.

6. Click on the **Create Address** button to enter the address for the site.

7. Enter the following details for the site address:

   ❑ Enter **United Kingdom** in the **Country** field

   ❑ Enter **Hertford Road** in the **Address Line 1** field

   ❑ Enter **Welwyn** in the **Town / City** field

   ❑ Enter **Herts** in the **County** field

   ❑ Enter **AL6 0JB** in the **Postal Code** field

8. In the **Business Purpose** region, select **Bill To** as the purpose and click on the **Primary** checkbox.

9. Click on the **Add Another Row** button.

10. Select **Ship To** in the **Purpose** field and click on the **Primary** checkbox.

11. Select **(Site Bill To)** as the **Bill To Location**.

12. Click on the **Finish** button.

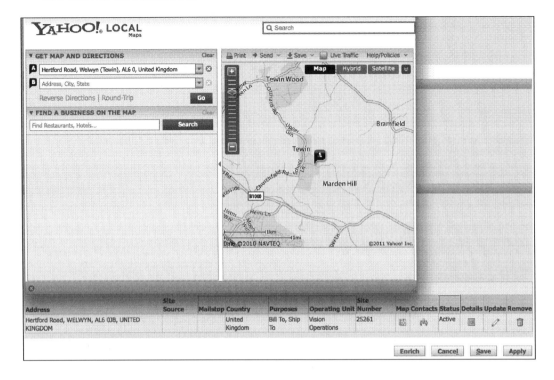

13. In the **Accounts** tab, select the **Hertford Road, WELWYN, AL6 0JB** address.

14. Click on the **Map** icon to view where the **Company** is located.

15. Click on the **Details** icon.

16. The **Site Details** tab is displayed.

Adding contacts

Let's look at how to add a contact:

1. Select the **Communication** tab.

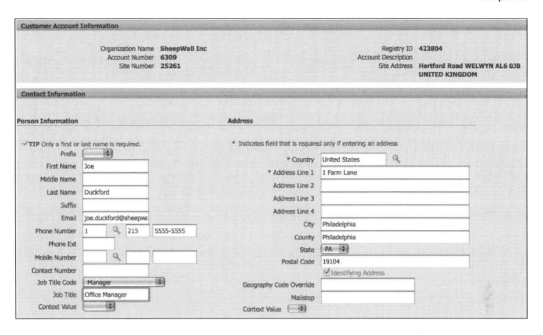

2. Click on the **Create Contact** button.

3. Enter the following information for the contact in the **Personal Information** section:

   ❑ Select **Mr** in the **Prefix** field

   ❑ Enter **Joe** in the **First Name** field

   ❑ Enter **Duckford** in the **Last Name** field

   ❑ Enter **joe.duckford@sheepwall.com** in the **Email** field

   ❑ Enter **1-215-5555-5555** in the **Phone Number** field

   ❑ Select **Manager** in the **Job Title Code** list

   ❑ Enter **Office Manager** in the **Job Title** field

4. Enter the following information in the **Address** section:

   ❑ Enter **United States** in the **Country** field

   ❑ Enter **1 Farm Lane** in the **Address Line 1** field

   ❑ Enter **Philadelphia** in the **City** field

   ❑ Enter **Philadelphia** in the **County** field

   ❑ Enter **PA** in the **State** field

   ❑ Enter **19104** in the **Postal Code** field

5. Click on the **Apply** button.

Adding profile details

1. Create **Profile** at the site level.

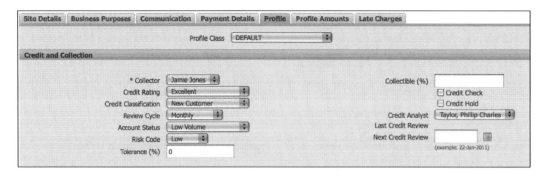

2. Click on the **Profile** tab.

3. Review the details; some of the data is defaulted from the **Customer** header.

4. Enter the following details:

   ❏ Enter **Jamie Jones** in the **Collector** field

   ❏ Enter **Excellent** in the **Credit Rating** field

   ❏ Enter **New Customer** in the **Credit Classification** field

   ❏ Enter **Monthly** in the **Review Cycle** field

   ❏ Enter **Low Volume** in the **Account Status** field

   ❏ Enter **Low** in the **Risk Code** field

   ❏ Enter **Taylor, Philip Charles** in the **Credit Analyst** field

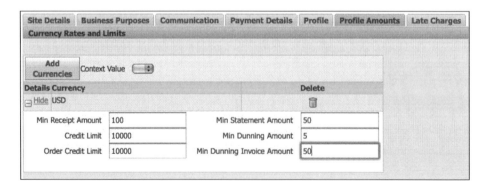

5. In the **Profile Amounts** tab, select **USD** as the currency.

6. Enter the following details in the **Details Currency** region:

   ❑ Enter **100** in the **Min Receipt Amount** field

   ❑ Enter **10000** in the **Credit Limit** field

   ❑ Enter **10000** in the **Order Credit Limit** field

   ❑ Enter **50** in the **Min Statement Amount** field

   ❑ Enter **5** in the **Min Dunning Amount** field

   ❑ Enter **50** in the **Min Dunning Invoice Amount** field

7. Click on the **Apply** button and close the form.

Entering sales orders

Orders can be imported from an external source, for example, a web order can be interfaced with Order Management. Sheepwall Inc. has requested to purchase an ACME laptop (Item number PRD20007 held in inventory). The laptop comes with a special warranty (Item number PRD99999 a service Item). In this recipe, we will enter a sales order for Sheepwall Inc. with two lines.

Getting ready

Log in to Oracle E-Business Suite R12 with the username and password assigned to you by the system administrator. If you are working on the Vision demonstration database, you can use OPERATIONS/WELCOME as the USERNAME/PASSWORD.

We also need the Item to be created in Inventory.

How to do it...

Let's list the steps required to create the order:

1. Select the **Order Management** responsibility.

2. Navigate to **Orders, Returns | Sales Order**.

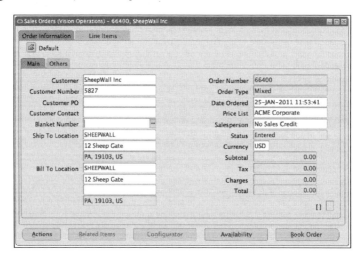

3. Select the **Main** tab.

4. Enter **SheepWall Inc** in the **Customer** field, the **Ship To Location** and the **Bill To Locations** are automatically populated.

5. In the **Order Type** field, select **Mixed**.

6. In the **Price List** field, select **ACME Corporate**.

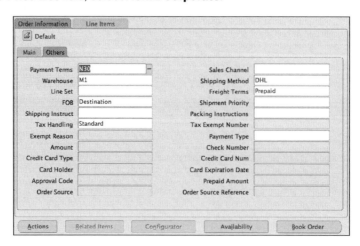

7. Select the **Others** tab.

8. Select **N30** as the **Payment Terms**.
9. Select **M1** as the **Warehouse** where the goods will be held.
10. Select **Standard** as the **Tax Handling** method.
11. Select **DHL** as the **Shipping Method**.
12. Select **Prepaid** as the **Freight Terms**.

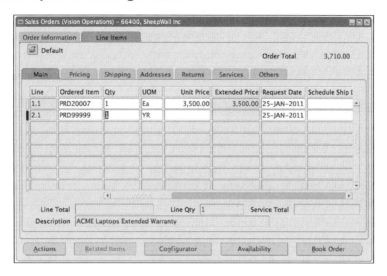

13. Select the **Line** tab and enter the line details.
14. Enter **PRD20007** in the **Ordered Item** field.
15. Enter **1** as the quantity in the **Qty** field and the price automatically defaults from the price list.

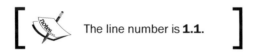

The line number is **1.1**.

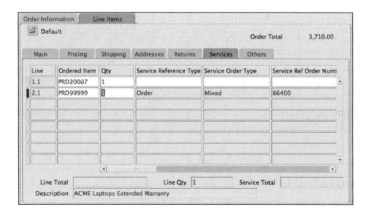

16. Select the next line. The line number automatically defaults to **2.1**.

17. Enter **PRD99999** as the **Ordered Item**.

18. Enter **1** as the **Qty** and select **YR** as the **Unit of Measure (UOM)**.

19. Select the **Services** tab.

20. Enter **Order** in the **Service Reference Type** field.

21. Enter **Mixed** in the **Service Order Type** field.

22. Enter the order number **66400** in the **Service Ref Order Number** field.

23. Enter **1** in the **Service Ref Line Number** field, the line number relating to the service Item.

24. Enter **1** in the **Service Ref Shipment Number** field.

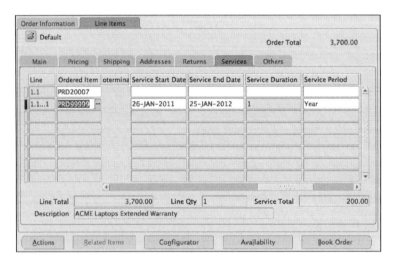

25. Enter a **Service Start Date** of **26-JAN-2011**.

26. Select a **Service Period** of **Year**.

27. Enter a **Service Duration** of **1**.

28. The **Service End Date** of **25-JAN-2012** is entered automatically.

29. Click on the **Book Order** button.

30. The **Status** of the **Order** is changed from **Entered** to **Booked**.

How it works...

An order consists of two main parts, the Order Header and the Order Lines. An order requires a customer and Items. Once the order is entered and booked, the workflow engine determines the flow of the order. The header has its workflow and each line has its own workflow. The line workflows need to be completed before the header flow can be closed.

Details entered in the order header include the following:

1. A Bill to and a Ship to address, and the details.
2. Order Type—this could be Order, Return, or a combination of both called Mixed.
3. A price list and a sales person.
4. Shipping details.

Key details entered on the Line include the following:

1. Line Items.
2. Price of the Items based on the price list.
3. The line types–this determines the line flow that will be called by the workflow engine.

When we enter order data in the **Order Management** form, some of the mandatory data is entered automatically based on the defaulting rules.

Let's view the defaulting rules for the **Price List**:

1. Select the **Order Management** responsibility.
2. Navigate to **Setup | Rules | Defaulting**.

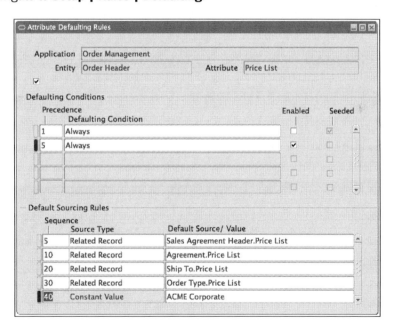

3. Press the *F11* function key to enter the Query Mode.
4. In the **Entity** field, enter **Order Header** and press *Ctrl+F11*.
5. The defaulting rules for the header attributes are displayed.

6. Select the **Price List** attribute.

7. Click on the **Defaulting Rules** button.

8. The defaulting conditions and the **Defaulting Sourcing Rules** are displayed.

9. The defaulting rule for the **Constant Value** is **ACME Corporate**.

There's more...

Let's look at other methods of entering an order.

Entering orders quickly

An order can be entered quickly using the Quick Sales Order Entry window:

1. Select the **Order Management** responsibility.

2. Navigate to **Orders, Returns | Quick Sales Order**.

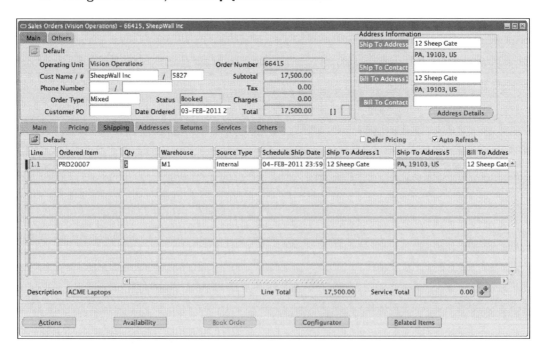

3. In the **Cust Name / #** field, enter **SheepWall Inc**, and press the *Tab* key to automatically search for and enter the customer name.

4. In the **Order Type** field, enter **Mixed**.

5. Select the **Ordered Item** field in the **Main** tab, and enter **PRD20007**.

6. Enter **5** in the **Qty** field.

7. Click on the **Book Order** button.

8. The defaulting rules are used to populate the details of the order.

9. The order is booked.

See also

Creating Items recipe in Chapter 1, Creating Items in Inventory

Creating Customers recipe in this chapter

Adding Items to price list

Items sold to our customers need to have a price. And the price is added to a price list. In this recipe, we will add an Item to a price list.

Getting ready

Before an Item can be added to a price list, we need to have an Item.

How to do it...

Let's add an Item to a price list:

1. Navigate to **Purchasing | Advanced Pricing | Price Lists | Price List Setup**.

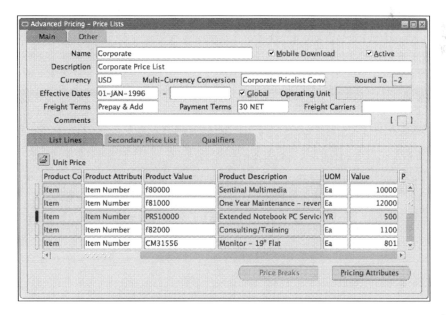

2. Press the *F11* function key to enter the Query Mode.

3. In the **Name** field, enter **Corporate** and press *Ctrl* and *F11* key.

4. The details of the **Corporate Price List** are displayed.

5. In the **List Lines** tab, click on the **Product Context** field.

6. Click on the **New** icon.

7. Select **Item** in the **Product Context** field.

8. Select **Item Number** in the **Product Attribute** field.

9. In the **Product Value** field, enter **PRS10000**.

10. Select **YR** as the **UOM**.

11. In the **Value** field, enter **500**.

12. Save the record.

How it works...

Order management uses a pricing engine to determine the price of an Item based on rules set up in Advanced Pricing. When an Item is selected, the pricing engine calculates the price based on the values entered in the price list.

The price may contain some modifiers (changes to the price) and qualifiers (the entity qualified to use the changes). Modifiers and qualifiers are applied to the base price. An example of a modifier is a discount applied to the price and a qualifier could be the order type.

There's more...

Now let's look at some other options, and some general information that is relevant to this task.

Applying a discount to the price

Let's apply a 20 percent discount to an Item's price. We will also use the Order Organizer to find the order:

1. Select the **Order Management** responsibility.

2. Navigate to **Orders, Returns | Order Organizer**.

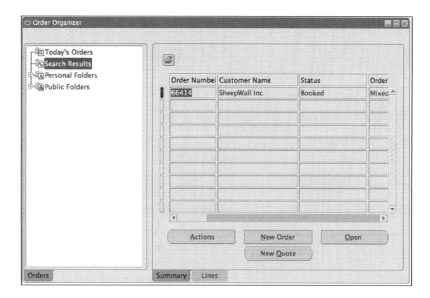

3. In the **Order Number** field, enter **66414** and click on the **Find** button.

4. Click on the **Open** button to view the **Order**.

5. Select the **Line Items** tab.

6. Select Line **1.1** and click on the **Actions** button.

7. Select **View Adjustment** and click on the **OK** button.

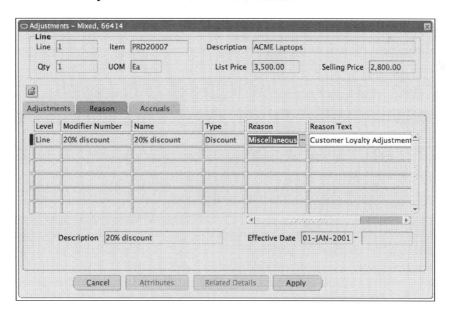

8. Select the **Modifier Number** field and select **20% discount**.

9. The **20% discount** is applied to the **Price** and the price is modified from **$3,500** to **$2,800**.

10. Select the **Reason** tab, and select **Miscellaneous**.

11. In the **Reason Text**, enter **Customer Loyalty Adjustment**.

12. Click on the **Apply** button to apply the discount.

Viewing modifiers

Let's view the modifier applied to an Item:

1. Navigate to **Purchasing | Advanced Pricing | Modifiers | Modifier Setup**.

2. Press the *F11* function key to enter the Query Mode.

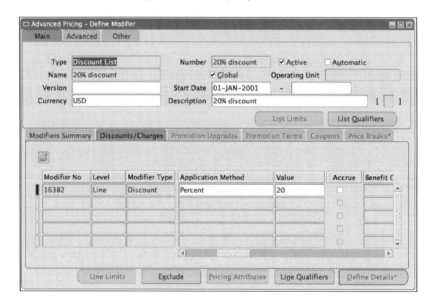

3. In the **Number** field, enter **20% discount** and press *Ctrl + F11*.

4. The details of the 20 percent modifier are displayed.

5. Close the form.

Mass adding of Items to a price list

Let's add a group of Items to a price list:

1. Navigate to **Purchasing | Advanced Pricing | Price Lists | Add Items to Price List**.

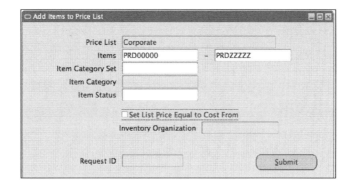

2. In the **Price List Field**, select **Corporate**.

3. Enter Item numbers **PRD0000 – PRDZZZZZ.**

4. Click on the **Submit** button.

5. The Items are added to the **Price List**.

Adjusting the price of Items

Let's adjust the price for a number of Items:

1. Navigate to **Purchasing | Advanced Pricing | Price Lists | Adjust Price List**.

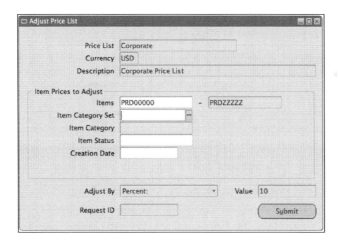

2. In the **Price List** field, select **Corporate**.

3. Enter Item numbers **PRD00000 – PRDZZZZZ.**

4. Select **Adjust By Percent** and enter the **Value** as **10**.

5. Click on the **Submit** button.

6. The **Items** are adjusted in the **Price List**.

See also

Creating Items recipe in Chapter 1, Creating Items in Inventory

Reviewing Order Management workflow

The workflow engine is used to control the processing of orders. And the type of order will determine the workflow that is called. Though seeded workflows are available with Oracle Order Management, you can customize a flow to suit your particular business requirements.

How to do it...

Let's view the progress of an order using workflow:

1. Select the **Order Management** responsibility.

2. Navigate to **Orders, Returns | Sales Order**.

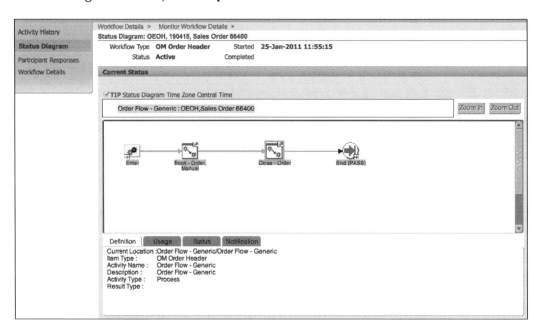

3. Press the *F11* function key to enter the Query Mode.

4. In the **Order Number** field, enter **66400** and press *Ctrl + F11*.

5. Select the **Line Items** tab.

6. Select Line number **1.1**.

7. From the menu, select **Tools | Workflow Status**.

8. Click on the **Status Diagram** link on the left navigation or the **View Diagram** button to view the progress of the order.

How it works...

The flow of the order is controlled by a workflow. This is represented in a diagram format behind the scenes. The workflow engine manages the route for the processing of an order type. Order Types are specified in the Transaction Types.

There's more...

Let's look at how the order calls the workflow behind the scenes.

Transaction Types

Let's review the Transaction Types for the Mixed Order Type:

1. Navigate to **Setup | Transaction Types | Define**.

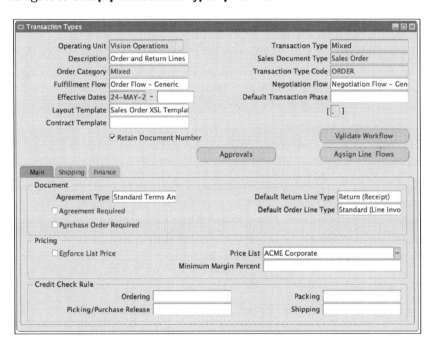

2. Press the *F11* function key to enter the Query Mode.
3. In the **Transaction Type** field, enter **Mixed** and press *Ctrl+F11*.
4. The details of the **Mixed** transaction type are displayed.

5. **Order Category** can contain a value of **Order**, **Return**, or **Mixed**. **Mixed** is a combination of an **Order** and a **Return** for the line Items.

6. Select **Order Flow – Generic** as the **Fulfillment flow**. This is the workflow called by the order header.

7. Click on the **Assign Line Flows** button to view the line workflows assigned to the header. This is called depending on the line type selected. The **Order** can have multiple lines. All the lines need to be completed before the order can be closed.

8. The **Main** tab contains three regions, namely, **Document**, **Pricing**, and **Credit Check Rule.** The **Main** tab details the default options used when an **Order** is created. For example, the default line type for an **Order** is **Standard (Line Invoicing)**.

9. The **Shipping** tab includes the defaults for **Shipping**. For example, shipping method **DHL**.

10. The **Finance** tab contains information that will affect the interface to the finance applications.

Creating Drop Ship orders

Some Items are not usually held in stock and can only be ordered when required by the supplier.

In this recipe, we will enter an order for a special Item not held in Inventory and raise a purchase order to the supplier to deliver the goods directly to the customer.

Sheepwall Inc. wants to purchase an ACME Special Laptop (PRD20006). We don't hold stock for the Item in Inventory, but we order it directly from Acacia Office Supplier, who will send it directly to our customer.

In this recipe, we will also use the Quick Sales Order Entry form to enter the sales order.

How to do it...

Let's list the steps required to create the Drop Ship order:

1. Select the **Order Management** responsibility.

2. Navigate to **Orders, Returns | Quick Sales Order**.

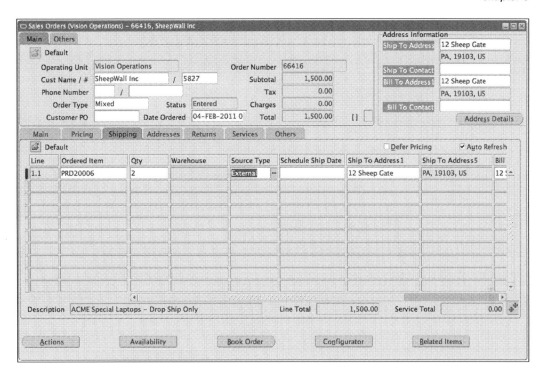

3. In the **Cust Name / #** field, enter **SheepWall**.

4. In the **Order Type** field, enter **Mixed**.

5. Select the **Ordered Item** field in the **Main** tab and enter **PRD20006**.

6. Enter **2** in the **Qty** field.

7. Select the **Shipping** tab and change the **Source Type** to **External**.

8. Click on the **Book Order** button.

9. The defaulting rules are used to populate the details of the order.

Line	Ordered Item	Qty	UOM	Request Date	Unit Price	Price List	Whse	Status
1.1	PRD20006 ...	2	Ea	04-FEB-2011 01:21	750.00	ACME Corpc		Booked

10. The order is booked.

11. The **Order Line** also has a booked status.

Line	Ordered Item	Qty	UOM	Request Date	Unit Price	Price List	Whse	Status
1.1	PRD20006	2	Ea	04-FEB-2011 01:21	750.00	ACME Corpc		Awaiting Receipt

12. The workflow engine runs in the background and moves the line to the status of **Awaiting Receipt**.

13. The **Requisition** created from Order Management needs to be imported to purchasing.

Let's run the requisition import program. This program can be automated and scheduled to run at a specific frequency:

1. Navigate to **Orders, Returns | Requisition Import**.

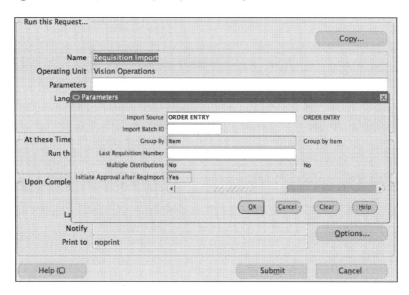

2. Click on the **Submit a New Request** button.

3. Select the **Single Request** option.

4. Click on the **OK** button.

5. In the **Submit Request** form, **Requisition Import** has been pre populated in the **Name** field.

6. Select the **Import Source** of **ORDER ENTRY**, in the **Import Source** field.

7. Accept the defaults.

8. Click on the **OK** button.

9. Click on the **Submit** button.

10. The Requisition is created and the goods are autosourced from the supplier **Acacia Suppliers**. The purchase order is also created.

Let's find the sales order from the Quick Order Organizer and view the details of the Drop Ship Purchase Order:

1. Navigate to **Orders, Returns | Quick Order Organizer**.

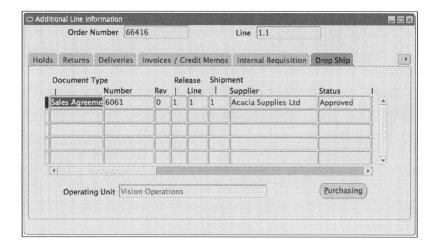

2. In the **Order Number** field, enter **66416**.

3. Click on the **Find** button. The **Order** details are displayed.

4. Click on the **Open** button to display the **Order** details.

5. Click on the line Item **1.1**.

6. Click on the actions button and select the **Additional Line** Information from the displayed list.

7. Select the **Drop Ship** tab to view the **Purchase Order** details. The **PO** number is **6061**.

8. Click on the **Purchasing** button to view the **Purchase Order**.

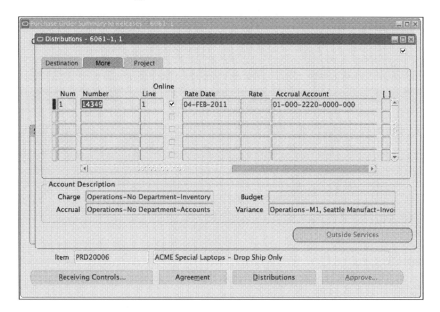

Once we receive a confirmation that the customer **SheepWall** has received the goods, we can then receive the goods in **Purchasing**:

1.   Navigate to **Purchasing | Receiving | Receipts**.

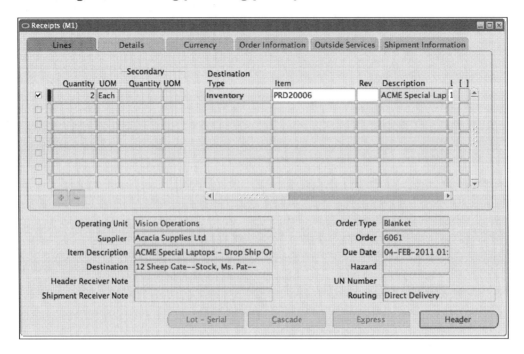

2.   In the **Purchase Order** field, enter **6061**, and in the **Release** field, enter **1**.
3.   Click on the **Find** button.
4.   Select the line to receive.
5.   In the **Sub Inventory** field, enter the **Drop Ship Subinventory**.
6.   Save the record.

Line	Ordered Item	Unit Price	Extended Price	Price List	Whse	Payment Terms	Shipping Metho	Status
1.1	PRD20006	750.00	1,500.00	ACME Corp		N30	DHL-Parcel-Exp	Shipped

The Workflow should now set the status of the Order line to Shipped. Let's review the line status:

1.   Navigate to **Orders, Returns | Quick Order Organizer**.
2.   In the **Order Number** field, enter **66416**.
3.   Click on the **Find** button. The **Order** details are displayed.
4.   Click on the **Open** button to display the **Order** details.

5. Click on the line Item **1.1**.

6. The line status is now shipped.

Line	Ordered Item	Qty	UOM	Request Date	Unit Price	Price List	Whse	Status
1.1	PRD20006	2	Ea	04–FEB–2011 01:21	750.00	ACME Corp(		Closed

7. Once the Order is shipped, the Workflow background engine will generate the customer's invoice and close the order.

How it works...

Drop Ship orders in Order Management are identified from the Source Type of External. This then routes the workflow to follow a specific path to fulfill the order.

In this recipe, a Blanket Purchase Order is already in place, with auto sourcing rules for the orders for the Item PRD20006 to be sourced automatically from Acacia Suppliers Limited. Once the purchase requisition is generated from Order Management, the Purchase order will be created as a release against the Blanket Purchase Order and sent to the supplier based on the rules.

The supplier receives the purchase order and sends the goods directly to the customer. After the supplier notifies us that the goods have been shipped, we can generate an invoice to the customer once we receive a confirmation of the shipment. The supplier can notify us through an **Advance Shipment Notice** (**ASN**) or through Invoice.

See also

Entering Sales Order recipe in this chapter

Creating Purchase Orders recipe in Chapter 2, Purchasing Items in Procurement

Receiving Items recipe in Chapter 2, Purchasing Items in Procurement

Reviewing Order Management workflow in this chapter

Creating Back-to-Back orders

Customers may request Items that are not in stock and need to be ordered from a supplier to replenish stock.

In this recipe, we will create an order for goods that are not in stock, but need to be ordered from a supplier.

How to do it...

Let's list the steps required to create the Back-to-Back order:

1. Select the **Order Management** responsibility.

2. Navigate to **Orders, Returns | Quick Sales Order**.

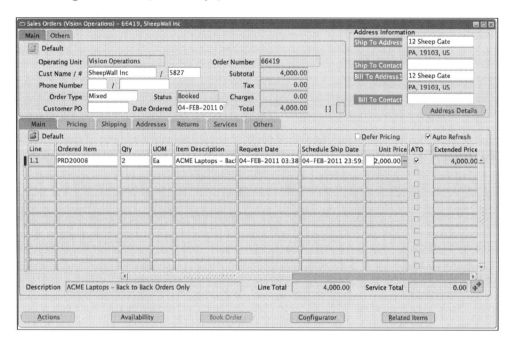

3. In the **Cust Name / #** field, enter **SheepWall**.

4. In the **Order Type** field, enter **Mixed**.

5. Select the **Ordered Item** field in the **Main** tab and enter **PRD20008**.

6. Enter **2** in the **Qty** field.

7. View the **ATO** box by selecting **Folder | Show Field** and select **ATO** in the displayed field.

8. Ensure that the **ATO** box is checked.

9. Click on the **Book Order** button.

10. The defaulting rules are used to populate the details of the order.

Line	Ordered Item	Qty	UOM	Request Date	Unit Price	Price List	Whse	Status
1.1	PRD20008	2	Ea	04–FEB–2011 03:38	2,000.00	ACME Corpc	M1	Supply Eligible

11. The order is booked.

12. The **Order Line** is also in the status of booked.

13. The **Status** is now **Supply Eligible**.

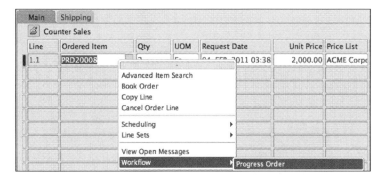

14. *Right-click* on the line and select **Workflow | Progress Order**.

15. In the **Eligible Activities** window, select **Create Supply Order – Eligible**.

Line	Ordered Item	Qty	UOM	Request Date	Unit Price	Price List	Whse	Status
1.1	PRD20008	2	Ea	04–FEB–2011 03:38	2,000.00	ACME Corpc	M1	External Req Requested

16. Click on the **OK** button.

17. The status of the order now changes to **External Req Requested**.

Let's run the **Requisition Import** to create the requisition:

1. Navigate to **Orders Returns | Requisition Import**.

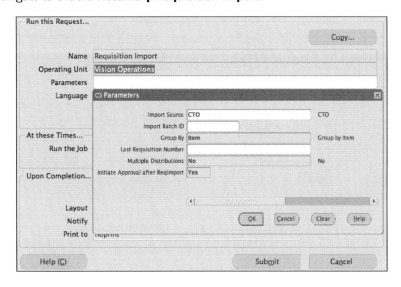

2. Select **CTO** as the **Import Source**.

3. Leave the other default values.

4. Click on **OK** and then the **Submit** button.

The workflow should now set the status of the order line to **Shipped**. Let's review the line status:

1. Navigate to **Orders, Returns | Quick Order Organizer**.

2. In the **Order Number** field, enter **66419**.

3. Click on the **Find** button. The **Order** details are displayed.

4. Click on the **Open** button to display the order details.

5. Click on the line Item **1.1**.

Line	Ordered Item		Qty	UOM	Request Date	Unit Price	Price List	Whse	Status
1.1	PRD20008	...	2	Ea	04-FEB-2011 03:38	2,000.00	ACME Corpc	M1	External Req Open

6. The line status is now **External Req Open**.

Let's find the PO requisition:

1. Navigate to **Purchasing | Requisitions | Requisition Summary**.

Number	Description	Approval Status	Creation Date	Currenc	Total	Preparer
14352		Approved	04-FEB-2011 03:5	USD	1,900.00	Stock, Ms. Pat

2. Enter **CTO** in the **Import Source** field.

3. Click on the **Find** button.

4. The requisition is displayed in the **Requisition Headers Summary** window.

5. The **Approval Status** is **Approved**.

Let's use the Buyer Work Center to create the purchase order. We can also use AutoCreate within Purchasing:

1. Navigate to **Purchasing | Buyer Work Center | Requisitions**.

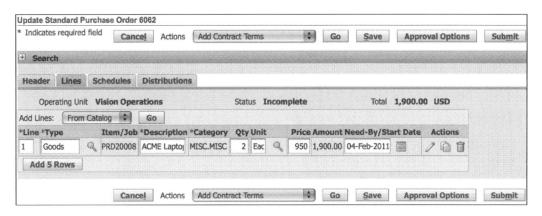

2. In the **Demand Workbench**, enter **14352** as the **Requisition Number**.

3. Click on the **Go** button.

4. The requisition's details are displayed.

5. Select the requisition and click on the **Add** button.

6. The requisition is added to the **Document Builder**.

7. Click on the **Create** button to create the **Purchase Order**. Note that the supplier is automatically selected based on sourcing rules.

8. Click on the **Lines** tab to review the **Purchase Order**.

9. Click on the **Submit** button to submit the **Purchase Order** for approval.

10. The workflow should now set the status of the **Order** line to **PO Open**.

Let's review the line status:

Line	Ordered Item	Qty	UOM	Request Date	Unit Price	Price List	Whse	Status
1.1	PRD20008	2	Ea	04–FEB–2011 03:38	2,000.00	ACME Corp	M1	PO Open

11. Navigate to **Orders, Returns | Quick Order Organizer**.

12. In the **Order Number** field, enter **66419**.

13. Click on the **Find** button. The order details are displayed.

14. Click on the **Open** button to display the order details.

15. Click on the line Item **1.1**.

16. The line **Status** is now **PO Open**.

Let's receive the goods in our Inventory:

1. Navigate to **Purchasing | Receiving | Receipts**.

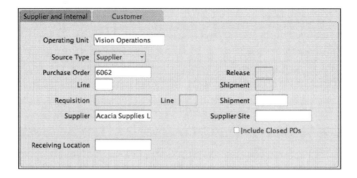

2. In the **Purchase Order** field, enter **6062**.

3. Click on the **Find** button.

4. Select the line to receive.

5. In the **Sub Inventory** field, enter the **FGI Subinventory**.

6. Save the record.

7. The workflow should now set the status of the order line to **Awaiting Shipping**.

Let's review the line status.

Line	Ordered Item	Qty	UOM	Request Date	Unit Price	Price List	Whse	Status
1.1	PRD20008 ...	2	Ea	04–FEB–2011 03:38	2,000.00	ACME Corp	M1	Awaiting Shipping

8. Navigate to **Orders, Returns | Quick Order Organizer**.

9. In the **Order Number** field, enter **66419**.

10. Click on the **Find** button. The Order details are displayed.

11. Click on the **Open** button to display the Order details.

12. Click on the line Item **1.1**.

13. The line **Status** is now **Awaiting Shipping**.

How it works...

Back-to-Back orders, links sales orders, and purchase orders are mainly used as a Replenish-to-Order process for Items that are normally stocked in inventory.

The requisition for a back-to-back must be identified as a **Configure-to-Order** (**CTO**). This allows the purchase order to be created automatically from the requisition and sent to the supplier. The supplier receives the purchase order and fulfills the order. The Items are recorded in inventory and a reservation is automatically made against the sales order line.

See also

Entering Sales Order recipe in this chapter

Creating Requisitions for Items in Chapter 2, Purchasing Items in Procurement

Creating Purchase Orders in Chapter 2, Purchasing Items in Procurement

Receiving Items in Chapter 2, Purchasing Items in Procurement

Reviewing Order Management Workflow recipe in this chapter

Creating a return

Items can be returned to the business from the customer based on a number of reasons, for example, damaged goods. In this recipe, we will look at how to enter the details or a returned Item. The customer needs to return one of the laptops (PRD20006) on Order 66417.

How to do it...

Let's list the steps required to create a return:

1. Select the **Order Management** responsibility.
2. Navigate to **Orders, Returns | Sales Order**.

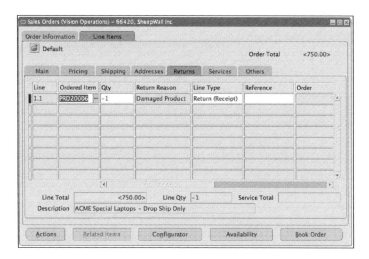

3. Enter the **SheepWall** in the **Customer** field.

4. Select the **Order Type** of **Return Only**.

5. Enter **ACME Corporate** in the price list.

6. Select the **Lines Items** tab.

7. In the **Ordered Item** field, enter **PRD20006**.

8. In the **Qty** field, enter **1**, the value changes to **-1**, to represent a return.

9. Select the **Returns** tab and enter **Damaged Product** in the **Return Reason** field. Note that the **Line Type** is **Return (Receipt)**.

10. Save the record.

11. Click on the **Book Order** to book the order number **66420**.

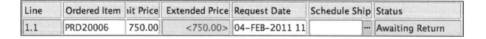

Line	Ordered Item	nit Price	Extended Price	Request Date	Schedule Ship	Status
1.1	PRD20006	750.00	<750.00>	04–FEB–2011 11	⋯	Awaiting Return

12. The line **Status** has now progressed to **Awaiting Return**. Once the goods have been received, they can be returned to inventory

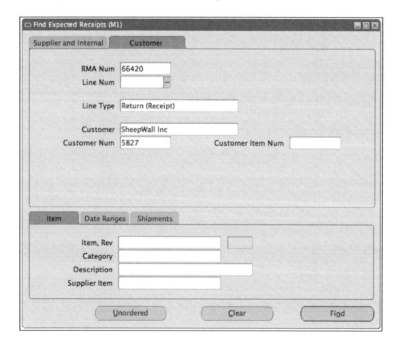

13. Navigate to **Purchasing | Receiving | Receipts**.

14. In the **Expected Receipts** form, select the **Customer** tab.

15. Enter the **RMA Num 66420**. This is the same as the order number.

16. Click on the **Find** button.

17. Select the line and enter the **DropShip Subinventory**.

18. Save the record.

Line	Ordered Item	Qty	UOM	Request Date	Unit Price	Price List	Whse	Status
1.1	PRD20006 ...	-1	Ea	04–FEB–2011	750.00	ACME Corpc	M1	Returned

19. The workflow should now set the status of the order line to **Returned**.

Let's review the line status:

20. Navigate to **Orders, Returns | Quick Order Organizer**.

21. In the **Order Number** field, enter **66420**.

22. Click on the **Find** button. The order details are displayed.

23. Click on the **Open** button to display the order details.

24. Click on the line Item **1.1**.

25. The line **Status** is now **Returned**.

See also

Entering a Sales Order recipe in this chapter

Receiving Items recipe in Chapter 2, Purchasing Items in Procurement

Applying holds

Computer Service and Consulting have a poor credit history and we have decided to suspend the account until this is fully reviewed. In this recipe, we will create an order for Computer Service and Consulting where the customer has been suspended.

How to do it...

Let's suspend the customer:

1. Select the **Order Management** responsibility.

2. Navigate to **Customers | Standard**.

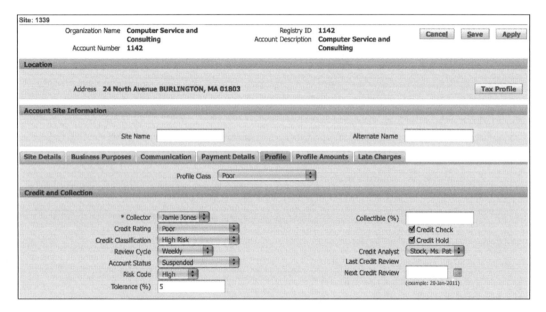

3. Enter **Computer Service%** in the **Name** field and click on the **Go** button.

4. Click on the **Computer Service and Consulting** link.

5. In the **Accounts** tab, select the details icon on the **24 North Avenue, BURLINGTON, MA 01803** line.

6. Select the **Profile** tab.

7. Select **Account Status** as **Suspended**.

8. Ensure that the **Credit Check** and the **Credit Hold** checkboxes are enabled.

9. Click on the **Apply** button.

10. Click on the **Save** button.

Let's now create a standard sales order for the customer:

1. Select the **Order Management** responsibility.
2. Navigate to **Orders, Returns | Sales Order**.

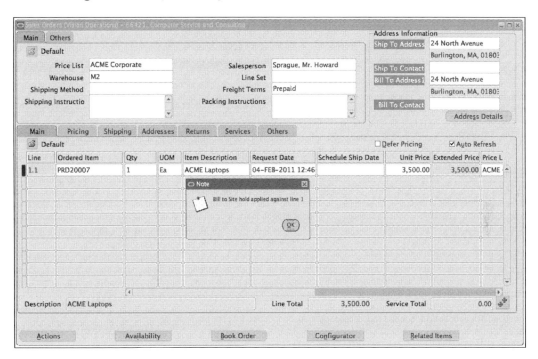

3. Enter **Computer Service and Consulting** in the **Customer** field.
4. Enter **Standard** as the **Order Type**.
5. In the **Main** tab, enter **PRD20007** in the **Ordered Item** tab.
6. Enter **1** in the **Qty** field.
7. Save the record and book the order.

8. A warning message is displayed to inform us that a hold is placed on the order.

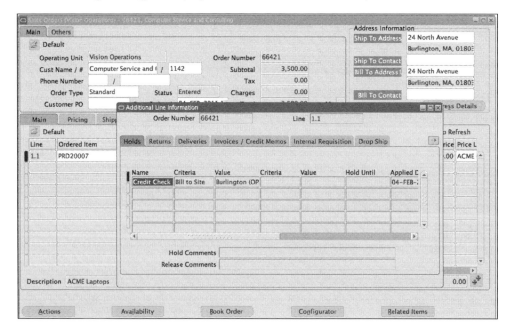

9. Select the **Actions** button.
10. Select **Additional Line Information** and select the **Holds** tab.
11. The details of the hold are displayed.

See also

Creating Customers recipe in this chapter

Entering sales orders recipe in this chapter

Releasing orders

Goods ordered by our customers need to be allocated and moved from the warehouse in preparation for shipping to the customer.

The key steps in the process are as follows:

▶ Run Pick Release for booked orders

▶ The orders are allocated and moved from the Subinventory and dropped into the staging area before shipping

In this recipe, we will look at how to release the order for shipment to our customers.

Getting ready

We will need a booked order that has the goods available in Inventory, with sales order lines in the Awaiting Shipping status before we can release the order for shipping.

How to do it...

Let's list the steps required to complete the task:

1. Select the **Order Management** responsibility.

2. Navigate to **Shipping | Release Sales Orders**.

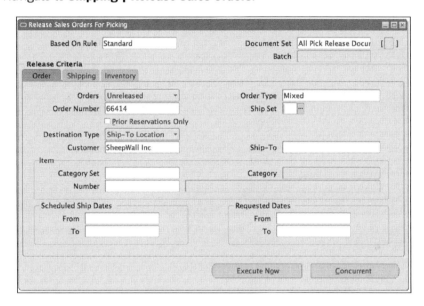

3. In the **Release Sales Orders** for the **Picking** form, enter **Standard** in the **Based On Rule** field. The **Document Set** field is auto populated.

4. In the **Order Number** field, enter **66414**, and the **Customer** name; and the **Order type** is automatically populated.

5. The **Shipping** tab is prepopulated based on the rule we selected.

6. Note that the **Auto Delivery** and the **Auto Pick** confirm are set to **Yes**.

7. The **Inventory** tab is prepopulated based on the rule we selected.

8. Note that **Auto Allocate** is set to **Yes**.

9. Click on the **Execute Now** button to pick release and pick confirm the order.

10. A message is displayed to confirm that the **Pick Release** has completed successfully.

11. Click on the **OK** button and close the form.

12. The workflow should now set the status of the order line to **Picked**.

Let's review the line status:

13. Navigate to **Orders, Returns | Quick Order Organizer**.
14. In the **Order Number** field, enter **66414**.
15. Click on the **Find** button. The order details are displayed.
16. Click on the **Open** button to display the order details.
17. Click on the line Item **1.1**.

Line	Ordered Item	Qty	UOM	Request Date	Unit Price	Price List	Whse	Status
1.1	PRD20007 ...	1	Ea	03–FEB–2011 12:47	2,800.00	ACME Corp	M1	Picked

18. The line status is now **Picked**.

How it works...

The release program is automated based on rules set up in the Release Rules Form. The rules can be a one, two, or three-step process:

1. The one-step process: No manual intervention; the allocation and the picking are done automatically. Auto Allocate from Inventory and Auto Pick Confirm for shipping are set to "Yes".

2. The two-step process: Manual intervention after auto allocation; this creates a move order that is automatically detailed. The reason for doing this could be that we may need to view the Pick Recommendation and change the Subinventory, quantity, the location, and some other details. We need to run the Transact Move Orders to Pick Confirm the inventory.

3. The three-step process: Manual allocation and Pick Confirm of the order.

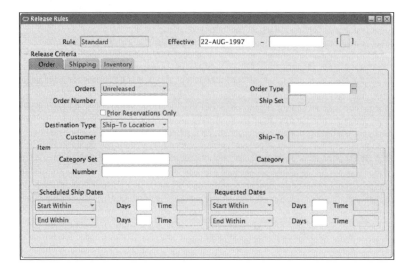

The release rules are set up in the **Shipping | Setup | Picking | Define Release Rules** form.

There's more...

Viewing the Pick Slip report

Let's view the Pick Slip report:

1. From the Menu, navigate to **View | Requests**.

2. In the **Find Requests** form, click on the **Find** button.

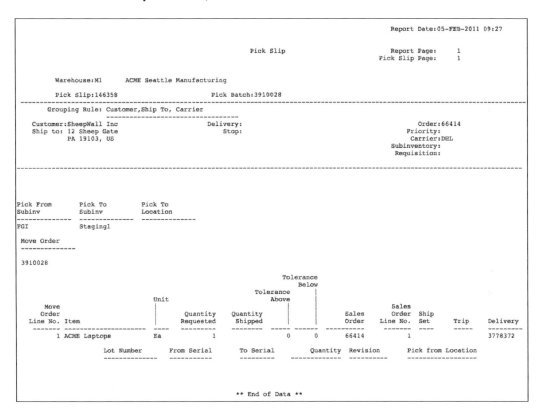

3. Select the **Request ID 5859851** for the **Pick Slip Report**.

4. Click on the **View Output** button.

5. The **Pick Slip** report for the goods is displayed.

See also

Entering Sales Orders recipe in this chapter

Shipping orders

Goods allocated and picked from the warehouse need to be packed and shipped to our customers.

The key steps in the process are:

▸ Find the order eligible for shipping

▸ The orders are then confirmed ready for shipping – "Ship confirmed" – the quantities in Inventory are adjusted based on the order and the sales order line are updated

In this recipe, we will look at how to create the shipment to our customers.

Getting ready

We need a booked order that has Picked status before we can ship the goods to our customer.

How to do it...

Let's list the steps required to complete the task:

1. Select the **Order Management** responsibility.

2. Navigate to **Shipping | Shipping Transactions**.

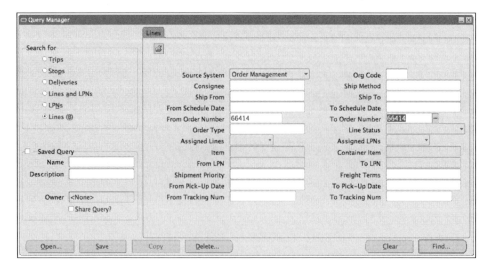

3. When the **Query Manager** window opens, enter **66414** in the fields **From Order Number** and **To Order Number**.

4. Change the **Line Status** field to blank.

5. Click on the **Find** button to find the order.

Detail	LPN	Item Name	Delivery	Line Status	Next Step	Exception	Order
3965480	☐	PRD20007	3778372	Staged/Pick Confirmed	Ship Confirm/Close Trip Stop	☐	66414

6. The **Shipping Transactions** window opens to display details of the order. The line status is **Staged/Pick Confirmed** and the **Next Step** is **Ship Confirm/Close Trip Stop**.

7. Click on the **Delivery** tab.

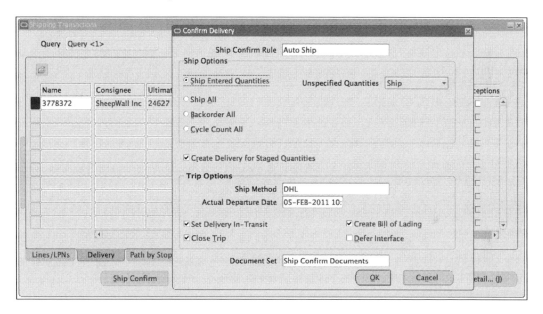

8. Click on the **Ship Confirm** button.

9. Accept all the defaults and click on the **OK** button.

10. A message is displayed to confirm that delivery was successful. Click **OK.**

11. Close the **Shipping Transactions** window.

Line	Ordered Item	Qty	UOM	Request Date	Unit Price	Price List	Whse	Status
1.1	PRD20007 ...	1	Ea	03-FEB-2011 12:47	2,800.00	ACME Corp	M1	Shipped

The workflow should now set the status of the order line to **Shipped**. Let's review the line status:

1. Navigate to **Orders, Returns | Quick Order Organizer**.

2. In the **Order Number** field, enter **66414**.

3. Click on the **Find** button. The Order details are displayed.

4. Click on the **Open** button to display the order details.

5. Click on the line Item **1.1**.

6. The line **Status** is now **Shipped**.

How it works...

The Ship Confirm window is used to confirm that the orders have been shipped out of Inventory to the customer. When we run the Ship Confirm, the system adjusts the quantities in Inventory and updates the sales order line status. The information is then transferred to Receivables for invoicing using the AutoInvoice rules.

There's more...

Now let's look at some other events happening behind the scenes.

Generated reports

The system generates reports and documents based on the rules setup. Some examples are Bill of Lading, Packing Slip, Commercial Invoice, Vehicle Load Sheet Details, and Interface Trip Stop.

1. From the **Menu**, navigate to **View | Requests**.

2. In the **Find Requests** form, click on the **Find** button.

```
                        Vehicle Load Sheet
                             Details
                       For Trip :  3132350

        Vehicle Type :                    Trip Status :  Closed
      Vehicle Number :                      Prior Trip :
            Carrier :  DEL                 Instructions :

            Location : 3455 108th Avenue                Status : Closed
                       Seattle,WA,98101
                       US

     Planned Arrival Date : 14-FEB-11        Actual Arrival Date : 05-FEB-11
   Planned Departure Date : 14-FEB-11      Actual Departure Date : 05-FEB-11

  Deliveries Picked Up:
       Load Sequence:                    Delivery Name: 3778372         Delivery Status: Closed
       Waybill Number:                       Customer: SheepWall Inc
       Gross Weight: 30                    Net Weight: 30                        Units: Lbs
       Items Picked Up:
       Load         Customer    Customer    Item                    Item
       Sequence     Product Seq Job         Number                  Description
       -----------  ----------- ----------- ----------------------  ----------------------------------
                                            PRD20007                ACME Laptops

  Deliveries Dropped Off:      *** No Deliveries Found ***

            Location : 12 Sheep Gate                   Status : Closed
                       ,PA,19103
                       US

     Planned Arrival Date : 14-FEB-11        Actual Arrival Date : 05-FEB-11
   Planned Departure Date : 14-FEB-11      Actual Departure Date : 05-FEB-11

  Deliveries Picked Up:       *** No Deliveries Found ***
  Deliveries Dropped Off:

       Load Sequence:                    Delivery Name: 3778372         Delivery Status: Closed
       Waybill Number:                       Customer: SheepWall Inc
       Gross Weight: 30                    Net Weight: 30                        Units: Lbs
       Items Dropped Off:
       Load         Customer    Customer    Item                    Item
       Sequence     Product Seq Job         Number                  Description
       -----------  ----------- ----------- ----------------------  ----------------------------------
                                            PRD20007                ACME Laptops

               ----- End of Report -----
```

3. Select the **Request ID 5859865** for the **Vehicle Load Sheet Details**.

4. Click on the **View Output** button.

5. The **Vehicle Load Sheet Details** for the goods are displayed.

Creating invoices

The customer needs to be invoiced for the goods. In this recipe, we will run Autoinvoice for all outstanding sales orders and view the generated invoice for the order number 66414.

Getting ready

The order needs to be shipped before we can create the invoice.

How to do it...

Let's create the invoice for all outstanding sales orders.

Let's list the steps required to complete the task:

1.   Navigate to **Receivables | Interfaces | AutoInvoice**.

2.   In the **Submit a New Request** form, click on the **OK** button.

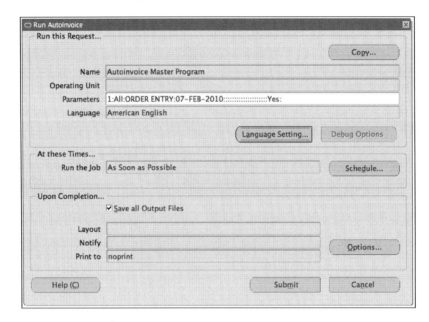

3.   In the **Autoinvoice Submit Request** form, select **Autoinvoice Master Program**.

4.   Select the **Import** source of **ORDER ENTRY** in the import source field.

5.   Enter **07-Feb-2011** in the **Default Date** field.

6.   Leave the defaults for all the other fields.

7.   Click on the **OK** button.

8.   Click on the **Submit** button.

Viewing the invoice details for order **66414**.

9.   Navigate to **Orders, Returns | Quick Order Organizer**.

10. In the **Order Number** field, enter **66414**.

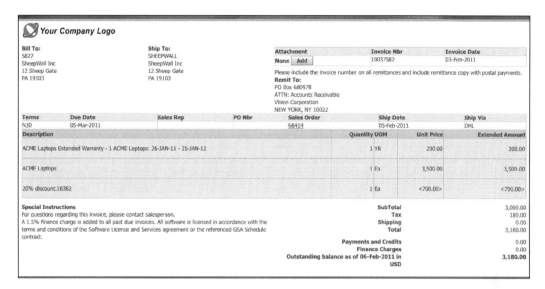

11. Click on the **Find** button. The Order details are displayed.

12. Click on the **Open** button to display the Order details.

13. Click on the line Item **1.1**.

14. Click on the **Actions** button and select the **Additional Order Information**.

15. Select the **Invoices / Credit Memos** tab.

16. Click on the **Invoice Details** button to view the details in Receivables.

How it works...

The shipping information is transferred to Receivables for invoicing using the Autoinvoice rules. The accounting information is then transferred to the General Ledger from Oracle Inventory and Oracle Accounts Receivable.

See also

Creating invoices recipe in Chapter 6, Receiving Funds in Receivables

6
Receiving Funds in Receivables

In this chapter, we will cover:

- ▶ Creating invoices
- ▶ Adjusting invoices
- ▶ Entering receipts
- ▶ Managing debts
- ▶ Reviewing receivables' accounting transactions

Introduction

Customers are billed for goods and services by an organization. Oracle Receivables creates an invoice for the bill and the customers pay the invoices. The receipts for the bill are entered and monitored in receivables. In this chapter, we will look at how to create invoices and record the receipts from customers. Let's start by looking at the receivables process.

The following diagram summarizes an example of the receivables process:

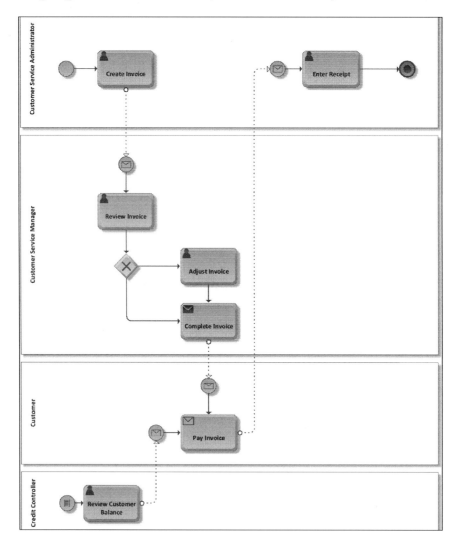

1. The **Customer Service Administrator** creates the invoice in Oracles receivables. Invoices can also be created and imported from other modules, for example, through order management, projects, service contracts, and other Oracle and non-Oracle systems.

2. The invoices are reviewed and adjusted if necessary by the **Customer Service Manager**. They are completed and sent to the **Customer**.

3. The **Customer** pays the invoice.

4. The **Customer Service Administrator** enters the receipt in receivables.

Let's start by looking at how to create an invoice.

Creating an invoice

Invoices can be imported from an external source or entered into Oracle Receivables manually. An invoice contains the information about the services or goods purchased from the organization. An invoice can contain a header, lines, and accounting information.

In this recipe, we will create a standard invoice for SheepWall Inc. This is for installation services. The service is for three hours at $100 per hour.

Getting ready

Log in to Oracle E-Business Suite R12 with the username and password assigned to you by the system administrator. If you are working on the Vision demonstration database, you can use OPERATIONS/WELCOME as the USERNAME/PASSWORD.

How to do it...

Let's list the steps required in creating an invoice:

1. Select the **Receivables** responsibility.

2. Navigate to **Transactions | Transactions**.

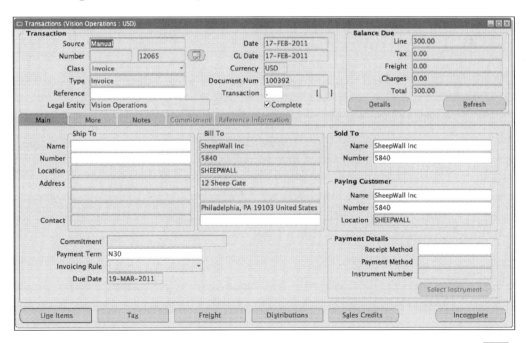

3. In the **Source** field, select **Manual**. The **Date** and the **GL Date** field are automatically populated.

4. In the **Class** field, select **Invoice**.

5. In the **Type** field, select **Invoice**.

6. In the **Bill To** region, enter **SheepWall Inc** in the **Name** field, and the **Location** and **Address** field are populated.

7. Save the record.

8. The transaction number **12065** is created: this is also the invoice number.

Let's enter the line Items.

1. Click on the **Line Items** button.

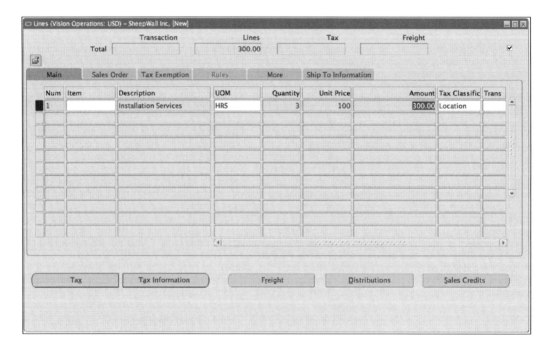

2. In the **Description** field, enter **Installation Services**.

3. In the **UOM** field, enter **HRS**.

4. In the **Quantity** field, enter **3**.

5. In the **Unit Price** field, enter **100**.

6. In the **Tax Classifications** field, enter **Location**.

Let's enter the distributions:

7. Click on the **Distributions** button.

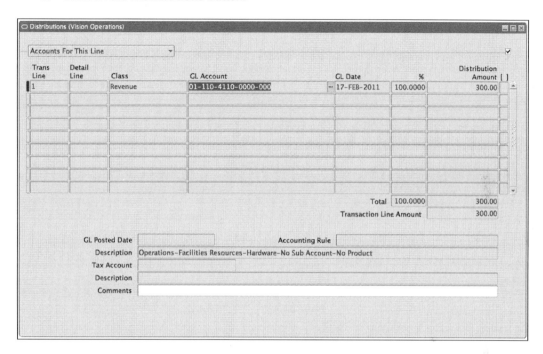

8. Enter **01-110-4110-0000-000** in the **GL Account** field. The accounting codes can also be generated using the autoaccounting rules.

9. Close the form and save the transaction.

10. Click on the **Complete** button to complete the transaction.

11. Click on the **View Invoice** icon to view the invoice.

How it works...

The transaction type field controls the accounting, customer balances, and GL postings. This is set up in the **Transaction Types** form:

1. Select the **Receivables** responsibility.

2. Navigate to **Setup | Transactions | Transaction Types**:

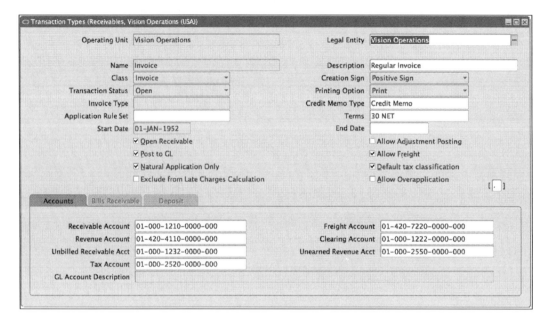

3. Press *F11* to enter the query mode.

4. In the **Name** field, enter **Invoice** and press *Ctrl+F11*.

Let's review some of the settings:

1. The **Legal** entity field identifies the default legal entity to use for the transaction type.

2. The **Name** of the transaction type identifies the transaction type and it is unique across receipt method, adjustment, and receivable activity.

3. The **Class** field identifies the transaction as an **Invoice**. We can use the **Transactions** form to create a **Chargeback**, **Credit Memo**, **Debit Memo**, **Deposit**, or **Guarantee**.

4. The **Creation Sign** can be either positive or negative. The creation sign cannot be changed once transactions are entered.

5. The **Transaction Status** field can be **Open**, **Closed**, **Pending**, or **Void**.

6. The AutoAccounting rules can use the accounts set up in transaction types. These values can also be overridden by the Subledger Accounting rules.

There's more...

Now let's look at some other transactions around the creation of an invoice.

Generating accounting

Let's generate and view the accounting transactions:

1. Navigate to **Tools | Create Accounting** in the menu:

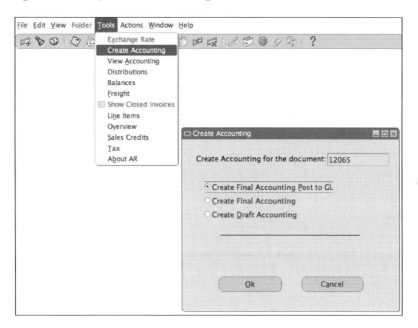

2. In the **Create Accounting** form, select **Create Final Accounting Post to GL**.

3. Click on the **Ok** button.

4. Click on **Ok** in the note displayed.

Let's view the accounting transactions:

1. Navigate to **Tools | View Accounting** in the menu.

2. Review the transactions.

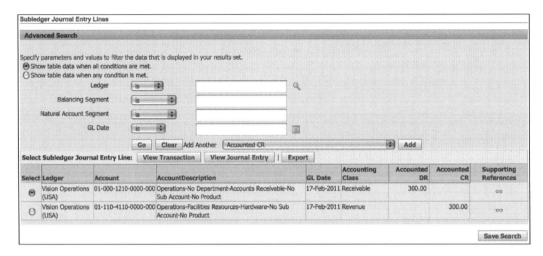

3. Note that the receivable account **01-000-1210-0000-000** is debited and the revenue account **01-110-4110-0000-000** is credited.

Entering Quick Transactions

Oracle Receivables enables us to enter invoice information quickly, using default values. Let's look at how to enter transactions using "Quick Transactions". We will create an invoice for the services of a Senior Consultant at the rate of $350 per hour for 10 hours:

1. Select the **Receivables** responsibility.

2. Navigate to **Transactions | Transactions Summary**.

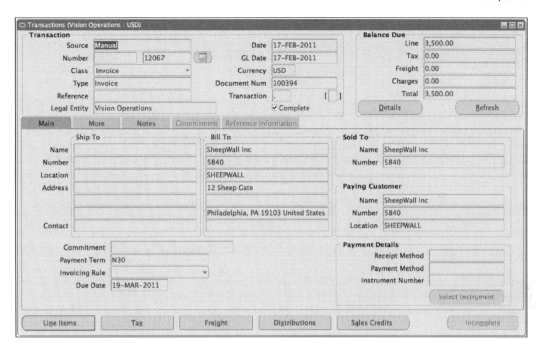

3. In the **Source** field, select **Manual**.

4. In the **Bill To Customer** field, enter **SheepWall Inc**.

5. In the **Class** field, enter **Invoice**.

6. Click on the **Open** button to display the **Transactions** page.

7. Click the **Line Items** button to enter invoice lines.

8. In the **Description** field, select **Senior Consultant**. The **UOM** of HRS and the **Price** of **350** are entered by default.

9. In the **Quantity** field, enter **10**.

10. Click the **Save** button to save the transaction.

11. The **Transaction Number** of **12067** is created.

12. Click on the **Complete** button to complete the transaction.

Entering deposits

Our customers can pay us in advance for goods or services. Let's look at how to enter a deposit of $500 for SheepWall Inc:

1. Select the **Receivables** responsibility.

2. Navigate to **Transactions | Transactions**.

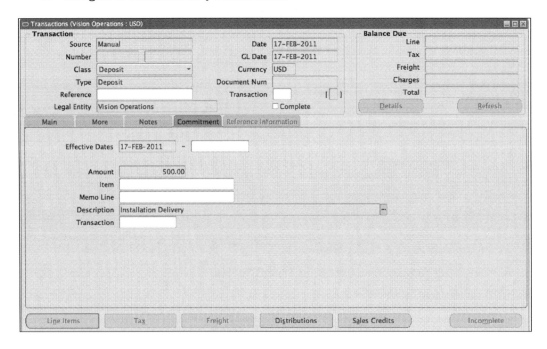

3. In the **Source** field, select **Manual**.

4. In the **Class** field, select **Deposit**.

5. In the **Type** field, select **Deposit**.

6. In the **Ship To: Name** field, enter **SheepWall Inc**.

7. Click the **Commitment** tab. This is used to specify the debit and credit accounts for the commitment.

8. In the **Amount** field, enter **500.00**.

9. In the **Description** field, enter **Installation Delivery**.

10. Click the **Save** button.

11. Click the **Complete** button.

Entering a credit memo

We are offering a 5 percent discount to our customer for invoice number 12065. Let's enter a credit memo for this transaction.

Search for the invoice number **12065**:

1. Select the **Receivables** responsibility.

2. Navigate to **Transactions | Transactions Summary**.

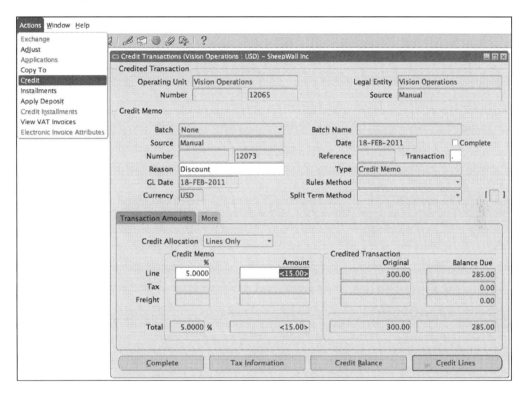

3. Press *F11* on the keyboard to enter the query mode.

4. In the **Number** field, enter **12065**.

5. Press *Ctrl+F11* to execute the query.

6. Navigate to **Actions | Credit**.

7. In the **Credit Memo** region, select **Discount** in the **Reason** field.

8. In the **Transaction Amounts** tab, select **Lines Only** in the **Credit Allocation** drop-down box. The credit can also be applied to specific lines by selecting the **Credit Lines** button.

9. In the **Credit Memo Region**, enter **5** in the % field; the amount of **<15.00>** is automatically populated in the **Amount** field.

10. The **Balance** due is also reduced to **285.00**.

11. Click on the **complete** button.

See also

Creating customers recipe in Chapter 5, Selling Items to Customers in Order Management

Defining Subledger Accounting recipe in Chapter 8, Defining Transactions for the General Ledger

Adjusting invoices

Invoices may need to be adjusted after they are complete.

In this recipe, we will enter an additional service amount of $5000 to the line for invoice number 12072. Adjustments may need to be approved based on the approval limits set for the user.

In this recipe, we will enter manual adjustments.

> Note: Searching for the invoice and clicking on the incomplete button, making the adjustment, and then clicking on the complete button can also be used to adjust invoices.

Getting ready

Login to Oracle E-Business Suite R12 with the username and password assigned to you by the System Administrator. If you are working on the Vision demonstration database, you can use OPERATIONS/WELCOME as the USERNAME/PASSWORD.

A transaction with a status of Complete is required before we can adjust it.

How to do it...

Let's create an adjustment:

1. Select the **Receivables** responsibility.
2. Navigate to **Transactions | Transactions Summary**.
3. Press *F11* on the keyboard to enter the query mode.
4. In the number field, enter **12072**.
5. Press *Ctrl+F11* to execute the query.

Let's create the adjustment:

1. Click the **Adjust** button.

2. In the **Activity Name** field, enter **Line Adjustment**:

3. Select the **Type** list, and select the **Line** list Item.

4. In the **Amount** field, enter **5000**.

5. A warning is displayed to indicate that we cannot approve this adjustment. Click on the **OK** button.

6. Select the **comments** tab and enter **Charges** in the **Reason** field.

7. Click the **Save** button.

Let's approve the adjustment:

1. Log in as an approver **CBAKER/WELCOME**.

2. Select the **Receivables** responsibility.

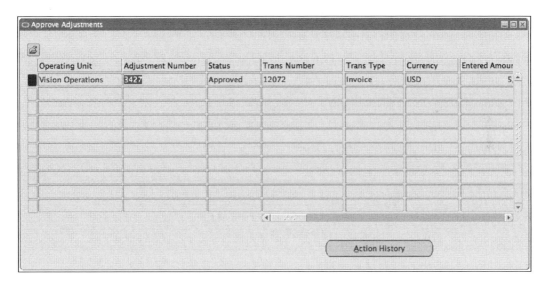

3. Navigate to **Control | Adjustments | Approve Adjustments**.

4. Click the **More** tab and enter **12072** in the **Transaction Number** field.

5. Click on the **Find** button.

6. In the **Status** field, enter a status of **Approved**.

7. Click the **Save** button.

How it works...

When an adjustment is applied to a transaction, the activity is assigned the accounts for the activity by receivables. Once the transaction is approved, the balance on the accounts will be applied and updated.

We can automatically approve adjustments, if they are within our approval limits; otherwise the adjustment will be placed in a status of pending approval. A user with the correct approval limit then approves the adjustment.

Let's review the approval limit of our user, **OPERATIONS**:

1. Navigate to **Setup | Transactions | Approval Limits**.

2. Press *F11* on the keyboard to enter the query mode.

3. In the **User Name** field, enter **OPERATIONS**.

4. In the **Document Type** field, select **Adjustment**.

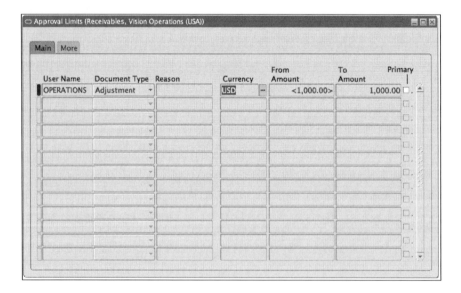

5. In the **Currency** field, enter **USD**.

6. Press **Control and F11** to run the query.

7. Notice that **OPERATIONS** can only approve an adjustment between **USD <1,000.00>** to **USD 1,000**.

8. Run the query again to view the approval limit of **CBAKER**.

9. **CBAKER** can approve between **USD <999,999,999.00>** to **USD 999,999,999.00**.

There's more...

Let's look at how to create revenue adjustments.

Adjusting revenue

Revenue accounting is used to adjust revenue and sales credits. Let's create an adjustment of $20 for unearned revenue.

1. Select the **Receivables** responsibility.

2. Navigate to **Control | Accounting | Revenue Accounting**.

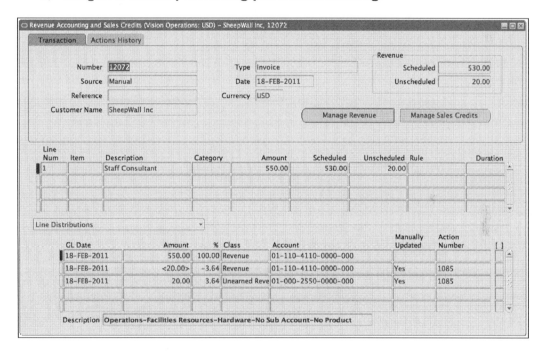

3. In the **Transaction Numbers** field, enter **12072**.

4. Click the **Find** button.

5. Select the **Transaction** tab in the **Revenue Accounting and Sales Credits Form**.

6. Click the **Manage Revenue** button. The **Manage Revenue Step 1** form is displayed. The form is used to modify, unschedule, or schedule revenue.

7. Select the **Unschedule Revenue** option and click the **Next** button.

8. In the **Manage Revenue Step 2** form, select **All** in the **Name** and the **Group** fields.

9. Click the **Next** button.

10. In the **Manage Revenue Step 3** form, select the **All Lines** option.

11. Click the **Next** button.

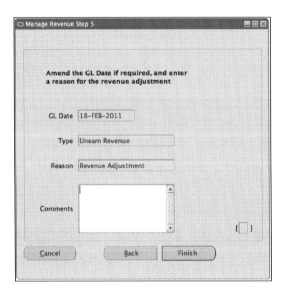

12. In the **Manage Revenue Step 4** form, select the **Amount** option and enter **20.00** in the field.

13. Click the **Next** button.

14. In the **Manage Revenue Step 5** form, select **Revenue Adjustment** as the reason.

15. Click the **Finish** button.

16. Click on the **Save** button to save the **Adjustment**.

Entering receipts

Payments received from customers are recorded in Oracle Receivables. Other non-invoice-based revenue can also be recorded, for example, bank interest. In this recipe, we will enter receipts.

Getting ready

Log in to Oracle E-Business Suite R12 with the username and password assigned to you by the system administrator. If you are working on the Vision demonstration database, you can use OPERATIONS/WELCOME as the USERNAME/PASSWORD.

How to do it...

Let's enter a standard receipt of $285 for invoice number 12065 from SheepWall Inc.

1. Select the **Receivables** responsibility.

2. Navigate to **Receipts | Receipts**:

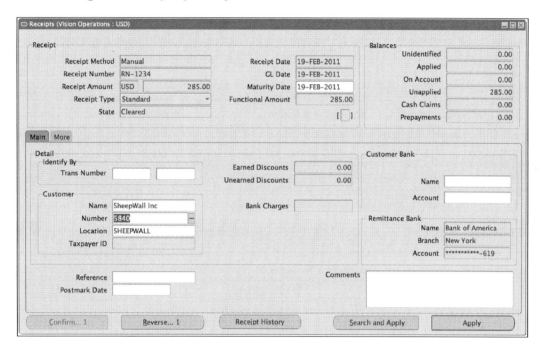

3. In the **Receipt Method** field, select **Manual**.

4. In the **Receipt Number** field, enter **RN-1234**.

5. In the **Receipt Type** field, select **Standard**.

6. In the **Receipt Amount** field, enter **285.00**.

7. Select the **Main** tab.

8. In the **Customer** region, select the **Name** field and enter **SheepWall Inc**.

9. Click the **Save** button to save the transaction.

Let's apply the receipt to invoice number **12065**:

1. Click the **Apply** button.
2. In the **Apply To** field, enter **12065**.

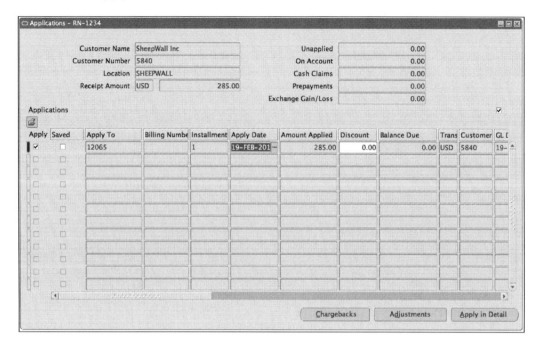

3. In the **Apply Date** field, select **19-Feb-2011**.
4. Click the **Save** button.

Let's generate and view the accounting transactions:

1. Navigate to **Tools | Creating Accounting** in the menu.
2. In the **Create Accounting** form, select **Create Final Accounting Post to GL**.
3. Click on the **Ok** button.
4. Click on **Ok** in the **Note** displayed.

Let's view the **Accounting Transactions**:

1. Navigate to **Tools | View Accounting** in the menu.
2. Review the transactions.
3. Note that the cash account **01-000-1110-0000-000** is debited and the receivable account **01-000-1210-0000-000** is credited.

How it works...

The receipt method is used to determine the required processing steps for accounting and remittance bank accounts for a receipt. This is set up in **Receipt Classes**. Let's look at the receipt classes:

1. Select the **Receivables** responsibility.

2. Navigate to **Setup | Receipts | Receipts Classes**:

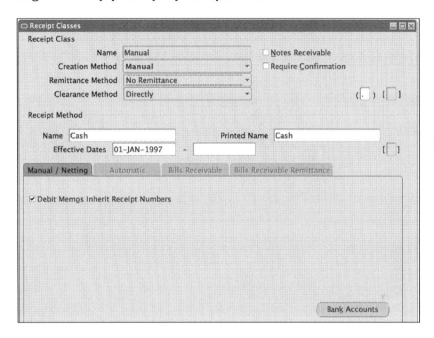

3. Press *F11*.

4. In the **Name** field, enter **Manual**.

5. In the **Creation Method** field, select **Manual**.

6. Press *Ctrl+F11* to execute the query.

7. Let's look at some of the fields:

  ❑ **Creation Method: Manual, Automatic** using the **Automatic Receipts** program, and **Bills Receivable** receipts

  ❑ **Remittance Method** determines the account for automatic receipts, **Standard/Factoring** remittance method

  ❑ **Clearance Method: Directly** (cleared at the time of receipt), **Automatic** (using the **Automatic Clearing** program), or **Matching** (manual matching **in Cash Management**)

  ❑ The **receipt method** region is used to assign the receipt class

8. Click on the **Bank Accounts** button.

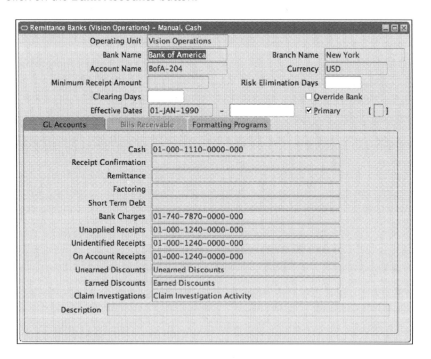

9. The **Bank** assigned to the **Receipt Class** is displayed.

There's more...

Let's look at some other types of receipts and reversing receipts.

Miscellaneous receipts

Non-invoice-related transactions such as investment and interest income are known as **miscellaneous receipts** in Oracle Receivables. Let's enter bank interest of $50, apportioned to two accounts with a split of 75 percent to 25 percent:

1. Select the **Receivables** responsibility.

2. Navigate to **Receipts | Receipts**.

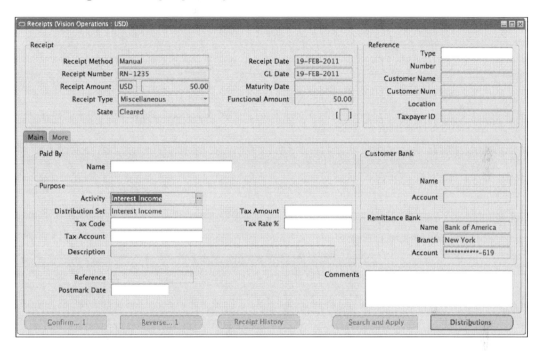

3. In the **Receipt Method** field, select **Manual**.

4. In the **Receipt Number** field, enter **RN-1235**.

5. In the **Receipt Amount** field, enter **50.00**.

6. In the **Receipt Type** field, select **Miscellaneous**.

7. In the **Activity** field, select **Interest Income**.

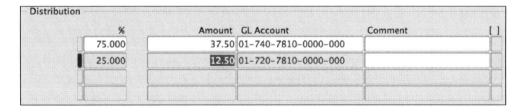

8. Click on the **Distribution** button.

9. In the % field, enter **75**. The **Amount** field automatically changes to **37.50**.

10. Enter **01-740-7810-0000-000** in the **GL Account** field.

11. Click on the second line and enter **25** in the % field.

12. Enter **01-720-7810-0000-000** in the **GL Account** field.

13. Click on the **Ok** button.

Reversing receipts

The bank has returned the receipt of $285, with a reason of "Non Sufficient Funds". Let's reverse the receipt:

1. Select the **Receivables** responsibility.

2. Navigate to **Receipts | Receipts**.

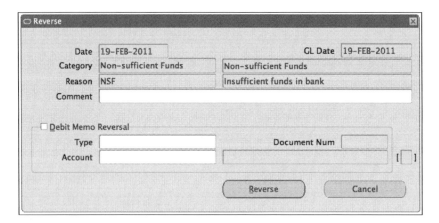

3. Press *F11* to enter the query mode.

4. In the **Receipt Method** field, enter **Manual**.

5. In the **Receipt Number** field, enter **RN-1234**.

6. Press *Ctrl+F11* to run the query.

7. The **Receipt** is displayed.

8. Click the **Reverse... 1** button.

9. The current date of **19-Feb-2011** autopopulates.

10. In the **Category** field, select **Non-Sufficient Funds**.

11. In the **Reason** field, select **NSF**.

12. Click the **Reverse** button. The transaction is saved.

Status History

Status	Date	GL Date	Amount	Rate	Functional Amount
Cleared	19–FEB–2011	19–FEB–2011	285.00		285.00
Reversed	19–FEB–2011	19–FEB–2011	285.00		285.00

Statement Number		Statement Date	
Line Number		Anticipated Value Date	
		Actual Value Date	

13. Click on the **Receipt History** button to review the **History**.

See also

Reconciling bank statements recipe in Chapter 7, Managing Cash

Managing debt

Customer debt is managed in receivables from advanced collections. This includes printing dunning letters, statements, and viewing outstanding bills. In this recipe, we will view aged debts.

Getting ready

Log in to Oracle E-Business Suite R12 with the username and password assigned to you by the System Administrator. If you are working on the Vision demonstration database, you can use OPERATIONS/WELCOME as the USERNAME/PASSWORD.

How to do it...

Let's view the transaction history and the aging bucket of SheepWall Inc:

1. Select the **Receivables** responsibility.

2. Navigate to **Collections | Collections**.

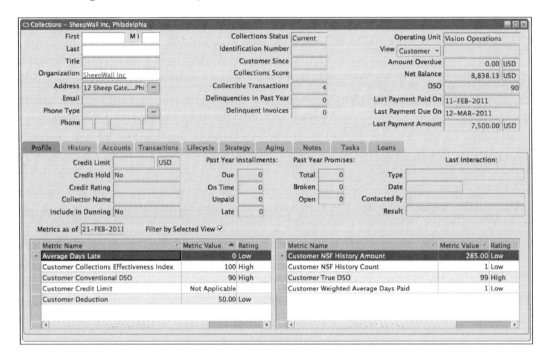

3 In the **Organization** field, enter **SheepWall Inc**.

4. The **History** tab shows the history of transactions between specific periods.

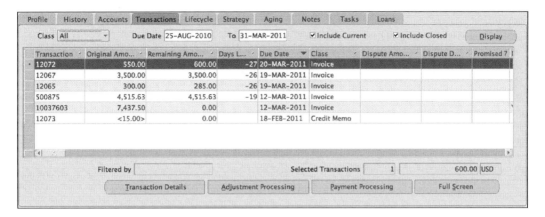

5. Click the **Transactions** tab to view the transactions between a specific period

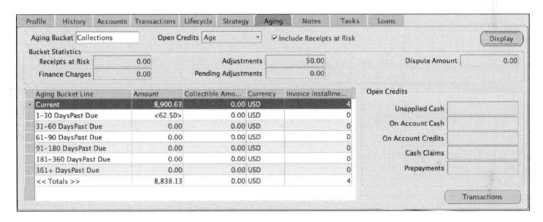

6. Click the **Aging** tab to view the **Aging Bucket** (the time periods to review the open transactions).

7. In the **Aging Bucket** field, select **Collections, Aging Type 7-Bucket**.

8. Click on the **Display** button to display the **7-Bucket Aging** account for **SheepWall Inc**.

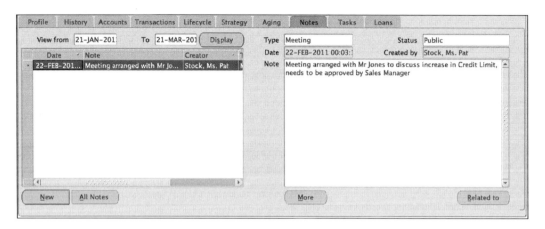

9. Click on the **Notes** tab to view notes recorded on the customer's account.

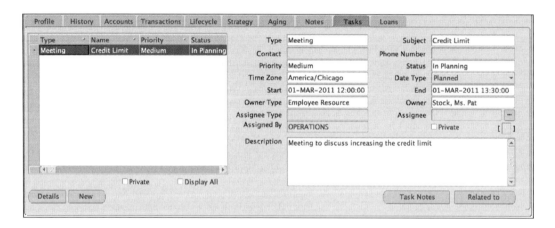

10. Click on the **Tasks** tab to view the tasks.

Reviewing Receivables' accounting transactions

In this recipe, we will transfer transactions to the General Ledger and review the accounting transactions generated.

Getting ready

Log in to Oracle E-Business Suite R12 with the username and password assigned to you by the system administrator. If you are working on the Vision demonstration database, you can use OPERATIONS/WELCOME as the USERNAME/PASSWORD.

How to do it...

Let's create accounting transactions for multiple transactions:

1. Select the **Receivables** responsibility.

2. Navigate to **Other | Requests | Run** or select **View | Requests** from the menu.

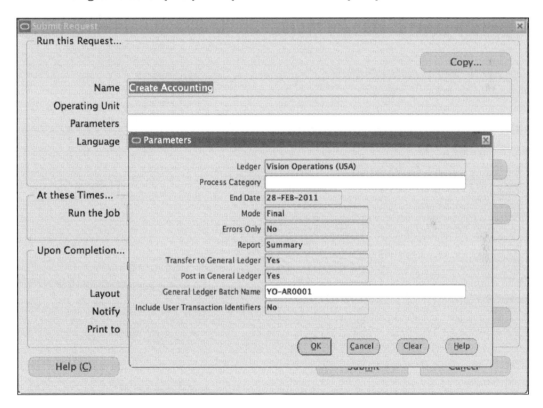

3. Click on the **Submit a New Request** button.

4. Select **Single Request** from the **Options**.

5. Click on the **OK** button.

6. In the **Submit Request** form, select **Create Accounting** from the list of values.

7. Select the **Parameters** field and select **Vision Operations (USA)** as the Ledger, enter **28-FEB-2011** as the **End Date**, select **Yes** as the parameter for **Post in General Ledger**, and enter **YO-AR0001** as the **General Ledger Batch Name**.

8. Accept the default values for the remaining fields.

9. Click on the **OK** button.

10. We can schedule the program to run periodically, for example, every month.

11. Click on the **Submit** button to submit the request.

Review the requests:

1. Navigate to **View | Requests** from the menu.

2. Click on the **find** button.

3. The **Create Accounting** program also spawns other programs to complete the transfer and posting of the journal in General Ledger.

Let's view the transactions from General Ledger:

1. Switch responsibilities by selecting **File | Switch Responsibility**.

2. Select the **General Ledger** responsibility.

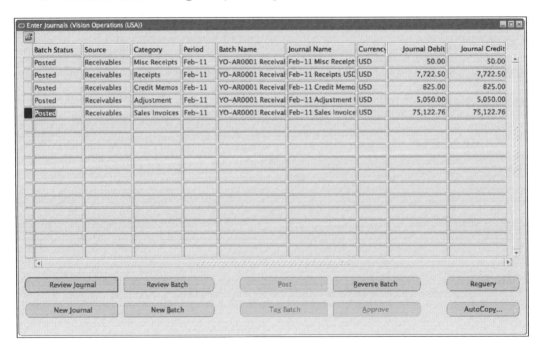

Batch Status	Source	Category	Period	Batch Name	Journal Name	Currency	Journal Debit	Journal Credit
Posted	Receivables	Misc Receipts	Feb-11	YO-AR0001 Receival	Feb-11 Misc Receipt	USD	50.00	50.00
Posted	Receivables	Receipts	Feb-11	YO-AR0001 Receival	Feb-11 Receipts USE	USD	7,722.50	7,722.50
Posted	Receivables	Credit Memos	Feb-11	YO-AR0001 Receival	Feb-11 Credit Memo	USD	825.00	825.00
Posted	Receivables	Adjustment	Feb-11	YO-AR0001 Receival	Feb-11 Adjustment	USD	5,050.00	5,050.00
Posted	Receivables	Sales Invoices	Feb-11	YO-AR0001 Receival	Feb-11 Sales Invoice	USD	75,122.76	75,122.76

Review Journal   Review Batch   Post   Reverse Batch   Requery

New Journal   New Batch   Tax Batch   Approve   AutoCopy...

3. Navigate to **Journals | Enter**.

4. Search for the journal by selecting the **Source** as **Receivables** and the **Period** as **Feb-11**.

5. Click on the **Review Journal** button to review the journal.

How it works...

Oracle Receivables uses the accounting event model defined in Subledger Accounting to determine the transactions that generate accounting transactions.

Now let's review the structure of the Event Model, which consists of Entities, Classes, Types, and Events:

1. Select the **Receivables** responsibility.

2. Navigate to **Setup | Financials | Accounting | Subledger Accounting | Subledger Applications | Accounting Methods Builder | Events | Event Model**.

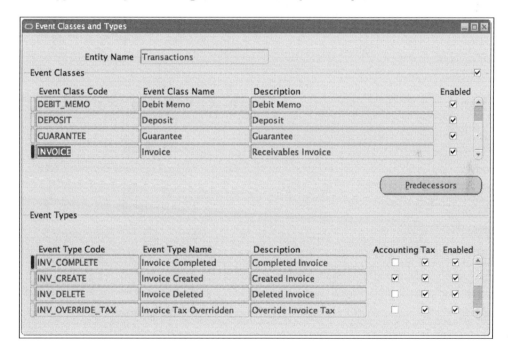

3. The **Event Model** consists of the various **Receivables Entities**.

4. Select the **Transactions Entity** and click on the **Event Classes** button.

5. Each **Event Class** also has its associated **Event Types**. The events are categorized into event types.

See also

Defining Subledger Accounting recipe in Chapter 8, Defining Transactions for the General Ledger

7
Managing Cash

In this chapter, we will cover:

- ▶ Creating bank accounts
- ▶ Entering bank statements
- ▶ Reconciling bank statements
- ▶ Creating cash forecasts
- ▶ Reviewing accounting transactions

Introduction

The liquidity of an organization is managed in Oracle Cash Management; this includes the reconciliation of the cashbook to the bank statements, and forecasting future cash requirements. In this chapter, we will look at how to create bank accounts, enter and reconcile bank statements, and create cash forecasts. Cash management integrates with Payables, Receivables, Payroll, Treasury, and General Ledger.

Let's start by looking at the cash management process:

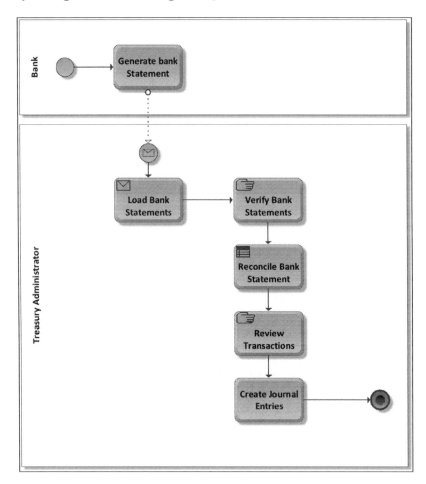

1. The **Bank** generates statements.

2. The statements are sent to the organization electronically or by post.

3. The **Treasury Administrator** loads and verifies the bank statement into cash management. The statements can also be manually entered into cash management.

4. The loaded statements are reconciled to the cash book transactions.

5. The results are reviewed, and amended if required.

6. The **Treasury Administrator** creates the journals for transactions in the General Ledger.

Creating bank accounts

Oracle Cash Management provides us with the functionality to create bank accounts. In this recipe, we will create a bank account for a bank called Shepherd Bank, for one of their branches called Kings Cross branch.

Getting ready

Log in to Oracle E-Business Suite R12 with the username and password assigned to you by the system administrator. If you are working on the Vision demonstration database, you can use OPERATIONS/WELCOME as the USERNAME/PASSWORD.

We also need to create a bank before we can create the bank account. Let's look at how to create a bank and the branch:

1. Select the **Cash Management** responsibility.

2. Navigate to **Setup | Banks | Banks**.

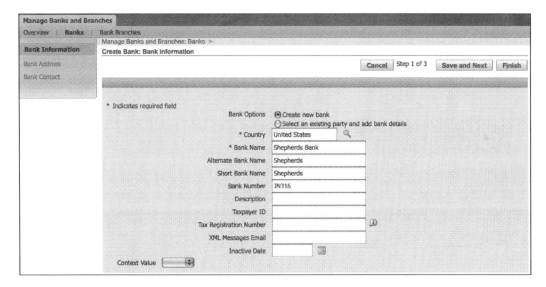

3. In the **Banks** tab, click on the **Create** button.

4. Select the **Create new bank** option.

5. In the **Country** field, enter **United States**.

6. In the **Bank Name** field, enter **Shepherds Bank**.

7. In the **Bank Number** field, enter **JN316**.

8. Click on the **Finish** button.

Let's create the branch and the address:

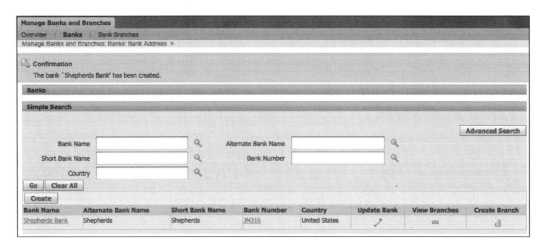

1. Click the **Create Branch** icon: The **Country** and the **Bank Name** are automatically entered.

2. Click on the **Continue** button.

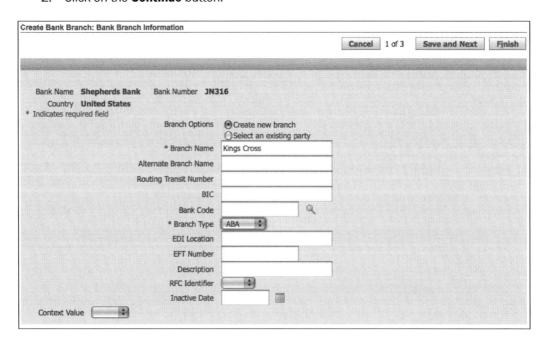

3. In the **Branch Name** field, enter **Kings Cross**.

4. Select **ABA** as the **Branch Type**.

5. Click on the **Save and Next** button to create the **Branch** address.

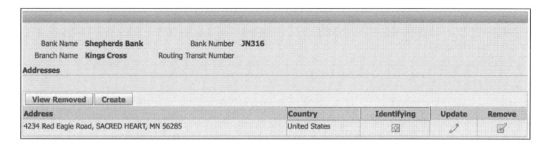

6. In the **Branch Address** form, click on the **create** button.
7. In the **Country** field, enter **United States**.
8. In the **Address Line 1** field, enter **4234 Red Eagle Road**.
9. In the **City** field, enter **Sacred Heart**.
10. In the **County** field, enter **Renville**.
11. In the **State** field, enter **MN**.
12. In the **Postal Code** field, enter **56285**.
13. Ensure that the **Status** field is **Active**.
14. Click on the **Apply** button.
15. Click on the **Finish** button.

How to do it...

Let's create the bank account:

1. Select the **Cash Management** responsibility.
2. Navigate to **Setup | Bank Accounts**.

3. In the **Manage Bank Accounts tab**, click on the **Create** button.
4. In the **Country** field, enter **United States**.
5. In the **Bank Name** field, enter **Shepherds bank**.
6. In the **Branch Name** field, enter **Kings Cross**.

7. Click on the **Continue** button.

8. Select **Vision Operations** for the **Bank Account Owner** field.

9. Select **Payables** and **Receivables** for the **Account Use** field and click on the **Next** button.

10. In the **Account Information** form, enter the following information:

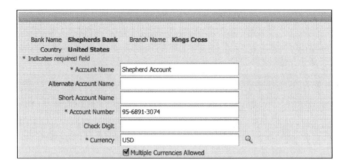

- ❑ In the **Account Name** field, enter **Shepherd Account**
- ❑ In the **Account Number** field, enter **95-6891-3074**
- ❑ In the **Currency** field, enter **USD**
- ❑ Select the **Multiple Currencies Allowed** option
- ❑ Click on the **Save and Next** button

11. In the **General Controls** form, enter the following information:

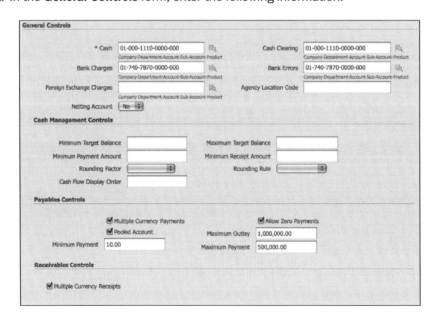

- ❑ In the **Cash** and the **Cash Clearing** fields, enter **01-000-1110-0000-000**
- ❑ In the **Bank Charges** and the **Bank Errors** fields, enter **01-740-7870-0000-000**
- ❑ In the **Payables Controls** region, select **Multiple Currency Payments**, **Allow Zero Payments**, and **Pooled Account**
- ❑ Enter **10.00** in the **Minimum Payment** field
- ❑ Enter **1,000,000.00** in the **Minimum Outlay** field
- ❑ Enter **500,000.00** in the **Maximum Payment** field
- ❑ Click on the **Save and Next** button

12. In the **Account Access** form, click on the **Add Organization Access** button.

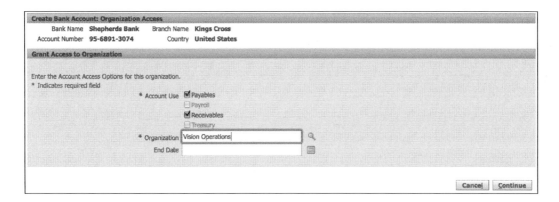

13. Select **Payables** and **Receivables** for the **Account Use** field.
14. Select **Vision Operations** for the **Organization** field and click on the **Continue** button.
15. Click on the **Apply** button.
16. Click on the **Save and Next** button.
17. Click on the **Finish** button, we should receive a confirmation that the account has been created.

There's more...

Loading bank statements electronically from the bank will enable us to automate the bank reconciliation process. We need to define the transaction codes that the bank will use to identify the different types of transactions on the statements.

Creating transaction codes

Let's create transaction codes that will be used by the bank:

1. Select the **Cash Management** responsibility.

2. Navigate to **Setup | Bank | Bank Transaction Codes**.

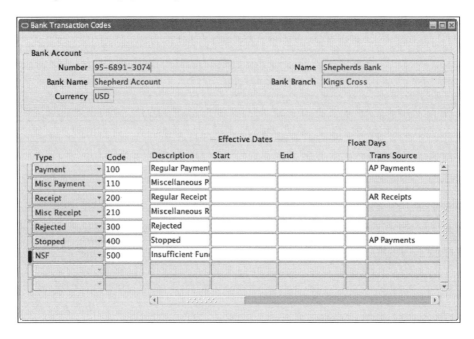

3. In the **Bank Transaction Codes** window, select the **95-6891-3074**, **Shepherd Account** bank account.

4. In the **Type** field select **Payment**.

5. Enter **100** in the **Code** field.

6. Enter **Regular Payment** in the **Description** field. The **Trans Source** of **AP Payments** is automatically entered.

7. Select the next line.

8. In the **Type** field, select **Misc Payment**.

9. Enter **110** in the **Code** field.

10. Enter **Miscellaneous Payment** in the **Description** field.

11. Select the next line.

12. In the **Type** field select **Receipt**.

13. Enter **200** in the **Code** field.

14. Enter **Regular Receipt** in the **Description** field. The **Trans Source** of **AR Payments** is automatically entered.

15. Select the next line.

16. In the **Type** field select **Misc Receipt**.

17. Enter **210** in the **Code** field.

18. Enter **Miscellaneous Receipt** in the **Description** field.

19. Select the next line.

20. In the **Type** field select **Rejected**.

21. Enter **300** in the **Code** field.

22. Enter **Rejected** in the **Description** field.

23. Select the next line.

24. In the **Type** field select **Stopped**.

25. Enter **400** in the **Code** field.

26. Enter **Stopped** in the **Description** field. The **Transactions Source** of **AP Payments** is automatically entered.

27. Select the next line.

28. In the **Type** field select **NSF**.

29. Enter **500** in the **Code** field.

30. Enter **Insufficient Funds** in the **Description** field.

31. Click on the **Save** icon, to save your work.

See also

Paying Invoices recipe in Chapter 3, Paying supplier Invoices in Payables

Entering receipts recipe in Chapter 6, Receiving Funds in Receivables

Entering bank statements

Bank statements are downloaded from the bank to a local directory. Once the file is received, the bank account balance and statement information can be loaded into the bank statement open interface tables, using the bank statement loader program or a custom loader program. The files can also be loaded automatically using an interface program or using the XML Gateway. Bank statements can also be entered manually.

In this recipe, we will look at how to enter bank statements.

Getting ready

The bank statement shown next has been loaded into the open interface table:

Date	Transaction	Description	Debit	Credit	Balance
		Opening Balance			0.00
03-Mar-11	Payment	Fixture Expert Inc		3,092.26	3,092.26
06-Mar-11	Deposit	GL Deposit	100,000.00		96,907.74
08-Mar-11	Payment	Consolidated Supplies		3,688.05	93,219.69
11-Mar-11	Payment	AP Bank Charges		30.00	93,189.69
11-Mar-11	Receipt	Bank Interest	37.52		93,227.21
14-Mar-11	Receipt	Advantage Corp	7,500.00		100,727.21
14-Mar-11	Receipt	Sheep Lamb Farmers	25,000.00		125,727.21
		Closing Balance	132,537.52	6,810.31	125,727.21

Let's review the transactions in the open interface:

1. Select the **Cash Management** responsibility.
2. Navigate to **Bank Statements | Bank Statement Interface Lines**.

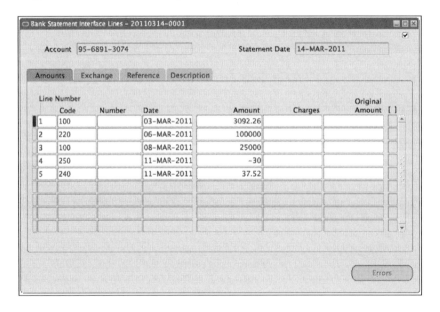

3. Select **95-6891-3074** in the **Account** field.
4. Click on the **Lines** button to view the transactions in the interface tables.

How to do it...

Let's list the steps required to automatically enter the bank statements from the import and AutoReconciliation program:

1. Select the **Cash Management** responsibility.

2. Navigate to **Other | Programs | Run**, or select **View | Requests** from the menu.

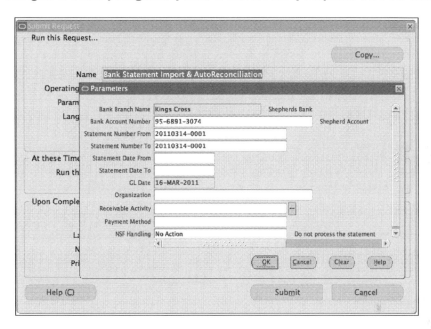

3. Click on the **Submit a New Request** button.

4. Select **Single Request** from the **Options**.

5. Click on the **OK** button.

6. In the **Submit Request** form, select **Bank Statement Import & AutoReconciliation** from the list of values. Please note that we could run the Bank Statement Import program, to run only the import.

7. Select the **Parameters** field, and select **Kings Cross** as the **Bank Branch Name**, select **95-6891-3074** as the **Bank Account Number**, and select **20110314-0001** as the parameter for the **Statement Number From** and the **Statement Number To** fields.

8. Accept the default values for the remaining fields.

9. Click on the **OK** button.

10. We can schedule the program to run periodically, for example, every day.

11. Click on the **Submit** button to submit the request.

Let's review the imported bank statements:

1. Navigate to **Bank Statement | Bank Statements and Reconciliation**.

2. The imported statement is displayed.

3. Click on the **Review** button.

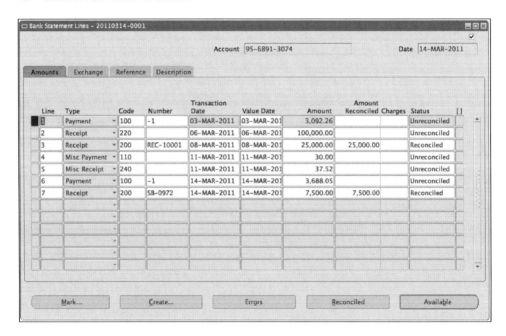

4. In the **Bank Statement** window, select the **Lines** button.

5. The imported lines are displayed.

How it works...

Bank statements can be imported automatically, using a SQL*Loader script against the bank file to populate the bank statement open interface. The bank statement information is then imported into the Bank Statement windows using the Bank Statement Import program.

There's more...

Now, let's look at how to enter statements manually.

Entering bank statements manually

Let's enter the bank statement for the 15th of March manually. The lines on the statement are as follows:

1. Payment of 213.80.

2. Receipt of 3,389.89 from A.C. Networks.

3. Credit of 7,500.00 for Non Sufficient Funds for the receipt from Advantage Corp.

4. Bank Transfer payment of 1,000.00.

5. Select the **Cash Management** responsibility.

6. Navigate to **Bank Statement | Bank Statements and Reconciliation**.

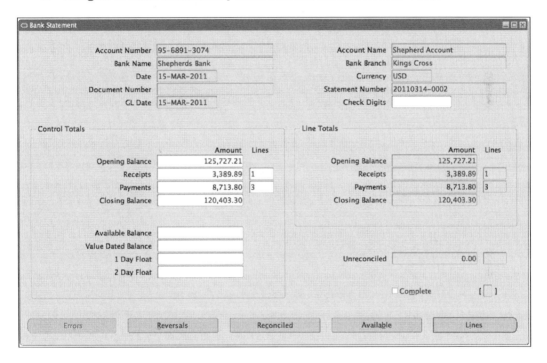

7. In the **Reconcile Bank Statements** window, click on the **New** button.

8. In the **Account Number** field, enter **95-6891-3074**, the other details are automatically entered.

9. In the **Date** field enter **15-MAR-2011**.

10. In the **Statement Number** field enter **20110314-0002**.

11. In the **Control Totals** region, let's enter control totals based on our bank statement.

12. The **Opening Balance** of **125,727.21** is entered based on the previous opening balance.

13. In the **Receipts** field, enter **3,389.89** and **1** in the **Lines** field.

14. In the **Payments** field, enter **8,713.80** and **3** in the **Lines** field.

15. The **Closing Balance** of **98,495.56** is entered automatically.

Let's enter the bank statement lines:

1. Click on the **Lines** button.

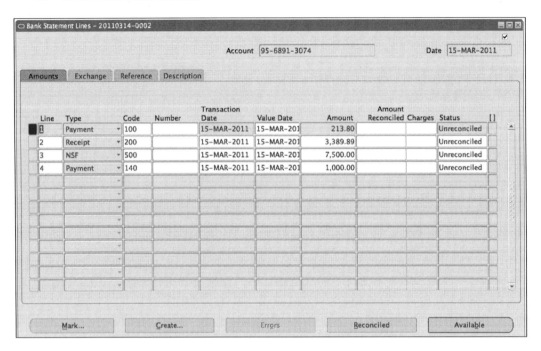

2. In the **Bank Statements Lines** form, enter **1** in the **Line** field.

3. Select **Payment** as the **Type**.

4. Enter **100** as the code.

5. In the **Transaction Date** field, enter **15-MAR-2011**.

6. In the **Amount** field, enter **213.80**.

7. Select the next line, and enter **2** in the **Line** field.

8. Select **Receipt** as the **Type**.

9. Enter **200** as the code.

10. In the **Transaction Date** field, enter **15-MAR-2011**.

11. In the **Amount** field, enter **3,389.89**.

12. Select the **Reference** tab, and enter **A.C. Networks**.

13. Select the next line, and enter **3** in the **Line** field.

14. Select **NSF** as the **Type**.

15. Enter **500** as the code.

16. In the **Transaction Date** field, enter **15-MAR-2011.**

17. In the **Amount** field, enter **7,500.00**.

18. Select the **Reference** tab, and enter **Advantage Corp**.

19. Select the next line, and enter **4** in the **Line** field.

20. Select **Payment** as the **Type**.

21. Enter **140** as the code.

22. In the **Transaction Date** field, enter **15-MAR-2011**.

23. In the **Amount** field, enter **1,000.00**.

24. Save the record.

Reconciling bank statements

After importing or entering the bank statements, we can run the AutoReconciliation program to automatically reconcile the bank transactions to the payables payments and receivables receipts. We can also run the bank statement import and AutoReconciliation program as we did in the previous recipe.

We can then review the AutoReconciliation execution report to identify and correct errors. We can rerun the AutoReconciliation program or perform a manual reconciliation, if necessary. In this recipe, we will review the results of the autoreconciliation program, and manually reconcile bank statements.

Getting ready

We need to have entered bank statements.

How to do it...

Let's list the steps required to reconcile bank statements:

1. Select the **Cash Management** responsibility.

2. Navigate to **Bank Statement | Bank Statements and Reconciliation**.

3. Navigate to the **Menu** and select **View | Find**.

4. In the **Account Number** field, enter **95-6891-3074**.

5. Click on the **Find** button.

6. Click on the **Review** button to view the status of your bank reconciliation.

7. Some of the lines have been autoreconciled.

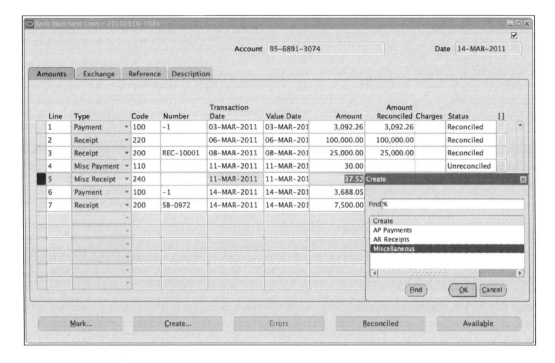

Let's manually reconcile the **Miscellaneous Receipt** for bank interest:

1. In the **Bank Statement Lines** window, select the **Misc Receipt** line.

2. Click on the **Create** button, and select **Miscellaneous**.

3. In the **Miscellaneous Receipts** window, enter **Interest Income** and click on the **OK** button.

4. In the **Method** field, enter **Manual – SB** (this is the receipt class for the **Bank Receipts**).

5. Click on the **Create** button.

6. A **Decision** box is displayed with the message **"Do you want to reconcile the receipt(s) to current statement line?"** click on the **Yes** button.

7. Save the record.

Let's manually reconcile the **Miscellaneous Payment** for **Bank Charges**:

1. In the **Bank Statement Lines** window, select the **Misc Payment** line.

2. Click on the **Create** button, and select **Miscellaneous**.

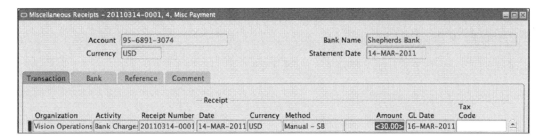

3. In the **Miscellaneous Receipts** window, enter **Bank Charges** and click on the **OK** button.

4. In the **Method** field, enter **Manual – SB** (this is the receipt class for the **Bank Receipts**).

5. Click on the **Create** button.

6. A **Decision** box is displayed with the message **"Do you want to reconcile the receipt(s) to current statement line?"** click on the **Yes** button.

7. All the lines are now reconciled.

8. Save the record.

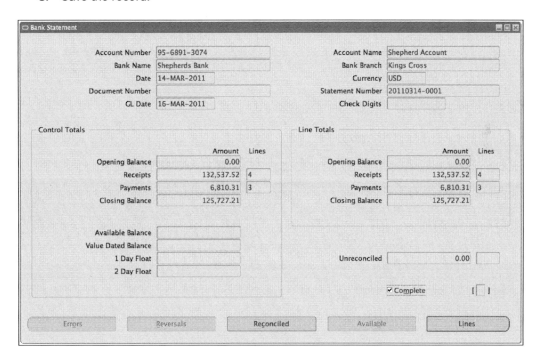

9. Click on the **Complete** checkbox to complete the reconciliation.

How it works...

The cash management reconciliation options are set up up in the system controls. The reconciliation controls region. The settings determine if:

▶ Only cleared transactions will be available for reconciliation

▶ Voided payments should be available for reconciliation

▶ Lines can be added to imported statements

The AutoReconciliation program performs validations when the bank statement information is loaded into the bank statement open interface tables. This includes validating:

▶ Bank statement header

▶ Control total

▶ Statement line

▶ Multicurrency

The matching order is determined when we create the bank account.

There's more...

Now, let's look at some other options that are relevant to reconciling bank statements.

Manual reconciliation

Let's manually reconcile some further transactions:

1. Select the **Cash Management** responsibility.

2. Navigate to **Bank Statement | Bank Statements and Reconciliation**.

Account Num	Statement Date	Statement Num	Complet	Opening Balance	Closing Balance	Account Name	Unreconciled Li
95-6891-3074	15-MAR-2011	20110314-0002	☐	125,727.21	98,495.56	Shepherd Acco	6

3. Navigate to the **Menu** and select **View | Find**.

4. In the **Account Number** field, enter **95-6891-3074**.

5. Click on the **Find** button.

6. Click on the **Review** button to view the status of the bank reconciliation.

7. In the **Bank Statement** form, select the **Lines** button.

Let's reconcile a payment already entered in accounts payable:

1. Select line 1 for **213.80**, click on the **Available** button.

2. Select the **Detail** option.

3. Enter **15-Mar-2011** in the **Date** field.

4. In the **Amount** field enter **213.80**.

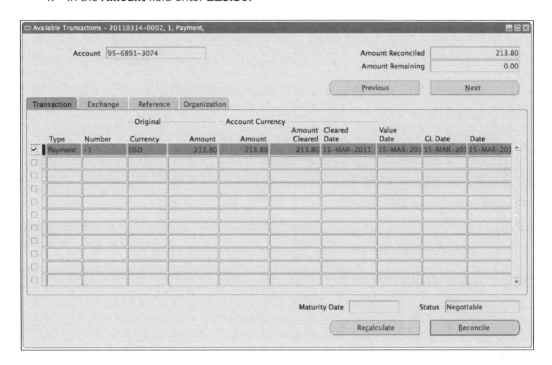

5. Click on the **Find** button.

6. Select the line and click on the **Reconcile** button.

7. The line is now reconciled.

Entering AR receipts

Let's reconcile a receipt not yet entered:

1. Select line 2 for **3,389.89**, click on the **Create** button.

2. Select **AR Receipts**.

3. Enter **Manual – SB** in the **Receipt Method** field.

4. Enter **CE-0001** in the **Receipt Number** field.

5. In the **Customer Name** field, enter **A. C. Networks**.

6. Click on the **Search and Apply** button in the **Search and Apply** form.

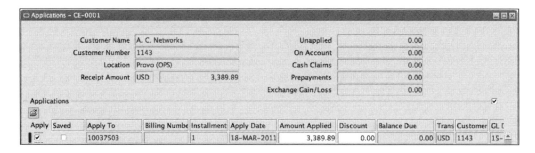

7. Select the **Apply** checkbox on the invoice number **10037503**.

8. Save the record.

9. Close the form, and the **Bank Statement Lines** will be displayed.

10. Select receipt line 2, click on the **Available** button.

11. Enter **CE-0001** in the **Number** field.

12. Click on the **Find** button.

13. Select the line, and click on the **Reconcile** button.

14. The line is now reconciled.

Entering AP payments

Let's reconcile a direct payment of $1,000.00:

1. Select line 4 for **1,000.00**, click on the **Create** button.

2. Select **AP Payments**, and the **Payments** form is displayed.

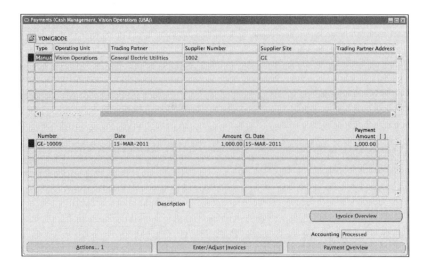

3. In the **Trading Partner** field select **General Electric Utilities**, and select **GE** for the **Supplier Site**.

4. In the **Payment Amount** field, enter **1,000.00**.

5. Select the **Payment Method** of **Wire**.

6. Select **Manual** as the **Payment Process Profile**.

7. Select **SB_Cheques** as the **Payment Document**.

8. The **Document Number** is automatically selected.

9. Click on the **Enter/Adjust Invoices** button.

10. Select the invoice **GE-10009**.

11. Save the record.

12. Click on the **Actions** buttons, and select the **Final Post** option.

13. Click on the **OK** button.

14. Close the form and we should be back at the **Bank Statements Line** form.

15. Click on the **Available** button, and search for the Item using the **Number 100000002**.

16. The document is displayed in the **Available Transactions** window.

17. Select the **Transaction** and click on the **Reconcile** button.

18. The line is now reconciled.

Reversing transactions

Let's reverse the receipt of $7,500 due to insufficient funds:

1. Select the reversal button from the **Bank Statement** page.

2. In the **Date** field, enter **14-Mar-2011**.

3. In the **Amount** field, enter **7,500** and click on the **Find** button.

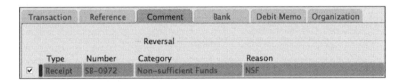

4. Select the **Transaction**.

5. Select the **Comment** tab, and select **Non-sufficient Funds** in the **Category** field and **NSF** in the **Reason** field.

6. Click on the **Reverse Receipt** button.

7. Close the form and select the **Lines** button.

8.   Select the **NSF** line and click on the **Available** button.

9.   Search for the Item using the amount **7,500** and the **Number SB-0972**.

10. The document is displayed in the **Available Transactions** window.

11. Select the **Transaction** and click on the **Reconcile** button.

12. The line is now reconciled.

See also

Paying Invoices recipe in Chapter 3, Paying Supplier Invoices in Payables

Entering receipts recipe in Chapter 6, Receiving Funds in Receivables

Creating cash forecasting

Cash forecasting is a tool that can be used to forecast the inflow and outflow of cash within the organization:

▶   **Inflows sources**: General Ledger, Sales, Order Management, Receivables, Treasury, Projects, and External Sources

▶   **Outflows sources**: General Ledger, Purchases, Payables, Payroll, Projects, Treasury, and External Sources

This can help the organization to plan liquidity requirements, and plan adequately. In this recipe, we will look at how to run cash forecast.

Getting ready

A cash forecast template is required. Let's look at a six month forecast template:

1.   Select the **Cash Management** responsibility.

2.   Navigate to **Cash Forecasting**.

Forecast Template: Six Month Forecast - VisionOps

Forecast Template Header

Template Name	**Six Month Forecast - VisionOps**
Description	**Six Monthly Buckets Forecast for Vision Operations**
Forecast By	**GL Periods**
Overdue Transaction	**EXCLUDE**
Cutoff Period	
Business Calendar	
Project Number From	
Project Number To	

Forecast Template Rows

Details Row Number	Source Type	Description
⊞ Show 2	Supplier Invoices	AP Invoices
⊞ Show 3	Customer Invoices	AR Invoices
⊞ Show 4	Purchase Orders	Purchase Orders
⊞ Show 5	Purchase Requisitions	Purchase Requisitions
⊞ Show 6	Sales Orders	Sales Orders

3. Select the **Forecast Templates** tab.

4. In the **Template Name** field, enter **Six Month Forecast – VisionOps**.

5. Click on the **Go** button.

6. The **Forecast Template** is displayed, click on the **Six Month Forecast – VisionOps** link.

7. The forecast is by **GL Periods** and **Overdue** transactions are excluded.

8. The row definitions are displayed, and this includes rows for **AP Invoices**, **AR Invoices**, **Purchase Orders**, **Purchase Requisitions**, and **Sales Orders**.

9. The columns are also displayed for the six months.

How to do it...

Let's run a cash forecast:

1. Select the **Cash Management** responsibility.

2. Navigate to **Cash Forecasting**.

3. Select the **Forecast Templates** tab.

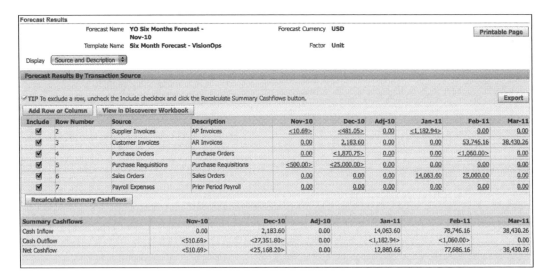

4. In the **Template Name** field enter **Six Month Forecast – VisionOps**.

5. Click on the **Go** button.

6. The **Forecast Template** is displayed, click on the **Run Forecast** icon.

7. In the **Forecast Name** field, enter **YO Six Months Forecast – Nov-10**.

8. In the **Calendar Name** field, enter **Accounting**.

9. In the **Forecast Currency** and the **Source Currency** fields enter **USD**.

10. In the **Start Period** field, enter **Nov-10**.

11. Select **Entered** in the **Source Currency Type**.

12. Click on the **Submit** button.

13. Review the forecast by selecting the link.

14. The forecast is displayed.

Reviewing accounting transactions

In this recipe, we will transfer transactions to the General Ledger and review the accounting transactions generated.

Getting ready

Log in to Oracle E-Business Suite R12 with the username and password assigned to you by the system administrator. If you are working on the Vision demonstration database, you can use OPERATIONS/WELCOME as the USERNAME/PASSWORD.

How to do it...

Let's list the steps required to complete the task:

1. Select the **Cash Management** responsibility.

2. Navigate to **Other | Programs | Run**, or select **View | Requests** from the menu.

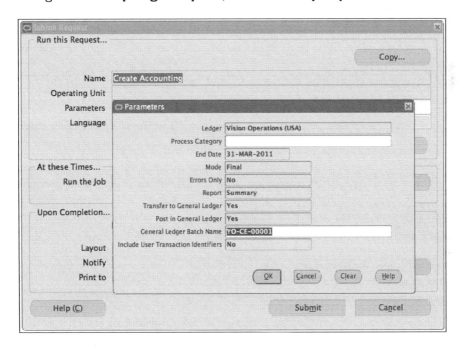

3. Click on the **Submit a New Request** button.

4. Select **Single Request** from the **Options**.

5. Click on the **OK** button.

6. In the **Submit Request** form, select **Create Accounting** from the list of values.

7. Select the **Parameters** field, and select **Vision Operations (USA)** as the **Ledger**, enter **31-MAR-2011** as the **End Date**, select **Yes** as the parameter for **Post in General Ledger**, and enter **YO-CE-00001** as the **General Ledger Batch Name**.

8. Accept the default values for the remaining fields.

9. Click on the **OK** button.

10. We can schedule the program to run periodically, for example, every month.

11. Click on the **Submit** button to submit the request.

12. Review the requests.

13. Navigate to **View | Requests** from the menu.

14. Click on the **find** button.

15. The **Create Accounting** program also spawns other programs to complete the transfer and posting of the journal in General Ledger.

There's more...

Now, let's review the transactions in General Ledger.

Viewing Transactions in General Ledger

Let's view the transactions from General Ledger:

1. Switch responsibilities by selecting **File | Switch Responsibility**.

2. Select the **General Ledger** responsibility.

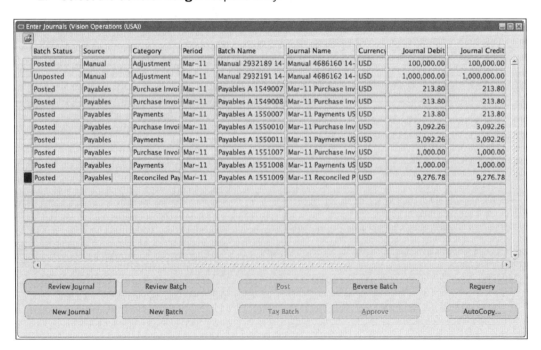

Batch Status	Source	Category	Period	Batch Name	Journal Name	Currency	Journal Debit	Journal Credit
Posted	Manual	Adjustment	Mar-11	Manual 2932189 14-	Manual 4686160 14-	USD	100,000.00	100,000.00
Unposted	Manual	Adjustment	Mar-11	Manual 2932191 14-	Manual 4686162 14-	USD	1,000,000.00	1,000,000.00
Posted	Payables	Purchase Invoi	Mar-11	Payables A 1549007	Mar-11 Purchase Inv	USD	213.80	213.80
Posted	Payables	Purchase Invoi	Mar-11	Payables A 1549008	Mar-11 Purchase Inv	USD	213.80	213.80
Posted	Payables	Payments	Mar-11	Payables A 1550007	Mar-11 Payments US	USD	213.80	213.80
Posted	Payables	Purchase Invoi	Mar-11	Payables A 1550010	Mar-11 Purchase Inv	USD	3,092.26	3,092.26
Posted	Payables	Payments	Mar-11	Payables A 1550011	Mar-11 Payments US	USD	3,092.26	3,092.26
Posted	Payables	Purchase Invoi	Mar-11	Payables A 1551007	Mar-11 Purchase Inv	USD	1,000.00	1,000.00
Posted	Payables	Payments	Mar-11	Payables A 1551008	Mar-11 Payments US	USD	1,000.00	1,000.00
Posted	Payables	Reconciled Pay	Mar-11	Payables A 1551009	Mar-11 Reconciled P	USD	9,276.78	9,276.78

Review Journal — Review Batch — Post — Reverse Batch — Requery

New Journal — New Batch — Tax Batch — Approve — AutoCopy...

3. Navigate to **Journals | Enter**.

4. Search for the journal, by selecting the **Period** as **Mar-11**.

5. Click on the **Review Journal** button to review the journal.

See also

Closing Payables recipe in Chapter 9, End of Period Processing

Closing receivables recipe in Chapter 9, End of Period Processing

8

Defining Transactions for the General Ledger

In this chapter, we will cover:

- ▸ Defining the chart of accounts
- ▸ Setting up the ledger
- ▸ Defining subledger accounting
- ▸ Defining E-Business Tax accounting

Introduction

Financial transactions are entered into ledgers. Oracle uses Subledgers (for example, Payables, Receivables, Assets, and Inventory) and the General Ledger to record the financial transactions. The transactions are entered in the Subledger and then transferred to the General Ledger through the Subledger Accounting engine. The General Ledger is used mainly to produce financial reports for decision-making.

The following diagram summarizes the process for transferring financial transactions from the Subledger to the General Ledger:

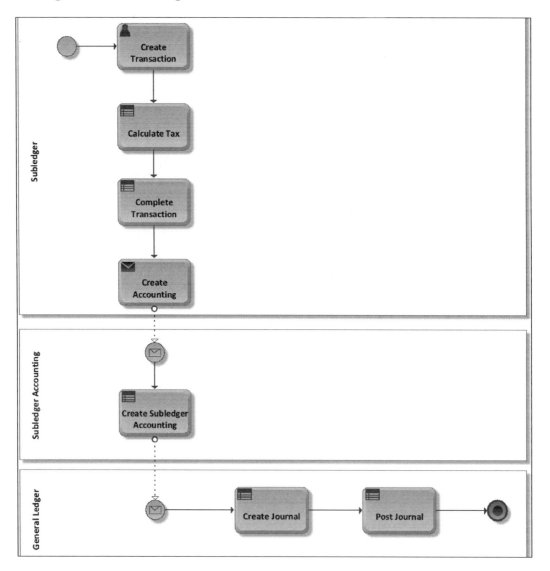

1. The transactions are entered in the **Subledger**, for example, in Payables.

2. Tax is calculated on the transactions based on the E-Business tax settings.

3. The transaction is completed and we run the **Create Accounting** program to transfer the transactions to the **General Ledger**.

4. The journals are created and posted in the **General Ledger**.

Defining the chart of accounts

An organization will require accounts to be set up before transactions can be entered. The chart of accounts defines the structure of the accounts: It can be defined to fit the requirements of the organization. The structure of the chart of accounts is called the **Accounting Key Flexfield** structure. The structure is made up of segments, and each segment is made up of values. In this recipe, we define the structure of the chart of accounts for ACME Corporation in the following order: Company, Department, Account, Product, and Spare segments.

For each of the segments we will enter the name, window prompt, and assign a segment column for the order of the segment and a Value Set. The Value Set determines the type of data that can be entered in the field.

Segment	Size	Qualifier	Default Value
Company	2	Balancing	01
Department	3	Cost Center	
Account	4	Natural Accounts	
Product	3		000
Spare	3		000

Getting ready

Log in to Oracle E-Business Suite R12 with the username and password assigned to you by the system administrator. If you are working on the Vision demonstration database you can use OPERATIONS/WELCOME as the USERNAME/PASSWORD.

How to do it...

Let's list the steps required to create the Accounting Structure. The **Key Flexfield Segments** page is used to define key Flexfields:

1. Select the **General Ledger** responsibility.

2. Navigate to **Setup | Financials | Flexfields | Key | Segments**:

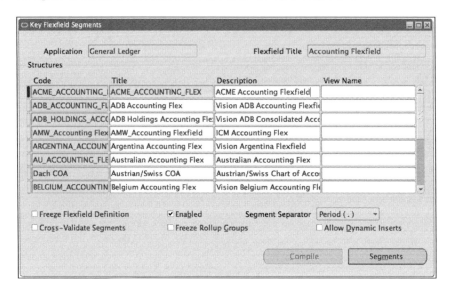

3. Press the *F11* key to enter the query mode.

4. Enter **General Ledger** in the **Application** field, and press *Ctrl+F11* to run the query.

5. Click in the **Code** field, and click on the **New** icon to create a new row. The **Code** for a structure is a developer key and is used by loader programs.

6. Enter **ACME_ACCOUNTING_FLEX** in the **Code** field; the title automatically defaults to the value we entered in the **Code** field.

7. Enter **ACME Accounting Flexfield** in the **Description** field.

Let's define the segments:

1. Click on the **Segments** button to display the **Segments Summary** page to define the segments.

2. Enter **1** in the **Number** field, and enter **Company** in the **Name** field. Company is automatically entered in the **Window Prompt** field.

3. In the **Column** field select **SEGMENT1** from the **List of Values**.

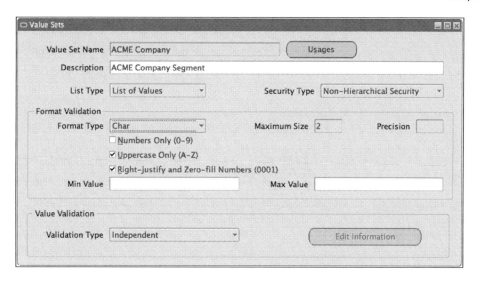

4. Click on the **Value Set** button to create a new value set.

5. In the **Value Set Name** field, enter **ACME Company**, and enter **ACME Company Segment** as the **Description**.

6. Select **List of Values** as the **List Type** and **Non-Hierarchical Security** as the **Security Type**.

7. In the **Format Validation** region, select **Char** as the **Format Type** as the field will contain characters. Enter **2** as the **Maximum Size** and enable the checkboxes for **Uppercase Only (A-Z),** and **Right-justify and Zero-fill Numbers (0001).**

8. In the **Validation Type** field select **Independent**.

9. Close the form.

10. Select the next line, and enter **Department** in the **Name** field; the **Window Prompt** is automatically entered.

11. In the **Column** field, select **SEGMENT2** from the **List of Values**.

12. In the **Value Set** field, select **Operations Department** from the **List of Values**.

13. Select the next line, and enter **Account** in the **Name** field; the **Window Prompt** is automatically entered.

14. In the **Column** field, select **SEGMENT3** from the **List of Values**.

15. In the **Value Set** field, select **Operations Account** from the **List of Values**.

16. Select the next line, and enter **Product** in the **Name** field; the **Window Prompt** is automatically entered.

17. In the **Column** field, select **SEGMENT4** from the **List of Values**.

18. In the **Value Set** field, select **Operations Product** from the **List of Values**.

19. Select the next line, and enter **Account** in the **Name** field; the **Window Prompt** is automatically entered.

20. In the **Column** field, select **SEGMENT5** from the **List of Values**:

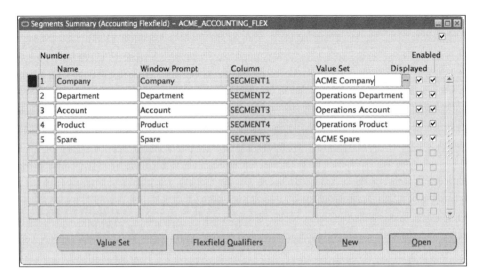

21. Click on the **Value Set** button to create a new value set.

22. In the **Value Set Name** field, enter **ACME Spare**, and enter **ACME Spare Segment** as the **Description**.

23. Select **List of Values** as the **List Type** and **Non-Hierarchical Security** as the **Security Type**.

24. In the **Format Validation** region, select **Char** as the **Format Type** as the field will contain characters. Enter **3** as the **Maximum Size** and enable the checkboxes for **Uppercase Only (A-Z)** and **Right-justify and Zero-fill Numbers (0001).**

25. In the **Validation Type** field, select **Independent**.

26. Close the form.

27. Click on the **Save** icon to save the record.

Let's assign the Flexfield qualifiers to the segments.

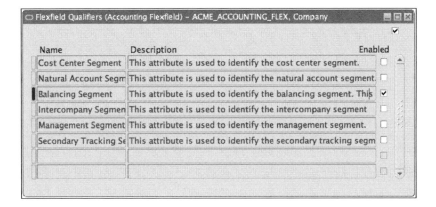

1. In the **Segments Summary** form, select the **Company** segment and click on the **Flexfield Qualifiers** button.

2. Select the enabled checkbox for the **Balancing Segment** row.

3. Click on the **Save** icon to save the record.

4. Select the **Department** row and click on the **Flexfield Qualifiers** button.

5. Select the enabled checkbox for the **Cost Center Segment** row.

6. Click on the **Save** icon to save the record.

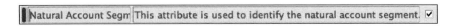

7. Select the **Account** row and click on the **Flexfield Qualifiers** button.

8. Select the enabled checkbox for the **Natural Account Segment** row.

9. Click on the **Save** icon to save the record.

Let's enter some default values for the segments:

1. Select the **Company** segment, and click on the **Open** button.

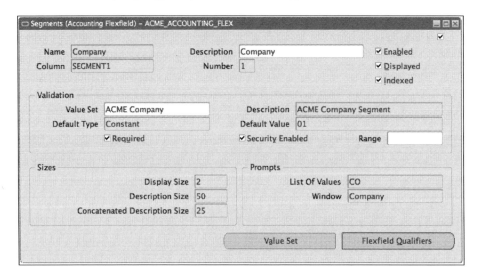

2. In the **Validation** region, select **Constant** as the **Default Type** and enter **01** as the **Default Value**.

3. In the **Prompts** region, enter **CO** in the **List Of Values** field.

4. Save the record.

5. Select the **Spare** segment, and click on the **Open** button.

6. In the **Validation** region, select **Constant** as the **Default Type** and enter **000** as the **Default Value**.

7. Save the record.

8. Close the form.

9. In the **Key Flexfield Segments** form, select **Period (.)** as the **Segment Separator**, and select the **Allow Dynamic Inserts** checkbox to allow us to automatically enter account combinations.

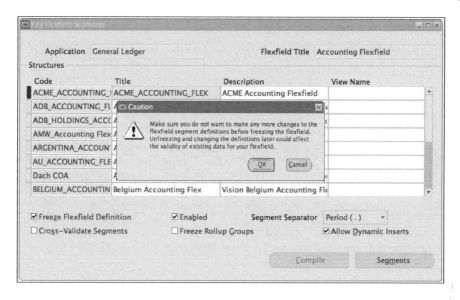

10. Click on the **Freeze Flexfield Definition**, and click on the **OK** button when a **Caution** message is displayed.

11. Click on the **Compile** button to compile the **Flexfield**.

12. Click on **OK** on the displayed note, and a note is displayed to confirm that the Flexfield view **GL_CODE_COMBINATIONS_KFV** has been created.

13. The page becomes read-only, once the Flexfield definition is frozen.

14. Close the form.

How it works...

The Accounting Flexfield has a number of sections called **segments** that contain separate fields. The values in the Flexfield are populated when a user clicks on a Flexfield. The Flexfield Qualifiers are used to assign qualifiers to key flexfield segments.

There's more...

Now, let's look at some additional tasks in setting up our chart of accounts.

Entering Flexfield values

Valid values must exist in a segment before we can use the segment. Let's enter values for the Company and Spare segments:

1. Select the **General Ledger** responsibility.

2. Navigate to **Setup | Financials | Flexfields | Key | Values**.

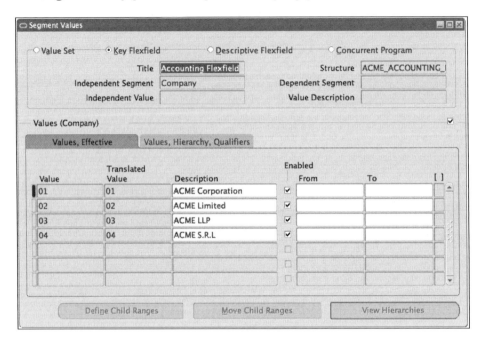

3. In the **Find Key Flexfield Segment** form, select **General Ledger** in the **Application** field.

4. Select **Accounting Flexfield** in the **Title** field.

5. Select **ACME_ACCOUNTING_FLEX** in the **Structure** field, and click on the **Find** button.

6. Select the **Values, Effective** tab.

7. Enter **01** in the **Value** field, and enter **ACME Corporation** in the **Description** field.

8. Enter **02** in the **Value** field, and enter **ACME Limited** in the **Description** field.

9. Enter **03** in the **Value** field, and enter **ACME LLP** in the **Description** field.

10. Enter **04** in the **Value** field, and enter **ACME S.R.L** in the **Description** field.

11. Click on the **Save** icon to save the record.

12. Select the **Independent Segment** tab, and click on the down arrow until the **Spare** segment is displayed.

13. Select the **Values, Effective** tab.

14. Enter **000** in the **Value** field, and enter **Default** in the **Description** field.

15. Click on the **Save** icon to save the record.

Entering natural account values

Natural accounts define the classification of the nominal ledger into Assets, Liabilities, Revenue, Expense, and Owner's Equity/Stock. Let's enter values for the following accounts:

Account	Account Number	Qualifier
Cash Account	1180	Asset
ACME Suspense	2999	Liability
ACME Retained Earnings	3311	Ownership / Stock
Special Consulting	4190	Revenue
Communications	7480	Expense
Special Expense	7490	Expense

1. Select the **General Ledger** responsibility.

2. Navigate to **Setup | Financials | Flexfields | Key | Values**.

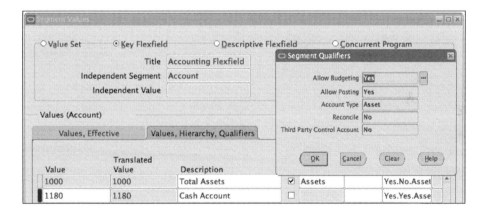

3. In the **Find Key Flexfield Segment** form, select **General Ledger** in the **Application** field.

4. Select **Accounting Flexfield** in the **Title** field.

5. Select **ACME_ACCOUNTING_FLEX** in the **Structure** field, and click on the **Find** button.

6. Select the **Values, Effective** tab.

7. Select the **Value** field and click on the **New Record** icon.

8. Enter **1180** in the **Value** field, and enter **Cash Account** in the **Description** field.

9. Select the **Values, Hierarchy, Qualifiers** tab.

10. Click on the **Qualifiers** field, and select **Asset** in the **Qualifiers** field; click on **OK**.

11. Save the record.

12. Select the **Value** field and click on the **New Record** icon.

13. Enter **2999** in the **Value** field, and enter **ACME Suspense** in the **Description** field.

14. Select the **Values, Hierarchy, Qualifiers** tab.

15. Click on the **Qualifiers** field, and select **Liability** in the **Qualifiers** field, click on **OK**.

16. Save the record.

17. Select the **Value** field and click on the **New Record** icon.

18. Enter **3311** in the **Value** field, and enter **ACME Retained Earnings** in the **Description** field.

19. Select the **Values, Hierarchy, Qualifiers** tab.

20. Click on the **Qualifiers** field, and select **Ownership/Stock** in the **Qualifiers** field, click on **OK**.

21. Save the record.

22. Select the **Value** field and click on the **New Record** icon.

23. Enter **4190** in the **Value** field, and enter **Special Consulting** in the **Description** field.

24. Select the **Values, Hierarchy, Qualifiers** tab.

25. Click on the **Qualifiers** field, and select **Revenue** in the **Qualifiers** field; click on **OK**.

26. Save the record.

27. Select the **Value** field and click on the **New Record** icon.

28. Enter **7480** in the **Value** field, and enter **Communications** in the **Description** field.

29. Select the **Values, Hierarchy, Qualifiers** tab.

30. Click on the **Qualifiers** field, and select **Expense** in the **Qualifiers** field; click on **OK**.

31. Select the **Value** field and click on the **New Record** icon.

32. Enter **7490** in the **Value** field, and enter **Special Expense** in the **Description** field.

33. Select the **Values, Hierarchy, Qualifiers** tab.

34. Click on the **Qualifiers** field, and select **Expense** in the **Qualifiers** field; click on **OK**.

35. Save the record.

Setting up the ledger

Before we can start to use General Ledger, we need to create a ledger. In this recipe, we will set up the ledger for a legal entity based in the United States. The ledger consists of four main parts:

- ▶ **Chart of Accounts**—The structure of the account—**ACME_ACCOUNTING_FLEX**.

- ▶ **Accounting Calendar**—The periods and the year for the financial transactions— Monthly Accounting.

- ▶ **Currencies**—The functional currency of the financial transactions. All the current ISO 4217 currencies are seeded with Oracle E-Business Suite—We will use USD (US Dollars).

- ▶ **Subledger Accounting Method**—The accounting standards applicable for the ledger —Standard Accrual.

The Accounting Setup Manager is used to set up the ledger.

How to do it...

Let's list the steps required to set up the ledger.

Let's create a Legal Entity:

1. Select the **General Ledger** responsibility.

2. Navigate to **Setup | Financials | Accounting Setup Manager | Accounting Setups**.

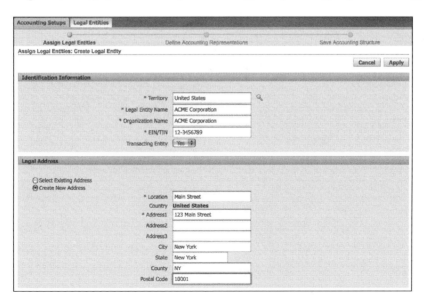

3. In the **Accounting Setups** form, click on the **Create Accounting Setup** button.

4. In the **Assign Legal Entities** form, click on the **Create Legal Entity** button.

5. In the **Identification Information** region, select **United States** as the **Territory**.

6. In the **Legal Entity Name** field, enter **ACME Corporation**.

7. In the **Organization Name** field, enter **ACME Corporation.**

8. Enter **12-3456789** in the **EIN/TIN** field.

9. Select **Yes** in the **Transaction Entity** list.

10. In the **Legal Address** field region, click on the **Create New Address** option.

11. In the **Location** field, enter **Main Street**.

12. In the **Address1** field, enter **123 Main Street**.

13. Enter **New York** in the **City** and **State** fields.

14. In the **County** field enter **NY**.

15. In the **Postal Code** field enter **10001**.

16. Click on the **Apply** button to create the Legal entity.

Let's set up the ledger:

1. In the **Create Accounting Setup | Assign Legal Entities** form, click on the **Add Another Row** button.

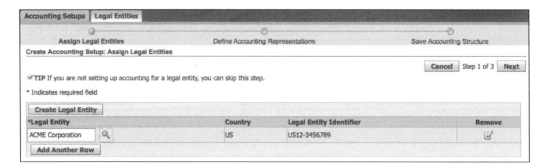

2. Enter **ACME Corporation** in the **Legal Entity** field and press the _Tab_ key on the keyboard. The **ACME Corporation** legal entity will be displayed with the country and the generated **Legal Entity Identifier**; assign the value **Yes** to the **LE: Generate Legal Entity Identifier**.

3. Click on the **Next** button to define **Primary Ledger** details.

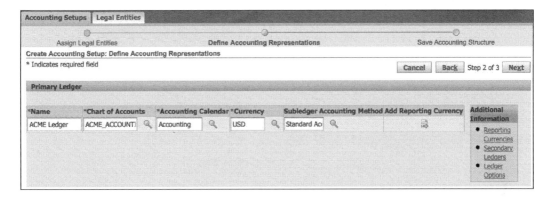

4. Enter the following in the **Define Accounting Representations** form:

5. In the **Name** field, select **ACME Ledger**.

6. In the **Chart of Accounts** field, select **ACME_ACCOUNTING_FLEX**.

7. In the **Accounting Calendar** field, select **Accounting**. This is the monthly calendar.

8. In the **Currency** field select **USD**.

9. In the **Subledger Accounting Method** field, select **Standard Accruals**.

10. Click on the **Next** button to review and save the **Accounting Structure**.

There's more...

Now, let's look at some additional setup options for setting up the ledger.

Reviewing the calendar

A calendar is required for the ledger. Once a calendar is opened, the period cannot be amended. Let's look at a calendar definition:

1. Select the **General Ledger** responsibility.

2. Navigate to **Setup | Financials | Calendar | Accounting**.

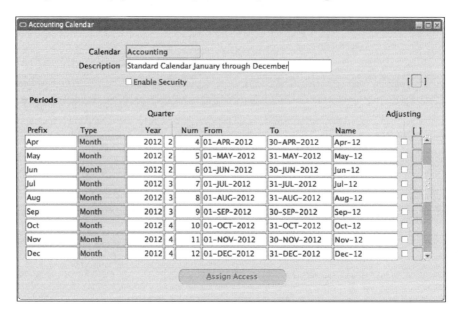

3. In the **Accounting Calendar** form, press *F11* to enter the query mode.

4. Enter **Accounting** in the **Calendar** field; press *Ctrl+F11*.

5. Review the **Calendar**; for example, note the period is month and the periods are for calendar months. You can also define other types of calendars with other periods, for example, weekly calendars.

Defining the ledger options

The ledger options define the default options used for the ledger, for example, the Accounting Calendar option, Year End processing option, Journal processing option, and the Currency Translation option. Let's define the following ledger options:

- First Ever Open Period–Dec-10

- Number of Future Enterable Periods–3

- Retained Earnings Account–01.000.3311.000.000

- Suspense Account–01.000.2999.000.000

- Rounding Differences Account–01.000.7870.000.000

- ▶ Default Period End and Average Rate Type–Corporate
- ▶ Cumulative Translation Adjustment Account–01.000. 3500.000.000

1. Select the **General Ledger** responsibility.

2. Navigate to **Setup | Financials | Accounting Setup Manager | Accounting Setups**.

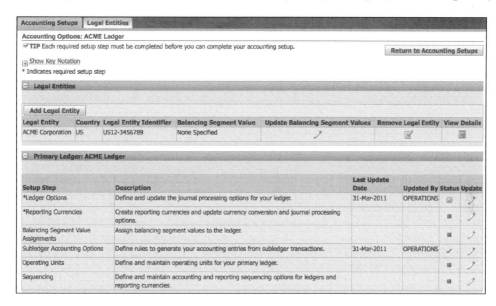

3. In the **Accounting Setups** form, enter **ACME** in the **Search by Legal Entity** field and click on the **Go** button.

4. Select the **Update Accounting Options** icon.

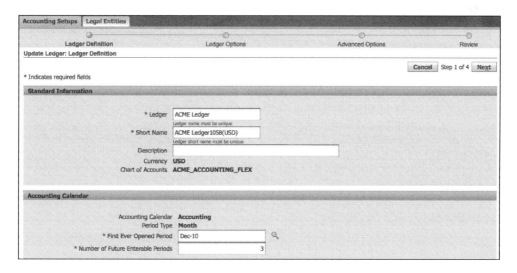

5. In the **Primary Ledger | ACME Ledger** region, select the **Update** icon in the **Ledger Options** step.

6. In the **Update Ledger | Ledger Definition form**, enter **Dec-10** in the **First Ever Open Period** field, and **3** in the **Number of Future Enterable Periods**.

7. Click on the **Next** button to enter the **Ledger Options**:

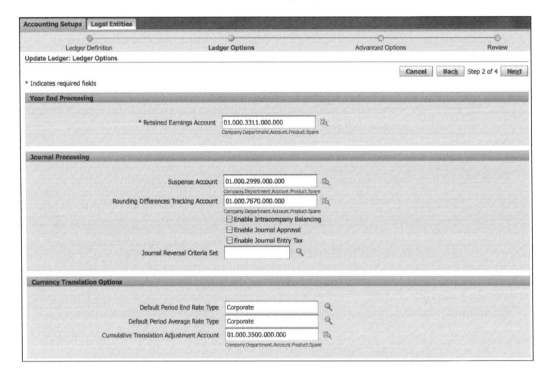

8. In the **Year End Processing** region, enter **01.000.3311.000.000** in the **Retained Earnings Account** field. The search form for the **Accounting Flexfield** will be displayed because the account combination has not been created.

9. Click on the **Create** button to create the account combination and click on the **Select** button.

10. In the **Journal Processing** region, enter **01.000.2999.000.000** in the **Suspense Account** field. The search form for the **Accounting Flexfield** will be displayed.

11. Click on the **Create** button to create the account combination and click on the **Select** button.

12. Enter **01.000.7870.000.000** in the **Rounding Differences Account** field. The search form for the **Accounting Flexfield** will be displayed.

13. Click on the **Create** button to create the account combination and click on the **Select** button.

14. In the **Currency Translation Options** region, select **Corporate** in the **Default Period End Rate Type** and **Default Period Average Rate Type** fields.

15. Enter **01.000. 3500.000.000** in the **Cumulative Translation Adjustment Account** field. The search form for the **Accounting Flexfield** will be displayed.

16. Click on the **Create** button to create the account combination and click on the **Select** button.

17. In the **Advanced Options** form, click on the **Next** button.

18. The **ACME Ledger** options now has a **Status** of **Complete.**

19. Click on the **Complete** button.

20. A warning message is displayed to notify the intention to save the setup options. Click on the **Yes** button.

21. The **General Ledger Accounting Setup Program** will be submitted.

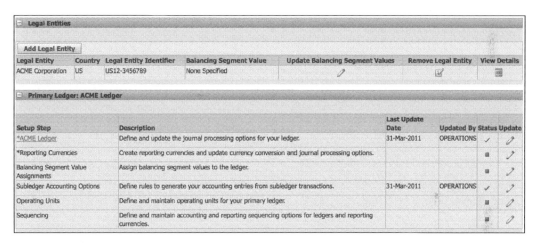

22. Click on the **Return to Accounting Setups** button.

23. The **Ledger Options Step** has now changed to **ACME Ledger**, and the **Update** button on the other steps are now enabled.

Creating the reporting currency

Reporting currencies will enable us to report on account balances in multiple currencies. Let's add a reporting currency of Euros (EUR) to our ledger:

1. Select the **General Ledger** responsibility.

2. Navigate to **Setup | Financials | Accounting Setup Manager | Accounting Setups**.

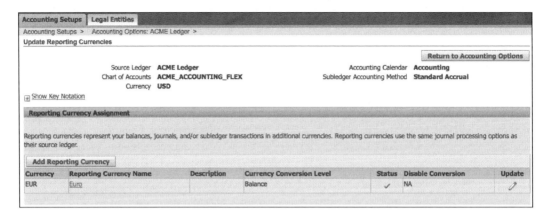

3. In the **Accounting Setups** form, enter **ACME%** in the **Search by Legal Entity** field and click on the **Go** button.

4. Select the **Update Accounting Options** icon.

5. In the **Primary Ledger | ACME Ledger** region, select the **Update** icon in the **Reporting Currencies** setup step.

6. In the **Add Reporting Currency** form, select **Balance** as the **Currency Conversion Level.**

7. Select **EUR** as the **Currency**.

8. Enter **Euro** as the **Reporting Currency Name** and **EUR** as the **Short Name.**

9. In the **Currency Translation Options** region, select **Corporate** as the **Period End Rate Type** and **Period Average Rate Type**.

10. Click on the **Apply** button.

11. Click on the **Complete** button.

Assigning the Balancing Segment Values (BSV) to the ledger

Balancing Segment Values can be used to track transactions that are not related to a legal entity. Balancing Segment Values needs to be assigned to legal entities in an accounting setup before we can assign a specific balancing segment value to the ledgers in the accounting setup.

Let's assign Balancing Segment Values to our legal entity and our ledger.

- ▸ ACME Corporation (01) to the legal entity
- ▸ ACME Limited (02) to the ledger
- ▸ ACME LLP (03) to the ledger

These are the valid values that can be used for the Subledger:

1. Select the **General Ledger** responsibility.

2. Navigate to **Setup | Financials | Accounting Setup Manager | Accounting Setups**.

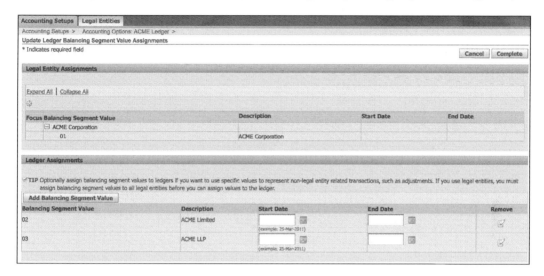

3. In the **Accounting setups** form, enter **ACME%** in the **Search by Legal Entity** field and click on the **Go** button.

4. Select the **Update Accounting Options** icon.

5. In the **Legal Entities** region, select the **Update Balancing Segment Value Assignments** icon.

6. Click on the **Add Balancing Segment Value** button, and select **01** from the list of values.

7. Click on the **Apply** button.

8. In the **Primary Ledger | ACME Ledger** region, select the **Update** icon in the **Balancing Segment Value Assignments** setup step.

9. In the **Ledger Assignments** region, click on the **Add Balancing Segment Value** button, and select **02** and **03** from the list of values.

10. Click on the **Complete** button.

Defining the operating units

Multiple operating units allow us to perform accounting transactions in one or more legal entities. Operating units are assigned to the primary ledger to separate Subledger transaction data. Let's define an operating unit for our ledger:

1. Select the **General Ledger** responsibility.

2. Navigate to **Setup | Financials | Accounting Setup Manager | Accounting Setups**.

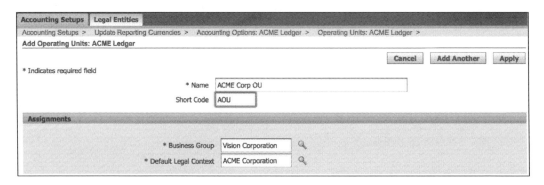

3. In the **Accounting Setups** form, enter **ACME%** in the **Search by Legal Entity** field and click on the **Go** button.

4. Select the **Update Accounting Options** icon.

5. In the **Primary Ledger | ACME Ledger** region, select the **Update** icon in the **Operating Units** setup step.

6. Click on the **Add Operating Unit** button.

7. In the **Name** field enter **ACME Corp OU**

8. Enter **AOU** in the **Short Code** field.

9. Enter **Vision Corporation** in the **Business Group** field.

10. Enter **ACME Corporation** in the **Default Legal Context** field.

11. Click on the **Apply** button.

12. Click on the **Complete** button.

Assigning the ledger to a responsibility

Let's create a GL responsibility called ACME GL Super User, and assign it to the OPERATIONS User:

1. Select the **System Administrator** responsibility.

2. Navigate to **Security | Responsibility | Define**.

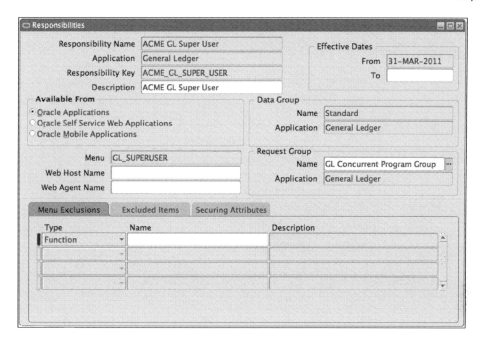

3. Enter **ACME GL Super User** in the **Responsibility Name** field.

4. Select **General Ledger** in the **Application** field.

5. Enter **ACME_GL_SUPER_USER** in the **Responsibility Key** field.

6. Enter **ACME GL Super User** in the **Description** field.

7. In the **Data Group** region select **Standard**, and **General Ledger** in the **Application** field.

8. Select **GL_SUPERUSER** in the **Menu** field.

9. Select **GL Concurrent Program Group** in the **Request Group** field.

10. Click on the **Save** icon to save the record.

Let's assign the responsibility to a user:

1. Navigate to **Security | User | Define**.

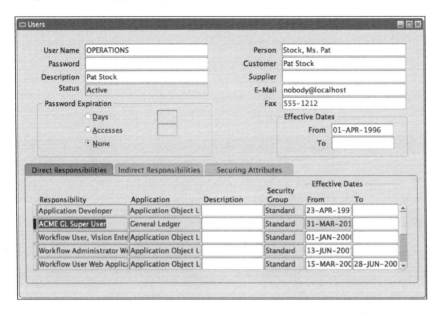

2. Press *F11* to enter the query mode.

3. Enter **OPERATIONS** in **User Name** field, and press *Ctrl+F11* to execute the query.

4. Select the **Direct Responsibilities Tab**, select the **responsibility** field.

5. Select the **New Record** icon to add an additional line to the responsibilities.

6. Enter **ACME GL Super User** in the **Responsibility** field

7. Click on the **Save** icon to save the record.

Let's assign the ledger to the GL responsibility:

1. Navigate to **Profile | System**.

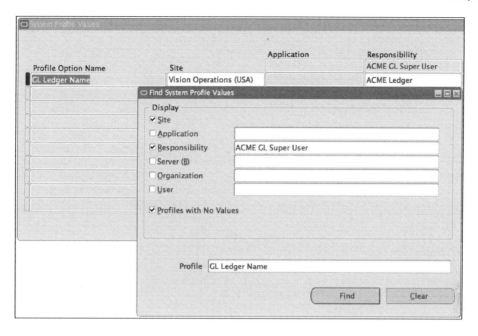

2. In the **Display** region, select **Responsibility** and enter **ACME GL Super User** in the **Responsibility** field.

3. In the **Profile** field, enter **GL Ledger Name**, and click on the **Find** button.

4. Enter **ACME Ledger** in the **Responsibility** field for the **GL Ledger Name** profile option.

5. Click on the **Save** icon to save the record.

Opening the first general ledger period

We need to open a period before we can start to enter transactions.

 Once the first period is opened, we cannot reverse this action.

1. Select the **ACME GL Super User** responsibility.

2. Navigate to **Setup | Open/Close**.

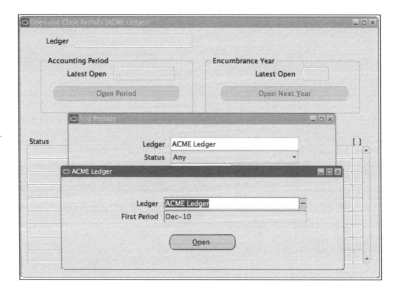

3. In the **Find Periods** form, click on the **Find** button.

4. The **First Open Period** form is displayed for the **ACME Ledger**.

5. Click on the **Open** button.

6. In the decision box, click on the **Yes** button to confirm that we want to open the first period.

7. The **Open Period** concurrent program starts to open the first period.

Let's review the opened periods:

1. Navigate to **Setup | Open/Close**.

2. In the **Find Periods** form, click on the **Find** button.

3. The **Open and Close Periods (ACME Ledger)** form displays the open periods.

Creating journals

Let's create a journal in the new ledger:

1. Select the **ACME GL Super User** responsibility.

2. Navigate to **Journal | Enter**.

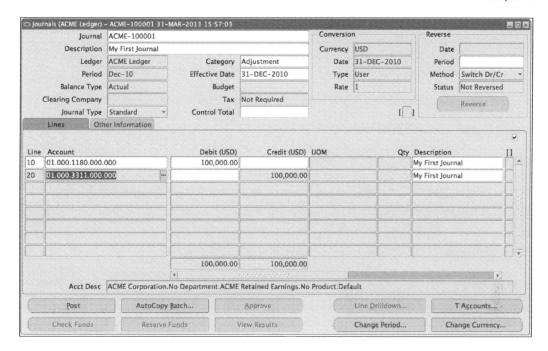

3. Click on the **New Journal** button.

4. In the **Journal** field enter **ACME-100001**.

5. Enter **My First Journal** as the **Description**.

6. Select the **Lines** tab, and enter **10** in the **Line** field.

7. Enter **01.000.1180.000.000** in the **Account** field and **100,000.00** in the **Debit** field.

8. Select the next line and enter **01.000.3311.000.000** in the **Account** field and **100,000.00** in the **Credit (USD)** field. The line number of **20** is automatically entered.

9. Click on the **Save** icon to save the record.

10. Click on the **Post** button to post the journal. Journals can also be posted using the concurrent program.

Defining Subledger accounting

When we record a transaction, Oracle Subledger Accounting Method identifies the associated Journal Line Types, Account Derivation Rules, and Journal Entry Descriptions to generate accounting events based on the Event Class Type.

At the end of the period, we run the **Create Accounting** program to generate Subledger journals in the Subledgers. The accounting transactions are transferred by journal entries from the Subledger to the appropriate ledgers in General Ledger.

In this recipe, we will look at how to define an accounting entry for a Payable transaction. We will demonstrate how any accounting distribution entered for the Miscellaneous expense type in Payables can be changed in Subledger Accounting Method to a special account distribution of **01-CEO-7490-0000-00014** in General Ledger.

The core steps are as follows:

- ▸ Create a Journal Type called Special Expense.
- ▸ Setup the Journal Lines Definition for the Special Expense.
- ▸ Create an Account Derivation Rule for the Special Expense Journal Line Type. This will use the account code of 01-CEO-7490-0000-00014 for the Special Expense Account.
- ▸ Set up the Application Accounting Definitions.
- ▸ Set up the Subledger Accounting Method.
- ▸ Assign the Subledger Accounting Method to the ledger.
- ▸ Create a payables invoice and create accounting to view the transactions.

How to do it...

Let's list the steps required to complete the task.

Create Journal Line Types:

1. Select the **Payables** responsibility.

2. Navigate to **Setup | Accounting Setups | Subledger Accounting Setup | Accounting Methods Builder | Journal Entry Setups | Journal Line Types**.

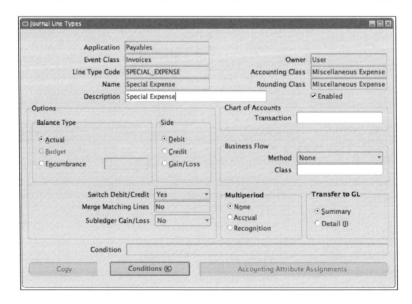

3. Click on the **New** button.

4. Select **Invoices** in the **Event Class** field and enter **SPECIAL_EXPENSE** in the **Line Type Code** field.

5. Enter **Special Expense** in both the **Name** field and the **Description** field.

6. Select **Miscellaneous Expense** in the **Accounting Class** and the **Rounding Class** fields.

7. Select **Actual** in the **Balance Type** region.

8. Select **Debit** in the **Side** region. The transaction is for a debit amount.

9. Select **Yes** from the **Switch Debit/Credit** drop-down list.

10. Select **No** in the **Merge Matching Lines** and the **Subledger Gain/Loss** fields.

11. Select **Summary** in the **Transfer to GL** region.

12. Click on the **Conditions(K)** button to enter the **Journal Line Type Conditions**.

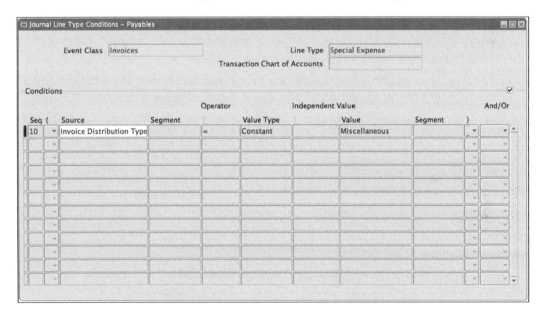

13. Enter **10** in the **Seq** field.

14. Select **Invoice Distribution Type** in the **Source** field.

15. Select **=** in the **Operator** field.

16. Select **Constant** in the **Value Type** field.

17. Select **Miscellaneous** in the **Value** field.

18. Save the record.

Let's set up the Journal Lines Definition.

1. Navigate to **Setup | Accounting Setups | Subledger Accounting Setup | Accounting Methods Builder | Methods and Definition | Journal Lines Definitions**.

2. In the **Journal Lines Definitions** form, select **Invoice** in the **Event Class** field, and click on the **Find** button.

3. Click on the **Copy Definition** button.

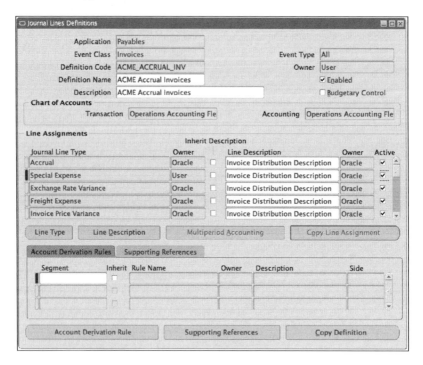

4. Enter **ACME_ACCRUAL_INV** in the **Definition Code** field.

5. Enter **ACME Accrual Invoices** in the **Definition Name** field.

6. Select **Operations Accounting Flex** in both the **Transaction** and the **Accounting** fields.

7. Select the **Copy Line Assignments** and **Display after Copy** checkboxes.

8. Click on the **Done** button.

9. In the **Journal Lines Definition** form, select a new line in the **Line Assignments** region.

10. Select **Special Expense** in the **Journal Line Type**.

11. Scroll to the **Miscellaneous Expense** Journal Line Type, and uncheck the **Active** checkbox.

12. Save your work.

Let's create an Account Derivation Rule for the Journal Line Type:

1. In the **Journal Lines Definitions** window, select **Special Expense** in the **Journal Line Type** field.

2. Click on the **Account Derivation Rule** button.

3. Click on the **New** button.

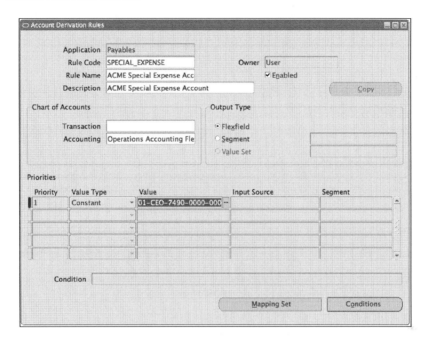

4. Enter **SPECIAL_EXPENSE** in the **Rule Code** field.

5. Enter **ACME Special Expense Account** in the **Rule Name** field.

6. Enter **ACME Special Expense Account** in the **Description** field.

7. Select **Operations Accounting Flex** in the **Accounting** field.

8. Select the **Flexfield** radio button.

9. Enter **1** in the **Priority** field.

10. Select **Constant** in the **Value Type** field.

11. Enter **01-CEO-7490-0000-00014** in the **Value** field.

12. Save the record and close the form.

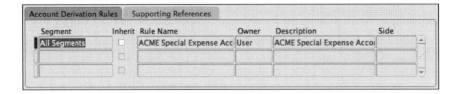

13. In the **Journal Lines Definitions** window, select the **Special Expense** type.

14. Select the **Account Derivation Rules** tab.

15. Select **All Segments** in the **Segment** field.

16. Select **ACME Special Expense Account** in the **Rule Name** field.

17. Save the record.

Let's set up the Application Accounting Definitions:

1. Navigate to **Setup | Accounting Setups | Subledger Accounting Setup | Accounting Methods Builder | Methods and Definitions | Application Accounting Definitions**.

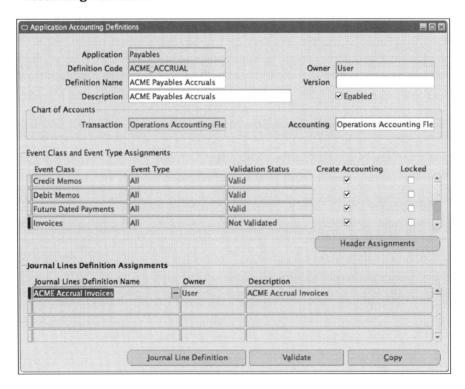

2. Enter **Accrual Basis** in the **Definition Name** field.

3. Click on the **Find** button.

4. Click on the **Copy** button to copy the definition to our new definition.

5. Enter **ACME_ACCRUAL** in the **Definition Code** field.

6. Enter **ACME Payables Accruals** in the **Definition Name** field.

7. Select **Operations Accounting Flex** in the **Accounting** and **Transaction** fields.

8. Deselect **Line Assignments**.

9. Click on the **Done** button.

10. In the **Journal Lines Definition Assignments** region, select **ACME Accrual Invoices** in the **Journal Lines Definition Name** field.

11. Click on the **Validate** button to validate the definition.

Let's set up the Subledger Accounting Method (SLAM) by copying and modifying an existing Subledger Accounting Method:

1. Navigate to **Setup | Accounting Setups | Subledger Accounting Setup | Accounting Methods Builder | Methods and Definitions | Subledger Accounting Methods**.

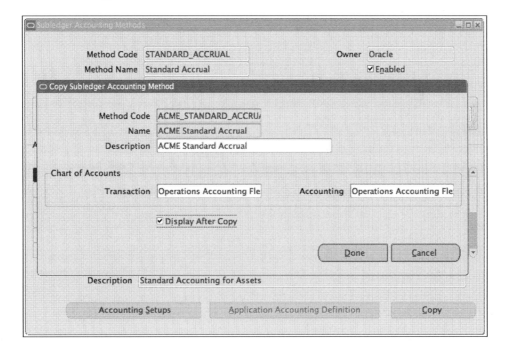

2. Enter **Standard Accrual** in the **Method Name** field, and click on the **Find** button.

3. Click on the **Copy** button to copy the **Subledger Accounting Method.**

4. Enter **ACME_STANDARD_ACCRUAL** in the **Method Code** field.

5. Enter **ACME Standard Accrual** in the **Name** field.

6. Enter **ACME Standard Accrual** in the **Description** field.

7. Select **Operations Accounting Flex** in the **Accounting** and the **Transaction** fields.

8. Click on the **Done** button.

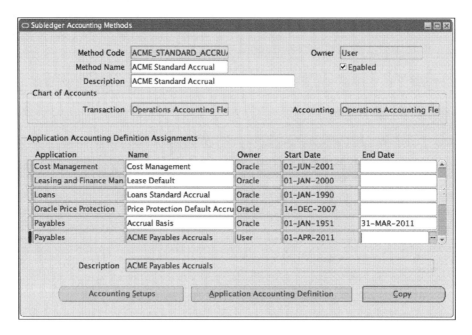

Let's enter an End Date to an existing Application Accounting Definition and add a new one:

1. Select the **Payables** line and enter an **End Date** of **31-MAR-2011**.

2. Add a new line and in the **Applications** field, select **Payables**.

3. Select **ACME Payables Accrual** in the **Name** field and enter **01-APR-2011** in the **Start Date** field.

4. Save the record and close the form.

Let's assign the Subledger Accounting Method to the Vision Operations (USA) ledger:

1. Navigate to **Setup | Accounting Setups | Ledger Setup | Define | Accounting Setups.**

2. Search for the **Vision Operations (USA)** ledger.

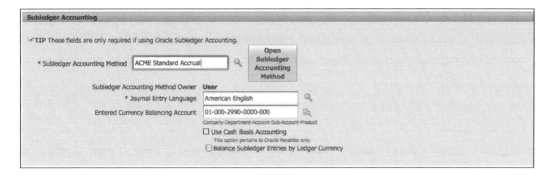

3. In the **Primary Ledger** region, click the **Update** icon in the ledger setup step.

4. In the **Subledger Accounting Method** region, change the **Subledger Accounting Method** to **ACME Standard Accrual**.

5. Click on the **Finish** button.

Let's create a Payables Invoice:

1. Select the **Payables** responsibility.

2. Navigate to **Invoices | Entry | Invoices.**

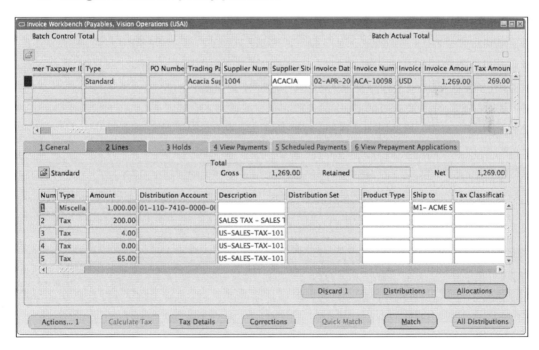

3. Select **Acacia Suppliers** in the **Trading Partner** field.

4. Enter **1,269.00** in the **Invoice Amount** field.

5. Select the **Lines** tab and select **Miscellaneous** in the **Type** field.

6. Enter **1,000.00** in the **Amount** field and **01-110-7410-0000-000** in the **Distribution Account** field.

7. Click on the **Calculate Tax** button to calculate the tax on the invoice.

8. Click on the **Actions... 1** button and select validate to validate the invoice.

Let's create the accounting and review the transactions:

1. Click on the **Actions... 1** button and select the **Create Accounting** checkbox.

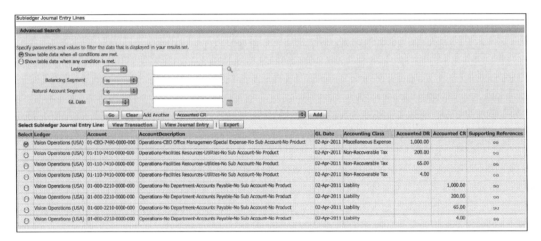

2. Select **Draft** in the **Mode** field.

3. Click on the **OK** button.

4. Select **Reports** on the **Menu**, and select **View Accounting**.

5. The Subledger journal entries are displayed in the **Results** region.

6. Observe that the **Miscellaneous Expense** shows the account **01-CEO-7490-0000-000.**

How it works...

The Subledger Accounting Method uses the Accounting Definition Assignment to determine the basis for determining the accounting transaction for a Subledger. The Event Class and the Event Type assignments classify the transaction types for the accounting rule and the possible actions for the accounting transaction.

The Account Derivation rules are assigned to the Application definition through the Journal assignment.

See also

Entering invoices, recipe in Chapter 3, Paying Suppliers Invoices in Payables

Defining E-Business Tax

Countries have a tax authority that regulates tax law. The laws have rules, which are set by the tax authorities. Rules determine the treatment of taxes set by the tax authorities. The rules are applicable within a boundary. Oracle E-Business Suite uses **E-Business Tax** (**EBTAX**) to calculate the tax on transactions based on rules.

The key steps in defining EBTAX are listed as follows:

- ▸ Create Tax Regime—the set of rules
- ▸ Create Tax
- ▸ Create Tax Status
- ▸ Create Tax Rate
- ▸ Create Tax Jurisdiction—boundaries where the tax is applicable
- ▸ Create Tax Account
- ▸ Create Defaulting Rules

In this recipe, we will look at the steps required to set up a new tax rule within a boundary for a tax authority.

Let's assume that the government has decided to introduce an additional Sales Tax of 20 percent to start on 01-APR-2011. In this recipe, we will define the new tax and enter a payables transaction for this new tax.

Getting ready

Login to Oracle E-Business Suite R12 with the username and password assigned to you by the system administrator. If you are working on the Vision demonstration database, you can use OPERATIONS/WELCOME as the USERNAME/PASSWORD.

How to do it...

Let's start by creating a transaction in payables to assess the current tax calculation:

1. Select the **Payables** responsibility.

2. Navigate to **Invoices | Entry | Invoices**.

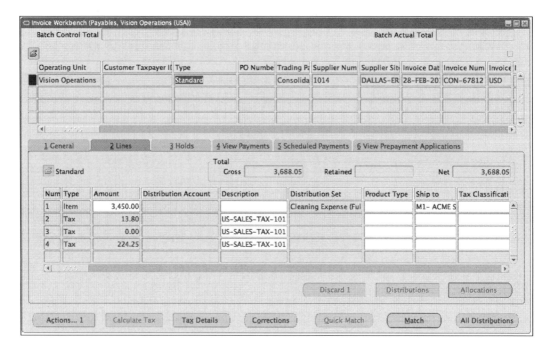

3. Select **Consolidated Suppliers** in the **Trading Partner** field.

4. Enter **3,688.05** in the **Invoice Amount** field.

5. Select the **Lines** tab and select **Item** in the **Type** field.

6. Enter **3,450.00** in the **Amount** field.

7. Click on the **Calculate Tax** button, to calculate the tax on the invoice.

8. Observe that three **Tax** lines of **13.80, 0.00**, and **224.25** are added to the **Tax** line.

The tax lines are added based on the default rules set up in E-Business Tax. Let's set up the new tax rules.

Let's create a Tax Regime:

1. Navigate to **Tax Configuration | Tax Regimes**.

2. Click on the **Create** button.

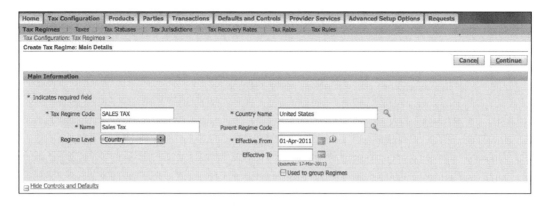

3. Enter **SALES TAX** in the **Tax Regime Code** field.

4. Enter **Sales Tax** in the **Name** field.

5. Select **Country** in the **Regime Level** field.

6. Select **United States** in the **Country Name** field.

7. Enter **01-APR-2011** in the **Effective From** field.

8. In the **Controls** and **Defaults** region, expand the **Show Controls and Defaults** link.

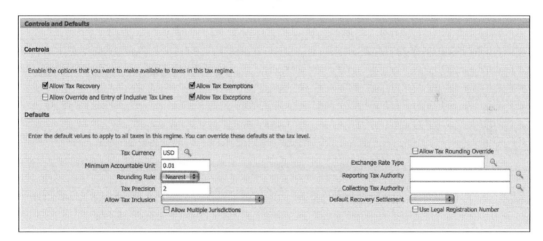

9. Enable the following fields in the **Controls** region:

   ❏ **Allow Tax Recovery**

   ❏ **Allow Tax Exemptions**

   ❏ **Allow Tax Exceptions**

10. In the **Defaults** region, enter the following information:

     ❑   Enter **USD** in the **Tax Currency** field

     ❑   Enter **0.01** in the **Minimum Accountable Unit** field

     ❑   Select **Nearest** in the **Rounding Rule** field

     ❑   Enter **2** in the **Tax Precision** field

11. Click on the **Continue** button.

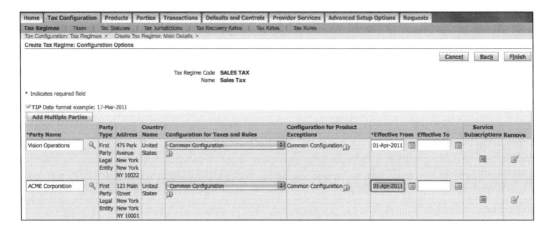

12. Select **Vision Operations** in the **Party Name** field.

13. Select **Common Configuration** in the **Configuration for Taxes and Rules.**

14. Enter **01-Apr-2011** in the **Effective From** field.

15. Select the next line.

16. Select **ACME Corporation** in the **Party Name** field.

17. Select **Common Configuration** in the **Configuration for Taxes and Rules.**

18. Enter **01-Apr-2011** in the **Effective From** field.

19. Click on the **Finish** button.

Let's create a Tax:

1. Navigate to **Tax Configuration | Tax Regimes**.

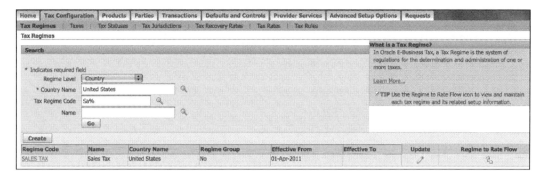

2. Enter **United States** in the **Country Name** field.

3. Enter **Sa%** in the **Tax Regime Code** field.

4. Click on the **Go** button.

5. Select the **Regime to Rate Flow** icon.

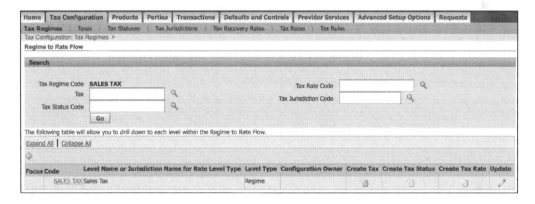

6. Select the **Create Tax** icon.

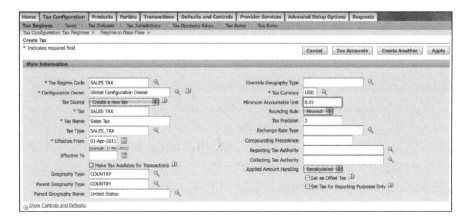

7. Select **SALES TAX** in the **Tax Regime Code** field.

8. Select **Global Configuration Owner** in the **Configuration Owner** field.

9. Select **Create a new tax** in the **Tax Source** field.

10. Enter **SALES TAX** in the **Tax** field.

11. Enter **Sales Tax** in the **Tax Name** field.

12. Enter **SALES_TAX** in the **Tax Type** field.

13. Enter **01-Apr-2011** in the **Effective From** field.

14. Select **COUNTRY** in the **Geography Type** and the **Parent Geography Type** fields.

15. Select **United States** in the **Parent Geography Name** field.

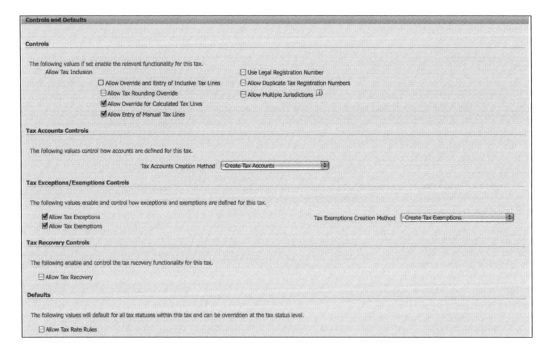

16. Expand the **Show Controls and Defaults.**

17. Enable the following tax controls:

    ❑ **Allow Override for Calculated Tax Lines**

    ❑ **Allow Entry of Manual Tax Lines**

    ❑ **Allow Tax Exceptions**

    ❑ **Allow Tax Exemptions**

18. Click on the **Apply** button.

Let's create a Tax Status:

1. Navigate to **Tax Configuration | Tax Statuses**.

2. Click on the **Create Tax Status** icon.

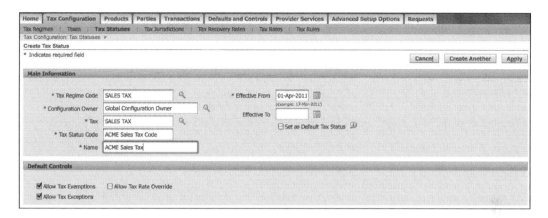

3. Enter **ACME Sales Tax Code** in the **Tax Status Code** field.

4. Enter **ACME Sales Tax** in the **Name** field.

5. Enter **01-Apr-2011** in the **Effective From** field.

6. Click on the **Apply** button.

Let's create a Tax Rate:

1. Navigate to **Tax Configuration | Tax Rates**.

2. Click on the **Create Tax Rate** icon.

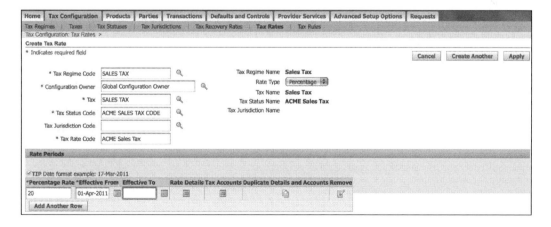

3. Enter **ACME Sales Tax** in the **Tax Rate Code** field.

4. Select **Percentage** in the **Rate Type** field.

5. Enter **20** in the **Percentage Rate** field.

6. Select the **Rate Details** icon.

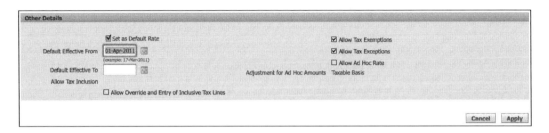

7. Select the **Set as Default Rate** checkbox.

8. Click on the **Apply** button.

Let's create a Tax Jurisdiction:

1. Navigate to **Tax Configuration | Tax Jurisdiction**.

2. Click on the **Create** button.

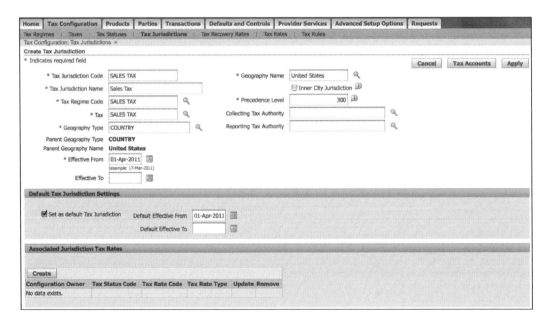

3. Enter **SALES TAX** in the **Tax Jurisdiction Code** field.

4. Enter **Sales Tax** in the **Tax Jurisdiction Name** field.

5. Enter **SALES TAX** in the **Tax Regime Code** field.

6. Enter **SALES TAX** in the **Tax** field.

7. Select **Country** in the **Geography Type** field.

8. Enter **01-Apr-2011** in the **Effective From** field.

9. Select **United States** as the **Geography Name**.

10. Enter **300** as the **Precedence Level**.

11. Enable the **Set as Default Tax Jurisdiction.**

12. Enter **01-Apr-2011** as the **Default Effective From** date.

13. Click on the **Apply** button.

Let's create the Tax Accounts:

1. Navigate to **Tax Configuration | Taxes**.

2. Search for the Tax.

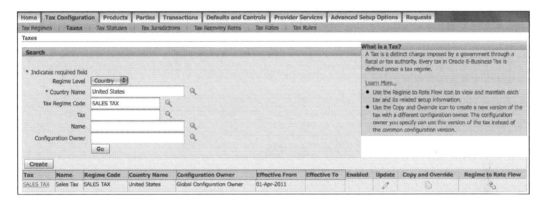

3. In the **Country Name** field, enter **United States**.

4. In the **Tax Regime Code** field, enter **SALES TAX**.

5. Click on the **Go** button.

6. Click on the **Update** icon.

7. Click on the **Tax Accounts** button.

8. Enter the ledger as **Vision Operations**.

9. Click on the **Create** button.

10. In the **Main Information** region, select **Vision Operations** from the list of values.

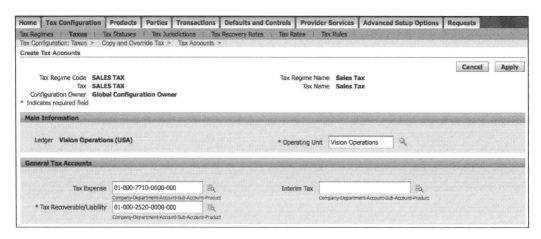

11. Enter tax accounts based on the following information:

   ❑ In the **Operating Unit** field, enter **Vision Operations**

   ❑ In the **Tax Expense** field, enter **01-000-7710-0000-000**

   ❑ In the **Tax Recoverable/Liability** field, enter **01-000-2520-0000-000**

12. Click on the **Apply** button.

Let's create the Default Rules:

1. Navigate to **Tax Configuration | Tax Rules**.

2. Let's search for the **Rule Type**.

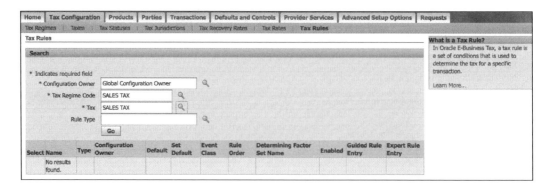

3. In the **Tax Rules** form, enter the following details:

   ❑ In the **Configuration Owner** field, enter **Global Configuration Owner**

   ❑ In the **Tax Regime Code** field, enter **SALES TAX**

   ❑ In the **Tax** field, enter **SALES TAX**

4. Click on the **Go** button.

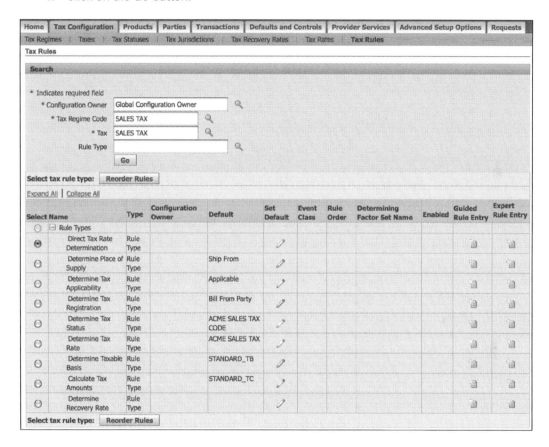

Let's enter tax rule defaults:

1. Click on the **Determine Place of Supply** option and click on the **Set Default** icon.

2. Select **Ship From** as the **Rule Type Default** and click on the **Apply** button.

3. Click on the **Determine Tax Applicability** option and click on the **Set Default** icon.

4. Select **Applicable** as the **Rule Type Default** and click on the **Apply** button.

5. Click on the **Determine Tax Registration** option and click on the **Set Default** icon.

6. Select **Bill From Party** as the **Rule Type Default** and click on the **Apply** button.

7. Click on the **Determine Tax Status** option and click on the **Set Default** icon.

8. Select **ACME SALES TAX CODE** as the **Rule Type Default** and click on the **Apply** button.

9. Click on the **Determine Tax Rate** option and click on the **Set Default** icon.

10. Select **ACME SALES TAX** as the **Rule Type Default** and click on the **Apply** button.

11. Click on the **Determine Taxable Basis** option and click on the **Set Default** icon.

12. Select **STANDARD_TB** as the **Rule Type Default** and click on the **Apply** button.

13. Click on the **Calculate Tax Amounts** option and click on the **Set Default** icon

14. Select **STANDARD_TC** as the **Rule Type Default** and click on the **Apply** button.

Let's make the Tax available for transactions:

1. Navigate to **Tax Configuration | Taxes**.

2. Enter **United States** in the **Country Name** field.

3. Enter **Sales Tax** in the **Tax Regime Code** field.

4. Click on the **Go** button.

5. Click on the **Update** icon.

6. Enable **Make Tax Available for Transactions**.

7. Select **Corporate** as the **Exchange** rate type.

Let's create a Payables invoice:

1. Select the **Payables** responsibility.

2. Navigate to **Invoices | Entry | Invoices**.

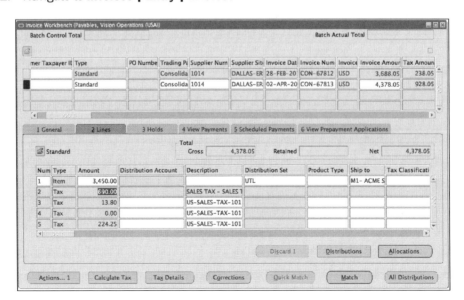

3. Select **Consolidated Suppliers** in the **Trading Partner** field.

4. Enter **4,378.05** in the **Invoice Amount** field.

5. Select the **Lines** tab and select **Item** in the **Type** field.

6. Enter **3,450.00** in the **Amount** field and **UTL** in the **Distribution Set** field.

7. Click on the **Calculate Tax** button to calculate the tax on the invoice.

8. Observe that an additional **Tax** line of **690.00** is added to the **Tax** line.

See also

Enter Invoices recipe in Chapter 3, Paying Supplier Invoices in Payables

9

End of Period Processing

In this chapter, we will cover:

- ► Closing Payables
- ► Closing Purchasing
- ► Closing Receivables
- ► Closing the Inventory
- ► Closing the General Ledger

Introduction

At the end of every period, accounting books need to be closed. In this chapter, we will look at the core steps required to close the financials periods.

The following diagram shows a typical period end process:

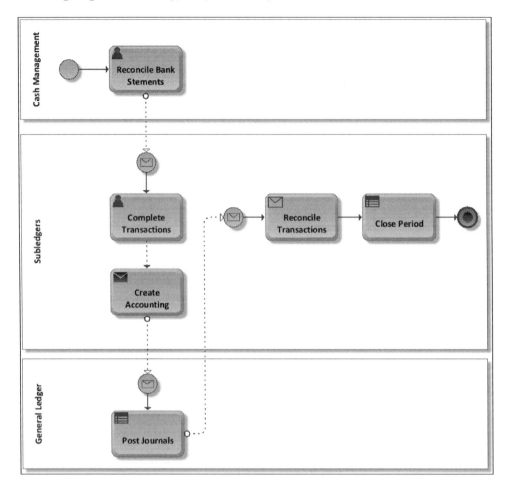

1. The bank statements are reconciled in **Cash Management**. Additional miscellaneous transactions are created.

2. All the transactions for the period are completed in the Subledger. All outstanding issues are resolved.

3. Run the Invoice Validation Report in Payables.

4. Review and resolve holds in Payables.

5. Run Purchasing Receipt Accruals.

6. Run Mass Additions Create for Assets.

7. Post Mass Additions.

8. Run Depreciation.

9. Create Accounting for transfers from the Subledgers to the General Ledger.

10. Run Payables Accounting Process to transfer to the General Ledger.

11. Run Receivables to transfer to the General Ledger.

12. Run Inventory to transfer to the General Ledger.

13. Post Journals in the General Ledger.

14. Run Journal Import.

15. Post Journals in the General Ledger.

16. Reconcile Subledgers to the General Ledger.

17. Reconcile Payables, Receivables, Assets, Cash Management, Order Management, and Inventory to the General Ledger.

18. Run Purchasing Period Accruals.

19. Close the periods.

20. Close the period in Payables.

21. Close the Purchasing period.

22. Close the Receivables period.

23. Close the Inventory period.

Closing Payables

At the end of a period, payables transactions are transferred to the General Ledger and Assets. In this recipe, let's close the payables period for March 2011.

Getting ready

Before we can close Payables, we need to complete the following:

1. Bank statements in Cash Management must be reconciled and all issues resolved.

2. Miscellaneous transactions are completed for transactions in Cash Management, for example, bank charges are entered in Payables from Cash Management.

3. Transactions for the period have to be completed. For example, invoices, prepayment, and payments.

4. Review the Uninvoiced Receipts Report from Purchasing for receipts not yet invoiced. When the receipt accrual is run from purchasing at the end of the period, journal entries are created for the amount of the receipt liabilities.

5. Ensure that eligible invoices are approved in readiness for payment.

6. Review and resolve holds placed on the invoices.

7. Complete all payment runs for outstanding invoices due for payment.

8. Run the Create Accounting program to transfer approved invoices and payments to the General Ledger.

How to do it...

Before we can close a period, we need to resolve all exceptions. Let's run the Period Close Exceptions Report for March 2011 to view the exceptions:

1. Select the **Payables** Responsibility.

2. Navigate to **Accounting | Control Payables Periods**.

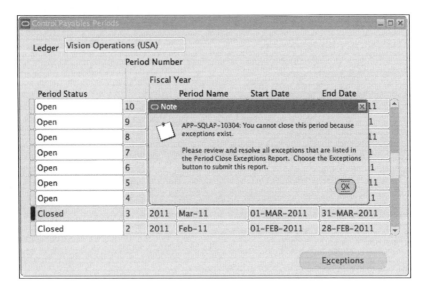

3. In the **Period Status** field, select **Closed** for the **Mar-11** period.

4. We receive a note to review the exceptions.

5. Click on the **OK** button.

6. Click on the **Exceptions** button.

7. In the decision box, select the review button.

8. The Concurrent Program is submitted. Click on the **OK** button.

ORACLE Payables   **Period Close Exception Report**   Report Date: 26-APR-2011
Company: Vision Operations (USA)   Page: 2 of 2

Operating Unit: Vision Operations

Unaccounted Invoices					
Supplier Name	Supplier Number	Invoice Number	Accounting Date	Currency	Invoice Amount
Acacia Supplies Ltd	1004	20110331-1	30-Mar-2011	USD	1,000.00
Advanced Network Devices	1013	ADV-001	27-Mar-2011	USD	2,672.50
Building Management Inc.	2012	BM-0091	27-Mar-2011	USD	2,170.00

View the **Period Close Exception Report**:

1. Select **View | Requests** from the **Menu**.

2. Click on the **Find** button to view the completed requests.

3. In the **Request** window, click on the **View Output** button.

4. The transactions that need to be reviewed are displayed.

Let's run the Create Accounting Program to account for the transactions:

1. Navigate to **Other | Requests | Run**.

2. Select **Single Request** in the **Submit a New Request** window and select the **OK** button.

3. In the **Name** field, enter **Create Accounting**.

4. Select **Vision Operations** in the **Ledger** field.

5. Enter **31-MAR-2011** in the **Date** field.

6. Click on the **Submit** button to submit the request.

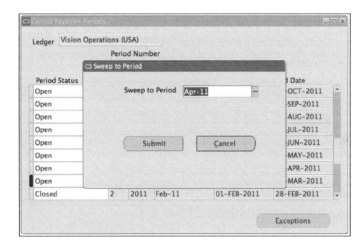

Let's sweep transactions to the next period:

1. Select the **Payables** responsibility.

2. Navigate to **Accounting | Control Payables Periods**.

3. In the **Period Status** field, select **Closed** for the **Mar-11** period.

4. We receive a note to review the exceptions.

5. Click on the **Ok** button.

6. Click on the **Exceptions** button.

7. In the decision box, select the Sweep button.

8. Select **APR-11** in the **Sweep to Period** field.

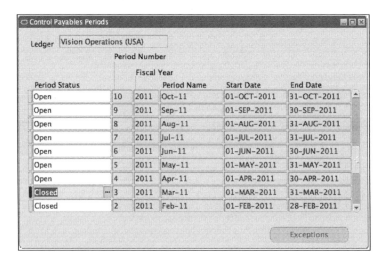

9. The **Concurrent Program** is submitted. Click on the **Ok** button.

10. The period status is set to **Closed**.

There's more...

After the journals are posted in the General Ledger, we need to reconcile the payables transactions to GL.

Reconciling Payables

Let's reconcile the Accounts Payable transactions to the General Ledger for the month of March 2011:

Report	Total Value
Previous Month Accounts Payable Trial Balance	X
Current Month Posted Invoice Register	X
Current Month Posted Payment Register	(X)
Current Month Accounts Payable Trial Balance	(X)
	Nil

Let's run the Accounts Payable Trial Balance at 28-FEB-2011:

1. Select the **Payables** responsibility.

2. Navigate to **Other | Requests | Run**.

3. Select **Single Request** in the **Submit a New Request** window and select the **OK** button.

4. In the **Name** field, enter **Accounts Payable Trial Balance**.

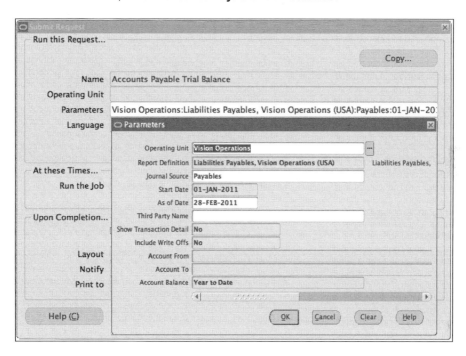

5. Select **Vision Operations** in the **Operating Unit** field.

6. Select **Liabilities Payables, Vision Operations (USA)** in the **Report Definition** field.

7. Enter **01-JAN-2011** in the **Start Date** field. The accounting period is from 01-Jan-2011.

8. Enter **28-FEB-2011** in the **As of Date** field.

9. Accept the defaults and click on the **OK** button.

10. Click on the **Submit** button to submit the request.

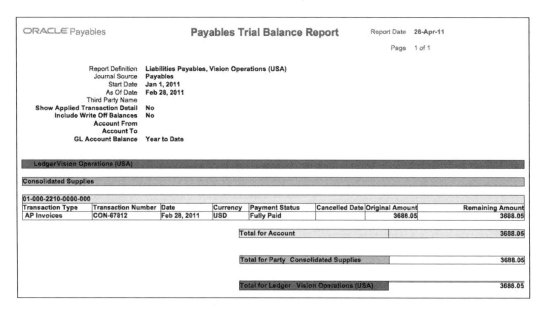

Let's view the Accounts Payable Trial Balance:

1. Select **View | Requests** from the **Menu**.

2. Click on the **Find** button to view the completed requests.

3. In the **Request** window, click on the **View Output** button.

4. The **Accounts Payable Trial Balance** is displayed with a total of **3688.05**.

Let's run the Posted Invoice Register for March 2011:

1. Navigate to **Other | Requests | Run**.

2. Select **Single Request** in the **Submit a New Request** window and select the **OK** button.

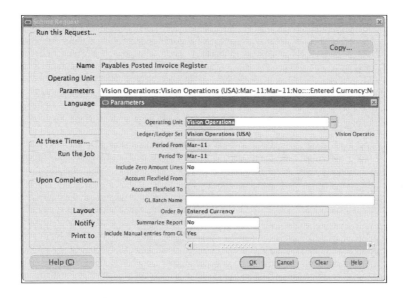

3. In the **Name** field, enter **Payables Posted Invoice Register**.

4. Select **Vision Operations** in the **Operating Unit** field.

5. Select **Vision Operations (USA)** in the **Ledger/Ledger Set** field.

6. Enter **MAR-2011** in both the **Period From** and **Period To** fields.

7. Select **Entered Currency** in the **Order By** field.

8. Accept all the other defaults.

9. Click on the **Submit** button to submit the request.

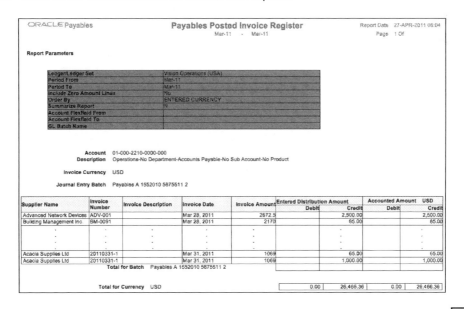

Let's view the Posted Invoice Register for March 2011:

1. Select **View | Requests** from the **Menu**.

2. Click on the **Find** button to view the completed requests.

3. In the **Request** window, click on the **View Output** button.

4. The **Posted Invoice Register** is displayed with a total of **26,466.36**.

Let's run the Posted Payment Register for March 2011:

1. Navigate to **Other | Requests | Run**.

2. Select **Single Request** in the **Submit a New Request** window, and select the **OK** button.

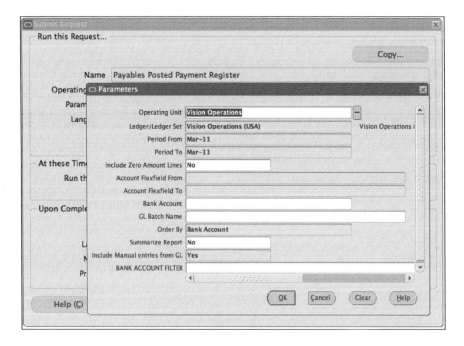

3. In the **Name** field, enter **Posted Payment Register.**

4. Select **Vision Operations** in the **Ledger** field.

5. Enter **MAR-2011** in the **Period From** and the **Period To** fields.

6. Accept all other defaults and click on the **OK** button.

7. Click on the **Submit** button to submit the request.

8. View the **Payables Posted Payment Register** report:

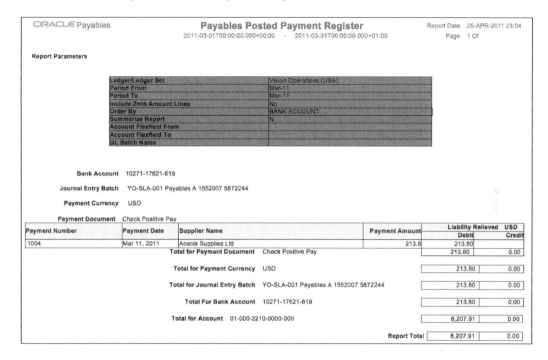

9. Select **View | Requests** from the **Menu**.

10. Click on the **Find** button to view the completed requests.

11. In the **Request** window, click on the **View Output** button to view the report.

Let's view the current month's Accounts Payable Trial Balance.

Let's run the Accounts Payable Trial Balance for Mar-11:

1. Navigate to **Other | Requests | Run**.

2. Select **Single Request** in the **Submit a New Request** window and select the **OK** button.

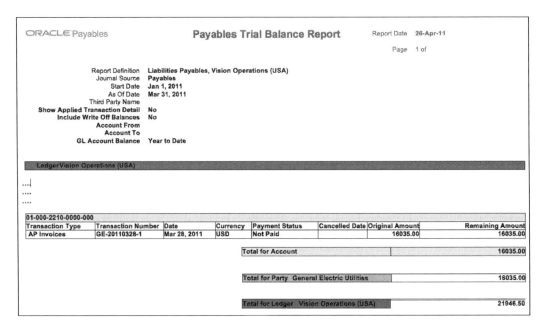

3. In the **Name** field, enter **Accounts Payable Trial Balance**.

4. Select **Vision Operations** in the **Ledger** field.

5. Enter **MAR-2011** in the **Date** field.

6. Click on the **Submit** button to submit the request.

Let's view the Accounts Payable Trial Balance:

1. Select **View | Requests** from the menu.

2. Click on the **Find** button to view the completed requests.

3. In the **Request** window, click on the **View Output** button to view the report, and complete the reconciliation.

Let's summarize the results:

Report	Value
Feb-11 Accounts Payable Trial Balance	3,688.05
Mar-11 Posted Invoice Register	26,466.36
Mar-11 Posted Payment Register	(8,207.91)
Mar-11 Accounts Payable Trial Balance	(21,946.50)
	Nil

Opening the next period

Open the next Oracle payables period:

1. Select the **Payables** responsibility.
2. Navigate to **Accounting | Control Payables Periods**.
3. In the **Period Status** field, select **Open** for the **Apr-11** period.

Closing Assets

At the end of every period, we need to run depreciation for each asset book. The depreciation run closes the period in Assets. Before we run depreciation for the period, we need to ensure that we run Mass Additions Create to transfer all asset transactions from Payables. We also need to complete all transactions, for example, complete all additions, adjustments, retirements, transfers, and retirements.

After we run depreciation for the period, we run the Create Accounting to transfer the transactions to the General Ledger and post the journals after review.

See also

Depreciating Assets recipe in Chapter 4, Managing Assets

Closing Purchasing

At the end of the purchasing period, we need to accrue for expense Items received from the supplier, but not yet invoiced before we close the period. In this recipe, we will close the period of March 2011 for Purchasing.

Getting ready

Before we can close Purchasing, we also need to:

1. Complete transactions for the period, including requisitions, purchase orders, releases, receipts, and returns.

2. Enter all receipts.

3. Complete the Payables Period-End Process.

How to do it...

Let's start by reviewing the uninvoiced receipts report, to review the receipts from our suppliers that have not yet been invoiced:

1. Select the **Purchasing** responsibility.

2. Navigate to **Other | Requests | Run**.

3. Select **Single Request** in the **Submit a New Request** window and select the **OK** button.

4. In the **Name** field, enter **Uninvoiced Receipts Report**.

5. Select **Mar-11** in the **Period Name** field.

6. Click on the **Submit** button to submit the request.

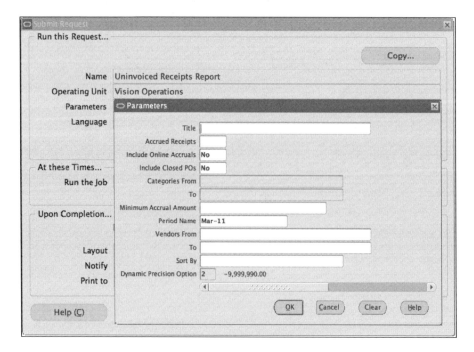

Let's view the Uninvoiced Receipts Report:

1. Select **View | Requests** from the **Menu**.
2. Click on the **Find** button to view the completed requests.
3. In the **Request** window, click on the **View Output** button.

Let's run the Receipt Accruals Program to account for the transactions. This will also create the period-end accruals for the un-invoiced expense receipts:

1. Select the **Purchasing** responsibility.
2. Navigate to **Other | Requests | Run**.

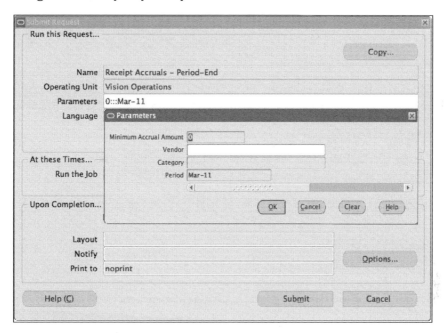

3. Select **Single Request** in the **Submit a New Request** window, and select the **OK** button.
4. In the **Name** field, enter **Receipt Accruals – Period End**.
5. Select **Mar-11** in the **Period Name** field.
6. Click on the **Submit** button to submit the request.
7. Close the PO Period.
8. Select the **Purchasing** responsibility.
9. Navigate to **Setup | Financials | Accounting | Control Purchasing Periods**.
10. Enter **2011** in the **Fiscal Year** field in the **Control Purchasing Periods** form.
11. Select **Closed** as the **Period Status** for **Mar-11**.

How it works...

The **Receipt Accruals - Period-End** report enables us to create period-end accruals for uninvoiced expense receipts. This creates a journal entry batch in the General Ledger for the receipt accruals, debiting the charge account and crediting the Expense AP Accrual Account.

Please note that this step is required if the Accrue Expense Items flag is set to Period End on the Accrual tabbed region of the Purchasing Options window for the Organization.

To reverse the accrual automatically in the next period, set the Profile option "GL: Launch Auto Reverse after Open Period" to Yes.

Closing Receivables

At the end of every period, receivables transactions need to be completed and reconciled. Transactions also need to be transferred to the General Ledger and the period closed. In this recipe, we will look at the process of closing the period of March 2011 for Receivables.

Getting ready

Prior to closing the period, the following steps need to be completed:

1. Reconcile Bank Statements in Cash Management and receivables adjustments processed, for example, bank interest.
2. Complete all transactions – invoice, adjustments, credits, reversals, and receipts.
3. Reconcile transactions – customer balances, transactions, receipts, and bank statements.
4. We can use the following formula to reconcile the Period-End balance:

	Value
Outstanding Balance at Start of Period	X
Transactions for the period	X
Adjustments for the period	X
Invoice Exceptions for the period	(X)
Applied Receipts for the period	(X)
Unapplied Receipts for the period	(X)
Period End Balance	(X)
	Nil

Run the following additional useful reports for reconciliation:

1. Journal Entries report
2. Aging report
3. Transaction Register
4. Adjustment Register
5. Invoice Exceptions
6. Applied Receipts
7. Unapplied and Unresolved Receipts Register
8. Aging report – last day
9. Post outstanding transactions to General Ledger
10. Print invoices
11. Subledger Period Close Exceptions report
12. Perform the end of period transactions for Order Management.

How to do it...

Run the revenue recognition program by following these steps:

1. Select the **Receivables** responsibility.
2. Navigate to **Control | Accounting | Revenue Recognition**.
3. Select **Single Request** in the **Submit a New Request** window and select the **OK** button.

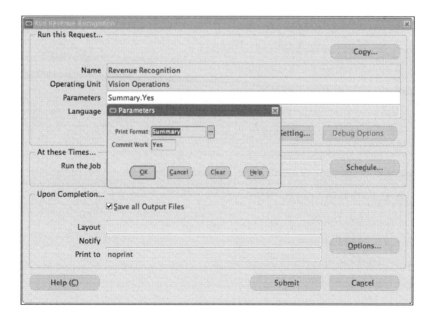

4. In the **Name** field, enter **Revenue Recognition**.

5. Accept the default parameters and click on the **OK** button.

6. Click on the **Submit** button to submit the request.

Run the AR to GL Reconciliation Report to compare the account balances in Receivables and the General Ledger. The report displays journal sources where discrepancies might exist. We can do this by carrying out the following steps:

1. Select the **Receivables** responsibility.

2. Navigate to **Control | Accounting | AR to GL Reconciliation**.

3. Select **Single Request** in the **Submit a New Request** window and select the **OK** button.

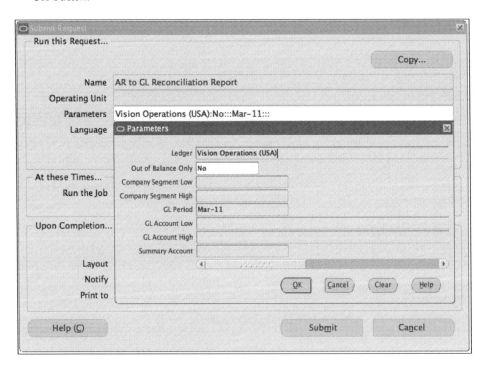

4. In the **Name** field, enter **AR to GL Reconciliation Report**.

5. Select **Mar-11** in the **Period Name** field.

6. Click on the **Submit** button to submit the request.

7. View the **AR to GL Reconciliation Report**.

8. Select **View | Requests** from the **Menu**.

9. Click on the **Find** button to view the completed requests.

10. In the **Request** window, click on the **View Output** button.

Now, let's close the receivables period:

1. Select the **Receivables** responsibility.

2. Navigate to **Setup | Financials | Accounting | Control Purchasing Periods**.

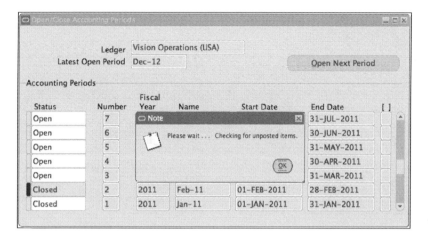

3. Enter **2011** in the **Fiscal Year** field in the **Control Purchasing Periods** form.

4. Select **Closed** as the **Period Status** for **Mar-11**.

There's more...

Order Management period end processes need to be completed prior to closing Receivables and Inventory.

Closing Order Management

We need to ensure that all orders have been processed in Order Management before closing Inventory. Order Management updates Inventory during the Ship Confirm process. The following is a summary of the steps required to close Order Management:

1. Complete all transactions – enter and book orders, confirm shipments, respond to workflow notifications, close orders.

2. Review Backorders and process cancelations.

3. Review Open Orders.

4. Review Orders on Hold using Outstanding Holds report.

5. Other useful reports.

6. Back Order Detail report.

7. Unbooked Orders report.

8. Canceled Orders report.

9. Review Workflow status.

10. Run Autoinvoice.

See also

Creating an Invoice recipe in Chapter 5, Selling Items to Customers in Order Management

Closing Inventory

At the end of a period Item, costs information needs to be transferred to the General Ledger before we can close the period. In this recipe, we will look at the process of closing inventory.

Getting ready

1. Complete all transactions – shipping, receipts, issues, and adjustments.

2. Check Interface managers for outstanding transactions.

3. Transfer transactions to the General Ledger using the Create Accounting – Cost Management Program.

4. Open the next period.

5. Close the Payables period.

6. Close the Purchasing period.

7. Close the Receivables period.

How to do it...

Close Inventory Period automatically transfers summary transactions to the GL interface table. The prior period needs to be closed before we can close the period. To accomplish this, carry out the following steps:

1. Select the **Inventory** responsibility.

2. Navigate to **Accounting Close Cycle | Inventory Accounting Periods**.

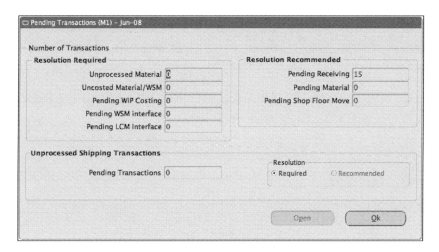

3. Select the period **Jun-08** and click on the **Pending** button to review the pending transactions.

4. Click on the **OK** button.

5. Click on the **Change Status** to change the status of the period to **Closed** by selecting **Closed (Irreversible)** in the options. Click on the **OK** button.

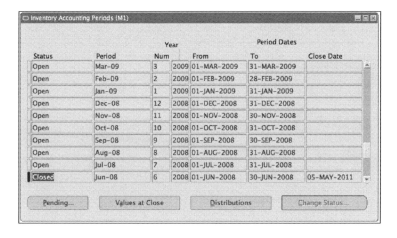

6. The pending transaction form is displayed. Click on the **Close** button to close the period

7. The **Period Close Reconciliation** report is generated by the close action.

8. Select the closed period and click on the **Values at Close** button to view the Inventory values of the Subinventories and the Cost Group.

Closing the General Ledger

An accounting period is closed in the General Ledger after all the accounting transactions have been completed for the period. The status of the period will determine whether transactions can be entered in the period. The status of the period can be Never Opened, Future Enterable, Open, Closed, or Permanently Closed. A Permanently Closed period cannot be reopened.

Getting ready

1. Complete all Subledger transactions – run the Create Accounting from the Subledgers to create the Subledger Accounting transactions. This populates the GL_JE_BATCHES, GL_JE_HEADERS, and GL_JE_LINES tables.

2. Import all Journals. This process populates the GL_INTERFACE tables.

3. Post all Journals. This updates the GL_BALANCES tables.

4. Run the Period Close Exception report in GL to ensure that there are no outstanding transactions in the Subledgers and GL.

5. Run the trial balance.

6. Perform reconciliations.

7. Reverse previous period accruals.

8. Enter Adjustments and Accruals and Post the journals.

How to do it...

1. Select the **General Ledger** responsibility.

2. Navigate to **Setup | Open/Close**.

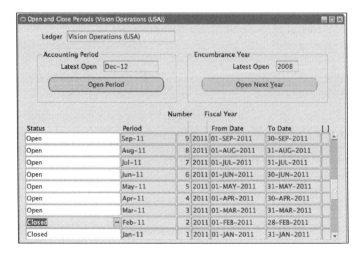

3. Click on the **Find** button.

4. Select the status field for the **Feb-11** period and change the status to **Closed**.

5. Click on the **Save** icon. This triggers a concurrent program to close the period.

6. A **Subledger Period Close Exception Report** is also created for transactions that need to be reviewed from the Subledger.

7. View the **Subledger Period Close Exception Report**.

8. Select **View | Requests** from the **Menu.**

ORACLE Subledger Accounting		**Subledger Period Close Exception Report**			Report Date	**05-May-11**	
		Period From **Feb-11**		Period To **Feb-11**		Page 3 of 4	
Feb 4, 2011	PO Delivery into Inventory	23619012	Unprocessed	04-FEB-11	M1	PRD20006	
Feb 4, 2011	PO Delivery into Inventory	23619018	Unprocessed	04-FEB-11	M1	PRD20008	

Journal Category	Receiving		Event Class	Receipt into Receiving Inspection		
Event Date	Event Type	Transaction Number	Status	Transaction Date	Organization Code	Item
Feb 4, 2011	Logical Receipt	4901363	Unprocessed	04-FEB-11	M1	PRD20006
Feb 4, 2011	Logical Receipt	4901365	Unprocessed	04-FEB-11	M1	PRD20006
Feb 4, 2011	Logical Receipt	4901367	Unprocessed	04-FEB-11	M1	PRD20006
Feb 4, 2011	Receipt into Receiving Inspection	4901369	Unprocessed	04-FEB-11	M1	PRD20008

Journal Category	Inventory		Event Class	Sales Order Issue		
Event Date	Event Type	Transaction Number	Status	Transaction Date	Organization Code	Item
Feb 5, 2011	Sales Order Issue	23619036	Unprocessed	05-FEB-11	M1	PRD20007
Feb 10, 2011	Sales Order Issue	23619997	Unprocessed	10-FEB-11	M1	PRD20007
Feb 10, 2011	Sales Order Issue	23620997	Unprocessed	10-FEB-11	M1	PRD20007
Feb 10, 2011	Sales Order Issue	23621010	Unprocessed	10-FEB-11	M1	PRD20007
Feb 10, 2011	Sales Order Issue	23621023	Unprocessed	10-FEB-11	M1	PRD20007
Feb 10, 2011	Sales Order Issue	23621036	Unprocessed	10-FEB-11	M1	PRD20007

Journal Source	Receivables					

Journal Category	Adjustment		Event Class	Adjustment		
Event Date	Event Type	Transaction Number	Status	Customer Name	Customer Number	Adjustment Number
Feb 22, 2011	Adjustment Created	3446	Incomplete	SheepWall Inc	5840	3446

Journal Category	Debit Memos		Event Class	Debit Memo		
Event Date	Event Type	Transaction Number	Status	Customer Name	Customer Number	Debit Memo Number
Feb 17, 2011	Debit Memo Created	12070	Final	SheepWall Inc	5840	12070

9. Click on the **Find** button to view the completed requests.

10. In the **Request** window, click on the **View Output** button.

See also

Defining subledger accounting recipe in Chapter 8, Defining Transactions for the General Ledger

Index

I

T

Tab key 303
TCA 186
Trading Community Architecture. *See* TCA
transaction codes
about 268
creating 268, 269

U

Unit of Measure (UOM) 13
Update Description button 43

V

Values at Close button 359
Value Set button 39
View Transaction button 180

W

Web Application Desktop Integrator. *See* ADI

Thank you for buying
Oracle E-Business Suite 12 Financials Cookbook

About Packt Publishing

Packt, pronounced 'packed', published its first book "*Mastering phpMyAdmin for Effective MySQL Management*" in April 2004 and subsequently continued to specialize in publishing highly focused books on specific technologies and solutions.

Our books and publications share the experiences of your fellow IT professionals in adapting and customizing today's systems, applications, and frameworks. Our solution-based books give you the knowledge and power to customize the software and technologies you're using to get the job done. Packt books are more specific and less general than the IT books you have seen in the past. Our unique business model allows us to bring you more focused information, giving you more of what you need to know, and less of what you don't.

Packt is a modern, yet unique publishing company, which focuses on producing quality, cutting-edge books for communities of developers, administrators, and newbies alike. For more information, please visit our website: www.PacktPub.com.

About Packt Enterprise

In 2010, Packt launched two new brands, Packt Enterprise and Packt Open Source, in order to continue its focus on specialization. This book is part of the Packt Enterprise brand, home to books published on enterprise software – software created by major vendors, including (but not limited to) IBM, Microsoft and Oracle, often for use in other corporations. Its titles will offer information relevant to a range of users of this software, including administrators, developers, architects, and end users.

Writing for Packt

We welcome all inquiries from people who are interested in authoring. Book proposals should be sent to author@packtpub.com. If your book idea is still at an early stage and you would like to discuss it first before writing a formal book proposal, contact us; one of our commissioning editors will get in touch with you.

We're not just looking for published authors; if you have strong technical skills but no writing experience, our experienced editors can help you develop a writing career, or simply get some additional reward for your expertise.

Oracle E-Business Suite R12 Supply Chain Management

ISBN: 978-1-849680-64-6   Paperback: 292 pages

Drive your supply chain processes with Oracle E-Business R12 Supply Chain Management to achieve measurable business gains with this book and eBook

1. Put supply chain management principles to practice with Oracle EBS SCM

2. Develop insight into the process and business flow of supply chain management

3. Set up all of the Oracle EBS SCM modules to automate your supply chain processes

4. Case study to learn how Oracle EBS implementation takes place

Oracle PeopleSoft Enterprise Financial Management 9.1 Implementation

ISBN: 978-1-849681-46-9   Paperback: 412 pages

An exhaustive book and ebook resource for PeopleSoft Financials application practitioners to understand core concepts, configurations, and business processes

1. A single concise book and eBook reference to guide you from PeopleSoft foundation concepts through to crucial configuration activities required for a successful implementation

2. Real-life implementation scenarios to demonstrate practical implementations of PeopleSoft features along with theoretical concepts

3. Expert tips for the reader based on wide implementation experience

Please check **www.PacktPub.com** for information on our titles

Getting Started with Oracle Hyperion Planning 11

ISBN: 978-1-849681-38-4   Paperback: 515 pages

Design, configure, and implement a robust planning, budgeting, and forecasting solution in your organization using Oracle Hyperion Planning with this book and eBook

1. Successfully implement Hyperion Planning—one of the leading planning and budgeting solutions—to manage and coordinate all your business needs with this book and eBook

2. Step-by-step instructions taking you from the very basics of installing Hyperion Planning to implementing it in an enterprise environment

3. Test and optimize Hyperion Planning to perfection with essential tips and tricks

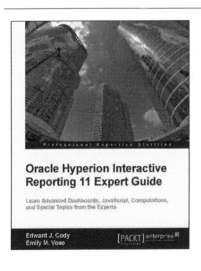

Oracle Hyperion Interactive Reporting 11 Expert Guide

ISBN: 978-1-849683-14-2   Paperback: 250 pages

Build advanced computations, dashboards, and scripting

1. Learn the best methods for data analysis, dashboards, and advanced techniques with this book and e-book

2. Explore dashboards and learn the methods used by developers to build advanced interfaces

3. Become an expert by mastering excellent concepts using the examples given in this guide

Please check **www.PacktPub.com** for information on our titles

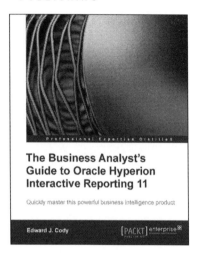

The Business Analyst's Guide to Oracle Hyperion Interactive Reporting 11

ISBN: 978-1-849680-36-3   Paperback: 232 pages

Quickly master the extremely robust and powerful Oracle Hyperion Interactive Reporting 11 tool with this book and eBook

1. Get to grips with the most important, frequently used, and advanced features of Oracle Hyperion Interactive Reporting 11

2. A step-by-step Oracle Hyperion training guide packed with screenshots and clear explanations

3. Explore the features of Hyperion dashboards, reports, pivots, and charts

Oracle Fusion Middleware Patterns

ISBN: 978-1-847198-32-7   Paperback: 224 pages

10 unique architecture patterns powered by Oracle Fusion Middleware in this book and eBook

1. First-hand technical solutions utilizing the complete and integrated Oracle Fusion Middleware Suite in hardcopy and ebook formats

2. From-the-trenches experience of leading IT Professionals

3. Learn about application integration and how to combine the integrated tools of the Oracle Fusion Middleware Suite - and do away with thousands of lines of code

Please check **www.PacktPub.com** for information on our titles

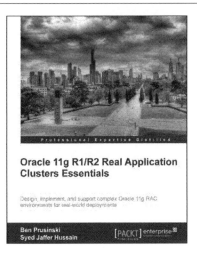

2625673R00204

Printed in Great Britain
by Amazon.co.uk, Ltd.,
Marston Gate.